Ain't Too Proud to Beg

Ain't Too Proud to Beg

LIVING THROUGH THE LORD'S PRAYER

Telford Work

WILLIAM B. EERDMANS PUBLISHING COMPANY
GRAND RAPIDS, MICHIGAN / CAMBRIDGE, U.K.

Published 2007 by

Wm. B. Eerdmans Publishing Co.

2140 Oak Industrial Drive N.E., Grand Rapids, Michigan 49505 /

P.O. Box 163, Cambridge CB3 9PU U.K.

www.eerdmans.com

Printed in the United States of America

11 10 09 08 07   7 6 5 4 3 2 1

Library of Congress Cataloging-in-Publication Data

Work, Telford.

Ain't too proud to beg: living through the Lord's prayer / Telford Work.

p.   cm.

Includes bibliographical references.

ISBN 978-0-8028-0393-1 (pbk.: alk. paper)

1. Lord's prayer.   I. Title.

BV230.W67   2007

226.9′606 — dc22

2007003699

"The Soulless World of Tom Wolfe" appeared in *The New Pantagruel.* "Will the Son of Man Find Faith on Earth When He Comes?" appeared as "Love Thyself" in *Books & Culture.* "Bible Stories You Didn't Outgrow: Jonah" appeared in *Word & World.*

To everyone who has prayed for me,
especially
my family,
Robert and Esther Vernon,
Pat Landis,
Paul Cedar,
Jonathan Wilson,
and
the ones who prayed in secret.
You know who you are,
and so does the Father.

Contents

CONTENTS

Acknowledgments

Many people deserve my thanks for their roles in this project. Sheryl Fullerton prodded me to conceive it in the first place. John Wilson supported it, and me, in the middle. Westmont College underwrote several of these chapters with two faculty development grants. Ben Patterson, Britta Phillips, Jonathan Wilson, Sarah Clark Elliot, Bob Hosack, Amy Reeves, Jon Pott, Michael Thomson, and several semesters' worth of students in my Christian doctrine classes read earlier drafts and offered helpful constructive criticism. Hope Community Church and Montecito Covenant Church invited me to preach and so inspired the sermons in the epilogue. First Presbyterian Church invited me to teach the essence of this book to an adult Sunday school class whose thoughtful reactions, responses, and suggestions helped me enrich several chapters. My colleagues Carter Crockett and Jeff Schloss responded with challenging and insightful comments to two chapters delivered as the Paul C. Wilt faculty lectures. Josh Nunziato, a student of mine and already an impressive theologian whose career you will want to follow, cheerfully compiled the indexes. Roger Van Harn at Eerdmans was a patient, supportive, and helpful editor.

I am just as profoundly indebted to the teachers and writers I have drawn on. I rarely cite my mentors at Fuller and Duke, but what they have shown me deserves grateful footnotes on practically every paragraph.

This book also happened while my family changed schools and moved repeatedly and while my wife, Kim, and I went through our first few years with four children: Jeremy, Daniel, Junia, and Benjamin. They were all patient with the hours of reading and writing that filled my summer, winter, and spring breaks. Just because they are used to it doesn't make it any less sacrificial.

Thank you all!

When You Pray . . .

Why I Am Writing a Book I Am Unqualified to Write

Be forewarned: this is a strange book. It is a series of remedial exercises in prayerful theology, in "living through" the Lord's Prayer.

For twenty years I have been a Christian, and I still feel like a stranger to prayer. Oh, I have prayed — by American standards, a lot. I bow my head at church and gladly say "Amen" to others' prayers. I often open classes with prayers. My family sings our thanks around the table at dinnertime. My wife and I pray with our kids after tucking them in at night. I speak out here and there during the day like Tevye in *Fiddler on the Roof.* In the car or walking to work I sometimes intercede for my family, friends, students, and strangers. These litanies can run from a few seconds to twenty minutes or more. (Some in my church consider that a sprint. With my family background, I consider it a marathon.) Yet despite all this I have not really become *familiar* with prayer. Instead, I have stuck to what I know. This is a personality trait of mine. I rarely order a new dish from a restaurant menu once I find a few I like. In the same way, I can easily pray conventional prayers for every one of the occasions on which I am already used to praying. But these are stock pieces from a narrow repertoire, not the adventurous discourses that really make for a *life* of prayer.

Even the stock pieces are too woodenly delivered. From childhood I thought of prayer as wimpy, and I have never quite shaken that impression. Even after my conversion to living faith the astonishing words of the Lord's Prayer would slip past me as I recited them. That changed too little as I entered my present career. How can a professor of Christian theology

xi

not have mastered five verses from the Gospel of Matthew (three in Luke!)? Believe me, it is possible.

In 2002, it was time to address the problem. Not by abandoning the stock pieces for a life of improvising, as some evangelicals do; in spirituality as in jazz, one begins not with long solos but with scales, chords, and standards. Not by developing a theology of prayer; for someone in my vocation that would just be an academic dodge. Not by writing a how-to guide for improving my "prayer-life"; not only do I obviously not know how to do that, but I am not sure a "prayer-life" is something we should have in the first place. Not by writing a commentary on the Lord's Prayer; those have been done by people far better equipped for the task. Rather, *it was time to pray*.

Specifically, it was time to pray and reflect just as I am: a sinner, a struggling but still tenacious believer, a fellow heir with Christ, a father and husband and friend, a no-longer-young white, male, Southern California evangelical in an era when such labels matter, a Christian whose graduate school years have convoluted his writing, a scholar whose fondness for writing on the Internet has made him too habituated to casual style, and — be warned, reader — a professor of Christian theology who will take *any* opportunity to exploit a "teachable moment" or dip into an intriguing question.

This book is the fallout from that effort. The subtitle captures at least four dimensions of my project.

First, we "live through" the Lord's Prayer in the same sense that, say, America lives by the American Way. The Lord's Prayer is the Lord's way; its agenda is the right agenda for the Father's children. When we pray it, it trains us in the way of the Lord Jesus, which is of course the only true way to live (John 14:6).

Because much of what I have been doing here is learning a way of life, I have intentionally left its chapters in essay form. "Essay" formally means a tentative or experimental effort from a limited or personal point of view. And prayerful theology is theology on the way rather than theology on arrival. That tactic will not seem promising to some, but I think it works out rather well.

Obviously, my remediation involved actually praying the Lord's Prayer. That entailed facing God in all my life, and facing life in all my prayers. Because Christian theology *is* my life, that meant praying theologically and theologizing prayerfully. Because teaching it is my vocation, the audience for these meditations is anyone (especially myself!) who might find this project a chance to learn something about how to be a Christian. Because no teacher is worthy of his or her subject, I set out with the same excited but queasy feeling I have when I teach a class for the first time, hoping my qualifications as an authority would develop as I proceeded. Because the gift of teaching is not restricted to teachers, I hope that learning in front of others inspires them to learn, pray, and teach for themselves.

My project left me open even to learning anew what a prayer really is. The theologian Ulrich Luz notes that the history of interpretation of the Lord's Prayer has taken three broad forms. The dogmatic reading, typified in the writings of Tertullian, reads the prayer as a summary of Christian doctrine. The ethical reading, typified by Gregory of Nyssa, takes the prayer as a guide to attaining the blessed life. The eschatological reading was pioneered by Albert Schweitzer and now dominates among biblical scholars. It sets the Lord's Prayer within Jesus' apocalyptic eschatology. It is as Jesus' way of anticipating the end of the world.[1]

I have some training in New Testament studies, and my readings tend to take the eschatological view. However, unlike many of my contemporaries, I can find no tension between an eschatological reading of the Lord's Prayer and ethical and theological readings. The pages that follow display no compelling reason to set Tertullian, Gregory, and the contemporary biblical studies guild in opposition to one another. Indeed, I think their concerns work together beautifully. However, this project has taught me that all three readings are vulnerable to a common error: They can impose *our* preconceived frameworks — be they cosmological, mystical, or historicist — upon the Lord's Prayer rather than run to it as *God's* way of transforming our thinking.

Why Prayer Does Not Come First (Nor Last)

Second, we "live through" the Lord's Prayer as, say, America lived through the wrenching changes of the Civil War and World War II. Jesus' prayer is a process through which our lives travel and are transformed. Prayer in Christ takes us places, places only Christ can take us, if we let it.

1. Ulrich Luz, *Matthew 1–7: A Continental Commentary* (Minneapolis: Augsburg, 1992), p. 375.

Letting it — protecting this project from being distorted by my own preconceptions and simply taking me where I already expected to go — called for a format that is as deliberately odd as prayer itself.

The Lord's Prayer acts as what liturgists call a "collect" (pronounced COL-lect). Like the middle of an hourglass, a collect very briefly draws together what has gone on so far in the worship service. It focuses and summarizes the past in order to transition to the future. Prayer is unpredictable because a collect is a catalyst of change. An example is the following collect for an Episcopal service that features a baptism. It caps off the previous phase of the liturgy so that worshippers can build upon it as they go on:

> Almighty God, by our baptism into the death and resurrection of your Son Jesus Christ, you turn us from the old life of sin: Grant that we, being reborn to new life in him, may live in righteousness and holiness all our days; through Jesus Christ our Lord, who lives and reigns with you and the Holy Spirit, one God, now and for ever. Amen.[2]

The collects of the *Book of Common Prayer* are amazing prayers, conveying divine truth with concise rhetorical elegance and moving us on from where we have been to where we should be next.

A collect never changes. However, what it does changes every time we say it. So it is with the Lord's Prayer. Praying it routinely might seem predictable and even boring, but in practice it proves to be the opposite. While it has a place in both the daily office and the Sunday liturgy, as an all-purpose prayer it can be said any time of day and in practically any Christian tradition. That means it does not just collect what comes before it in a structured worship service. It collects anything and everything. As Martin Luther put it:

> Whatever needs are in the world, they are included in the Lord's Prayer. And all the prayers in the Psalms and all the prayers which could ever be devised are in the Lord's Prayer.[3]

2. *The Book of Common Prayer* (New York: Church Hymnal Corporation, 1979), p. 254.
3. Quoted in John Dillenberger, ed., *Martin Luther: Selections from His Writings* (New York: Doubleday, 1962), p. 226.

In this book I put Luther to the test, and he passes. I collect a few prominent concerns from my recent life in the various petitions of the Lord's Prayer and offer them up in penitence and trust. I find out what is gold, silver, and precious stones that last, and what is wood, hay, and straw that burns in the fire of God's judgment (1 Cor. 3:10-15).

The *Didache,* a document from the Church of the first few generations after the apostles, advises Christians to pray the Lord's Prayer three times a day. That makes every morning an anticipation, every midday an examination, and every evening a celebration. In that spirit, every chapter in this book begins with reflection on needs to which that one part of the prayer awakened me. The heart of each chapter is unwritten: it is the praying itself. Each chapter then closes with an examination of that part of the Lord's Prayer that responds to the concerns laid out in the beginning and puts the prayer's lesson to fruitful use. The celebration comes in the epilogue, which gathers several sermons that could not have been written except as fruit of these months of prayerful theology.

Each petition really is its chapter's *heart,* in a strong metaphorical sense. From a maze of capillaries a distant force draws blood together in larger and larger streams until the corpuscles are gathered in its chambers: *Our Father . . . Amen.* Then the energized fellowship parts for new journeys to unpredictable and innumerable destinations. This endless circle of work literally keeps the body alive. And the distant force pushing us back meekly into God's presence for another meeting is the same pump that drives us out surging with enthusiasm.

Some might imagine that an organ of such small size — just a few phrases of a few words each — is inadequate for such a critical task, or that the monotony of its beating calls for embellishment. But we "do not heap up empty phrases as the Gentiles do; for they think they will be heard for their many words" (Matt. 6:7). The little auricles and ventricles of these pithy phrases are enough to provide for a whole body of vast needs and great size.

Or, to change metaphors, the Lord's Prayer is a halftime activity. It presupposes a game already in progress, a life already in play. Our team withdraws from field and fans to a place and a time for refreshment and renewal. We focus back on the coach's training and learn new lessons from our prior experiences. We may want to build on our successes: "Hallowed be your name." We may be celebrating a good first half but worried about giving back our gains in the second: "Deliver us from evil." Or we may be smarting from setbacks and wondering how to come back: "Forgive us our sins." Or we may just be disoriented and bewildered: "Your kingdom come, your will be done." Teammates gather, speak, listen, console, and reflect so that the past can orient them toward their future. An observer who misunderstands the game might think halftime is just a break, a diversion, a way to sell concessions, a lot of talk. But this little breather, used wisely, is a precious resource for transfiguring the whole game.

George Lindbeck proposed an influential typology of three popular conceptions of doctrine which will shape our understanding of the Lord's Prayer.[4] The first he calls "cognitive-propositionalist." It claims that our beliefs are like an intellectual system whose essence can be contained in valid or invalid logical statements. Such a conception would make the Lord's Prayer a resource for identifying qualities of God: The Father is our provider, our sovereign, our atonement, our judge, and so on. A sign that this approach is too narrow is that the only line of the Lord's Prayer that sounds anything like a proposition is the last — "for the Kingdom and the power and the glory are yours, now and for ever" — and that line is missing from the earliest biblical manuscripts. It is an addition probably crafted from the lines in 1 Chronicles 29:11-13 with which David blessed YHWH (the Divine Name, rendered "the LORD" in most Bibles, and sometimes transliterated as "Jehovah") at the funding of Solomon's temple. Even there it is not primarily a list of facts, but rather the warrant for a grand act of praise.[5]

Beginning each chapter with a verse from which "principles" are extracted or "applications" derived might appeal to theological conservatives who tend to be loyal to this vision of doctrine, but it would tend to twist the prayer's petitions into factoids. I do not want to give readers the impression that principles or even worldviews are what it is to live in Christ, or even that they are what theology is really about.

Lindbeck's second type, called "experiential-expressive," claims that our beliefs are basically expressions of something we feel at a level below human language. All our words are intrinsically limited and culture-bound attempts to give form to this elusive but universal experience of what Friedrich Schleiermacher called "absolute dependence." This concep-

---

4. George Lindbeck, *The Nature of Doctrine: Religion and Theology in a Postliberal Age* (Philadelphia: Westminster, 1984).

5. See below, "The Victory of God."

tion would make the Lord's Prayer little more than a formulaic articulation of convictions that derive from our own subjective experiences. A sign that this approach is flawed is that it gives the act of prayer much less to do than Jesus does. These petitions are demands, not feelings or attitudes. Furthermore, the Lord's Prayer does *not* sum up my experience. More often, it interrupts, criticizes, and overturns it.

Crafting chapters that begin in my own experience and culminate in the Lord's words might be popular among theological liberals who tend to be loyal to this way of living, but it would make Jesus my public relations representative, not my King. I do not want to give readers the impression that Christianity is just a name for one's mental attitude or outlook.

Lindbeck's third type sees doctrine as a "cultural-linguistic" system. It claims that what we say is what we do. Christian speech can work in every way language works. Our words of faith flow from all the ways we live and perform an unlimited variety of tasks. Some of Lindbeck's readers[6] have pointed out that these tasks of course include naming facts and putting words to experiences, which is why this third approach is both an umbrella over the first two approaches and a radical alternative to each. This conception sees the Lord's Prayer as, well, what I think it really is. Ludwig Wittgenstein said our concepts "arise out of the middle of" life.[7] So it is with this prayer's petitions. They belong at the center of this exercise, literally in the middle of each chapter.

To repeat: Each petition does not begin its chapter because prayer, like the Bible itself, does not represent the beginning of all our disciplined thinking. We *come* to prayer; or rather prayer comes to us. The Spirit finds us where we already are and transports us with Christ to the Father's throne. The petitions meet us estranged, impatient, needy, marred, hardened, harried, chastened, and resigned respectively; and the meeting reorients and even shocks us into a new world.

Each petition is not at the end of each chapter because prayer, like the Bible itself, is not merely an articulation of what we already sense. It is a radical challenge that sends us away renewed, transformed, and empow-

6. See George Hunsinger, "Postliberal Theology," in *The Cambridge Companion to Postmodern Theology,* ed. Kevin J. Vanhoozer (New York: Cambridge University Press, 2003), pp. 42-57; and Alister E. McGrath, *The Genesis of Doctrine: A Study in the Foundation of Doctrinal Criticism* (Grand Rapids: Eerdmans, 1997).

7. Ludwig Wittgenstein, *Remarks on Color,* trans. Linda L. McAlister and Margarete Schättle (Berkeley: University of California Press, 1977), p. 302.

ered. Tertullian called the Lord's Prayer "the foundation of further desires." He was saying that a community at prayer should begin with this standard text, and only then append requests of its own. That is a good strategy; I heartily recommend it. However, his point applies more broadly to prayer itself. It always finds us unprepared and somehow leaves us readied to receive and use what we had asked for.

To bifurcate each chapter with the prayer at its heart rings true to Scripture, true to liturgy, true to theology, and true to life. In theology a longstanding axiom holds that "the law of prayer is the law of belief" *(lex orandi lex credendi)*. We believe and teach according to the way we pray. Our assumptions inevitably inform our interpretation of the Lord's petitions, but ultimately the Lord's words restructure our theological, spiritual, and practical agenda. Each phrase determines the setting, the doctrines, and the lessons of its chapter. In Matthew the Lord's Prayer comes in the middle of the Sermon on the Mount. In Luke it is in an apparently random spot in the travel narrative between Jesus' Transfiguration and his triumphal entry. In traditional Sunday services it is almost always used before or after the breaking of Eucharistic bread, in daily services between the creed and the concluding prayers. (That makes it more of a seventh-inning stretch than a halftime, but it is still in the middle.)

The consistent difference between each chapter's first and second halves led me to the hypothesis that *prayer is transfiguring.* The Transfiguration is a figure for the Lord's Prayer in our lives.[8] Recall the scene in Luke 9:28-36: Jesus takes his disciples up the high mountain to pray, but they sleep. They awaken not to news of a change of plan, but to the plan's unveiling in true grandeur. Like Peter, James, and John, we too are weary from our efforts to keep up and our struggles to understand. He leads us up to pray. We awaken to see him as the Father does. The prayer rouses us with the only perspective in which our concerns are worth raising and leaves us humbly silenced, listening to him, and newly ready (if still a little reluctant) to descend and get on with our work.

As I prayed, investigated, and reflected upon each phrase in the Lord's Prayer, specific concerns in my life surfaced that it turned out to have been addressing. Jesus' words overturned these old concerns and supplied new ones by unveiling their true context: his Kingdom and righteousness. Each chapter uncovered a dilemma or question that was haunting me, not just

---

8. See below, Epilogue, "You Can Say That Again."

in my own field but more often in the intersections where life is more confusing and less predictable. It left me having learned something homely yet revolutionary, not just about that one area of concern but about the whole sweep of salvation still unfolding in our midst. Tertullian and Gregory of Nyssa and Albert Schweitzer can harmonize because the eschatological *is* the theological, *and* the spiritual, *and* the practical — *and* the anthropological, political, economic, sociological, biological, psychological, and so on. These chapters' individual lessons coalesced into a broader, more fundamental rediscovery of what Karl Barth called "the strange new world within the Bible,"[9] which has turned out to be my world all along. The pattern of transfiguring prayer fits the theological dogma that describes our Triune God, *and* the biblical economy of salvation in which we find the prayer, *and* the roles Jesus gave his disciples in his mission to reconcile all things through the blood of his cross.

As tempting as it is to offer a conclusion on "what I have learned from the Lord's Prayer," it would miss the point. If anything, I have learned that prayer is never finished. There can be no last word, because a prayer is only one moment in an eternal conversation. Once the point is fully grasped, it is time to move on. So the final chapter of this book, "Amen," simply gathers several sermons delivered over the span of this project that I consider fruit of the project as a whole. Sermons are incomplete, ephemeral, and local by nature. They too are moments in a conversation. That makes them fitting testimony to answered prayers. I offer them to confirm or disconfirm that this whole thing has worked and to display the new perspective my living, praying, reading, and thinking has given me.

These exercises — an intentionally modest word — were just an experiment to show whether and how faithful prayer brings integrity to our complex, incoherent, and inconsistent lives, redeeming our unholy acts and ordering our holy acts into a living sacrifice of praise. My analytical work is short on secondary sources but suffused with Scripture and fixed on the life, death, and resurrection of Jesus.[10] My hope and experience has been that the two halves of each chapter, and the bookends of the introduction and epilogue, would differ from one another like the "before" and

9. Karl Barth, "The Strange New World within the Bible," in *The Word of God and the Word of Man* (New York: Harper, 1957).

10. For those who would like a rationale for this approach I recommend John O'Keefe and R. R. Reno, *Sanctified Vision* (Baltimore: Johns Hopkins University Press, 2005).

"after" pictures of an advertisement and so testify to the power of the unseen process in the middle. If that has truly happened, I will consider my hypothesis confirmed.

Shortcomings I Am Not Sorry For

My approach committed me to a measure of awkwardness. I make no apologies when a chapter begins messily or in a place that seems to have little to do with prior chapters. My life is complicated, compartmentalized, and disorganized. It is not a hard life, but it is a fragmented one. I teach at a Christian liberal arts college where we proclaim the coherence of all things in Jesus Christ, but our departments think very differently and our bookshelves are full of books that want little to do with one another. My desk is cluttered and my thoughts are scattered. On a typical day there are minor crises at home, a smattering of e-mails waiting for me in my inbox, a pile of leftover unanswered ones, stacks of tasks left undone from yesterday (okay, last month), iTunes on my stereo, daunting parental challenges, a barrage of advertising, the constant lure of Internet weblogs and news sites, friends and family in need, classes and Bible studies to prepare, and a growing pile of books I wish I had time to read. This is the typical state I am in when God meets me; this is the chaos that faces the Holy Spirit who blesses me with his mysterious intercession. What you see is what he gets. Can the Lord's Prayer bring order to it? Is the risen Jesus really Lord of all this mess, or are we just thinking wishfully? Begging him to pull it all together and chronicling the results is one way to see.

I also make no apologies if the transition in the middle of a chapter is jarring. God is surprising. In fact, God is downright shocking. Encounters with God tend to be abrupt. Think of Abraham's visitors at Mamre, Moses' burning bush, the visions that sweep Isaiah and Daniel into the heavenly throne room, Mary's angelic visitation, the stranger who comes to John the Baptizer, and the power that leaves Simon the fisherman terrified of his sinfulness. God often breaks into our worlds like a Fellini character who walks suddenly into the foreground of a long shot. So it is also with prayer. One moment we are scurrying through the things that fill our day. Then we utter "Our Father" — and suddenly we are in the Spirit, like John the Prophet on the isle of Patmos looking on as Jesus removes the veil from his whole world.

Too extravagant a comparison? Then consider a more mundane metaphor: the moment you first hear the phone ring. You stop what you are doing (unless it is your cell phone ringing during class!), cut off whatever conversations are in progress as politely as possible, pick up the receiver, and enter a whole different space. From the first sound of the voice at the other end, you begin to learn whether a loved one got home all right, a faraway friend was thinking of you, an associate needs something, the thing you had been dreading is true after all, or your number just came up again on a telemarketer's screen. All the while your prior life hangs in suspension.

Such interruptions break into our lives so many times every day that we think nothing of them. Many prayers come and go as unremarkably as daily phone calls. Yet there are calls I will always remember, right down to the tone of the callers' voices: news of my father's sudden death, last-minute news of a scholarship, a scare only hours after my daughter's birth, and learning of the attacks on September 11. Sometimes I think Luke's story of the importunate friend at midnight (11:5-10) has it backwards: *God* is the persistent and unwelcome solicitor knocking at my door, and *I* am the one hiding in the bedroom. Of course prayer is jarring! Sometimes it leaves us terrified and sickened like the prophet Daniel, sometimes wildly rejoicing like the heavenly host, sometimes dumbstruck like Zechariah the priest. (I suppose it jars in the heavenly realms too.) Usually we are unmoved and apparently unaffected, resuming our normal lives as if nothing had just happened; yet it was still an interruption.

Here lies a third sense of the subtitle: we "live through" the Lord's Prayer in the sense that, say, America lived through the Great Depression. We struggle to survive the challenges it hands us: adoption, cosmic sanctification, disorienting immigration, cruciform discipleship, sometimes severe providence, costly forgiveness, and often disastrous deliverance. When I actually ponder what it is we are asking for, it becomes clear that this may be a mission for the weary and heavy laden, but it is not for the faint of heart.

Yet it is here that we can glimpse a paradoxical fourth sense of the subtitle: we also "live through" the Lord's Prayer as, say, America lived through the genius of James Madison and the Constitution's other framers. We survive by mean of the same challenges of this prayer that seem so threatening. Its petitions supply the struggles that save us by making us the truly human, truly personal people God intends us to be.

Consider Sunday mornings at the Work home. We have never been *early* to church, even when we attended nine o'clock worship at a Los Angeles church so packed that there were no parking spaces or Sunday school spots left well before the service started. My wife Kim and I would pull our sluggish children out of bed, hurry them past the dresser and the bathroom, and shove them into our minivan in order to get one of the scarce parking spaces within a block of the campus. The kids were surprised when we *weren't* doing seventy-five on the freeway offramp while they tied their shoes and munched the Eggo waffles that passed for breakfast. After parking, making nametags for the kids, and herding them into their different places we would enter the sanctuary. There, like the first blast of cold air from an office building on a hot day, the presence of the risen Christ would hit us. *Ahhhh!*

We only stay oriented through such transitions because we have learned to take the shock for granted. *Of course* God hears us. *Of course* he is here receiving our praise. *Of course* his Word is sharp and powerful. *Of course* this is his body and blood. It always is. Jesus is the same yesterday, today, and forever (Heb. 13:8).

This acclimation is not a bad thing. In fact, acclimation to God is the result of a life of ceaseless prayer, and the will of God for our perfect sanctification (1 Thess. 5:16-24). But it must be a certain kind of acclimation. The old must be relocated in the new, not the other way around. We must become familiar with the world of the prayer rather than domesticating the prayer to our world.

Over and over in this book, prayer created space that is eschatological. This is why theological and ethical readings of the Lord's Prayer ought not to conflict with our academic readings. The shift that goes on between the hubbub of common life and the petitions of common prayer is a move from absence to presence, from promise to fulfillment, from there to here, from then to now. In his lovely little book on the Lord's Prayer N. T. Wright says,

> Jesus didn't come simply to offer a new pattern, or even a new depth, of spirituality. Spiritual depth and renewal come, as and when they come, as part of the larger package. But that package itself is about being delivered from evil; about return from exile; about having enough bread; about God's kingdom coming on earth as it is in heaven. It's the Advent-package. Jesus was taking the enormous risk of saying that this package was coming about through his

own work. All of that is contained in the word "Father," used in this way, within this prayer.[11]

The Lord's Prayer begs for eternal salvation to come, *here, now.* As an artifact of authentic Christian life, it fuses present things, the last things, and the first things. It joins heaven and earth into a community that realizes the purposes of both. The fissure between each chapter's two halves is an eschatological earthquake. Calling on God to sanctify his name judges our witting and unwitting blasphemies. Pleading for our daily bread transforms the everyday economics of our earning, saving, and spending. Begging for a respite from temptation strips us of the vanities we rely on for our lives' meaning. Repeating these words herds us back behind the enfleshed Word and around his indwelling Spirit. By all means, let us become acclimated to that!

Finally, I make no apologies if the end of each chapter is unsatisfying. No one performance of the Lord's Prayer can be comprehensive. This text is open-ended as long as its Lord is still working through it. It is sometimes said that there is little original in the Lord's Prayer, and that practically all of it could be cribbed from Jewish sources.[12] Some see it as a lengthened Kaddish,[13] others a shortened Amidah. Yet even if it *is* all rehashed, Jesus' life and mission give it a new location and a definitive interpretation in both the gospels and our lives. Whenever we use the Lord's Prayer into a new context, including that of my own life between 2002 and 2005, the old becomes new. Let whatever has happened here be a challenge for readers and writer alike to return to it to obtain something more, infinitely more, than what is on these pages.

Besides, it is wrong to expect the Lord's Prayer simply to bring order to our willy-nilly lives. Our disruptive God might just as often use it to bring *disorder* to the habits of vice I have worked meticulously into "my Christian life." If disorientation results as the Holy Spirit uproots and plows before replanting, then there is no use apologizing for that either. Holy disruptions might leave us right where Luke's hearers are: suspicious that his power is bogus, worried that his mighty works are demonic, appreciative

---

11. N. T. Wright, *The Lord and His Prayer* (Grand Rapids: Eerdmans, 1996), p. 17.

12. Israel Abrahams, *Studies in Pharisaism and the Gospels* (Jersey City: Ktav, 1967), pp. 98-99.

13. See below, "Interlude."

for all the wrong reasons (Luke 11:14-28), but aroused and unsettled. In other words, finally fallow for the good news.

"Messy, jarring, unsatisfying" — what a book review that would be! Yet isn't it how prayer works? Doesn't it describe the lives of the prophets, apostles, and disciples?

I have a final non-apology to offer for these words. As I have already said, I am not very good at all this. Prayer takes practice. Following Jesus is both harder and easier than anyone expects at the outset. Fatigue, frustration, and dissatisfaction are to be expected, if not celebrated. They show we have room to grow. Perhaps there is a fifth sense of the subtitle to ponder here: we "live through" the Lord's Prayer in the sense that we endure it, as America lived through the unlamented seventies. We put up with the prayer's deadening familiarity and its permanent strangeness, with the uninspired group chanting that we fall into when it comes up in church, with all it seems to ignore about our ever-changing lives and our ever-mysterious Lord, and with all that never seems to happen no matter how many times we say it.

That does not seem like a very respectful way for a theologian, let alone a disciple, to talk. Yet there is a restlessness to this sense of "living through" that deserves respect. It drives us onward in the hope of something better, something more promising (or promised) than we already have. As you read, do you find yourself thinking "I can do better than this"? Then do it! I will consider these exercises in prayer and reflection a smashing success if they drive dissatisfied readers to exercises of their own, or at least to suit up and work out alongside me. Living through the Lord's Prayer is a job for everyone.

Let us pray. . . .

PART I

THE FIRST TABLET

CHAPTER 1

The Character of God

When you draw near to a town to fight against it, offer it terms of peace. If it accepts your terms of peace and surrenders to you, then all the people in it shall serve you at forced labor. If it does not submit to you peacefully, but makes war against you, then you shall besiege it; and when YHWH your God gives it into your hand, you shall put all its males to the sword. You may, however, take as your booty the women, the children, livestock, and everything else in the town — all its spoil. You may enjoy the spoil of your enemies, which YHWH your God has given you. Thus you shall treat all the towns that are very far from you, which are not towns of the nations here. But as for the towns of the these peoples that YHWH your God is giving you as an inheritance, you must not let anything that breathes remain alive.

Deuteronomy 20:10-16[1]

God Made Strange

September 11, 2001, caught me off guard.

To know how and why, it helps to know my background. I came to theology as an evangelical Protestant. Evangelicalism is a theological tradition

---

1. Here and elsewhere when I quote Scripture, I will use various translations but substitute "YHWH" for "the LORD," the more familiar way of rendering the Divine Name.

3

that develops largely through strenuous debates that erupt every decade or so. You can tell when an evangelical came to theological maturity by asking what battle was theologically formative: biblical inerrancy (1950s and 1960s), charismatic gifts (1970s), women's ordination (1980s), postmodernism (1990s), divine foreknowledge (2000), or homosexuality (today).[2] These and other issues leave their marks on evangelicals. We bear the scars and the loyalties of the age-old Reformed controversies over predestination, the constellation of Wesleyan accounts of sanctification, the ever-shifting maze of Adventist and Dispensational timelines of the future, the fallout from the fundamentalist-modernist controversy, and the crusades against evolution (currently reenacting the Children's Crusade, with about the same measure of success). To be a competent evangelical theologian demands that one be up on the issues at the heart of the evangelical zeitgeist.

Going with the theological flow is natural and nothing to be ashamed of. Yet it failed to address a grave weakness in my formation. Get me outside the familiar and I can be like a commuter who takes the wrong exit and ends up lost in her own town, or a tour guide disoriented by a question in the middle of his monologue. And evangelicalism failed really to familiarize me with many aspects of the faith. I love to teach the doctrines that are less controversial, less familiar, and less interesting to fellow evangelicals — Trinity, Incarnation, the church, and so on — in part because my students find them so shocking. These issues are newer to them than the old shibboleths. They remain more foreign to the people who worship next to me in church, and much more remote from their concerns. And every once in a while a question comes along that reminds me that their place in my own theological world is still precarious.

Just such a question arose recently: *What is the character of the God we worship?*

What jolted me with that question, and what has shaken my faith more than any other event in the past ten years, was a group of people who boarded airplanes full of hundreds of innocent travelers, "compassionately" slit the throats of the crew, and piloted those planes into skyscrapers filling with tens of thousands of workers from all nations and creeds and social circles. As they took the lives of these thousands of infidels, they shouted, "God is great!" and prepared for the paradise awaiting them.

---

2. A war memorial for the courageous is Gregory A. Boyd and Paul R. Eddy, *Across the Spectrum: Understanding Issues in Evangelical Theology* (Grand Rapids: Baker, 2002).

Lost in My Own Faith

As a student in philosophy I had of course weighed traditional and contemporary arguments for or against the existence of God. I had debated as an Arminian and a Calvinist whether God is just or whether justice is divine. I had contemplated the problem of evil. What I had never done was seriously entertain the question of whether the author of our universe could approve of *this* atrocity, this sickening metaphor of passenger jets and business offices turned into missiles and targets.

It was not that the answer had been obvious; it was that the question had not been pressed. The western world of September 10, 2001, was no longer really bothered by the question of whether God would sanction such horrors as the Holocaust or the Armenian Genocide. It was a settled issue. Fascists and ideologues from the century just banished, medievals who lived in a different world, tribalists in the Balkans or Rwanda whose theologies were just a cover for hatred, and a few crazies in Adventist splinter groups and militias on the fringes of the old American frontier might have believed such things. But they were obviously disturbed and, at any rate, they were marginal.

When the unimagined becomes real, worlds rise and fall. My old theological world collapsed not long after the Twin Towers did. I found myself lost in my own faith.

American society rapidly found its answers to September 11's questions. The novelist Tom Wolfe reports that the day barely registers in the consciousness of today's college students. Things have not gone so smoothly for me. Once events made the question thinkable, the answer turned out to be less obvious than I thought it would be. Osama bin Laden's flair for imagery resonates with images from Scripture. Disasters, psalms that curse, gruesome prophecies, ritual slaughters of whole towns, and apocalyptic carnage are all part of the story we Christians have told all along. My ways of subliminally smoothing them out no longer worked. The Word of God is now newly uncomfortable for me to read. When I read of Canaan and Assyria I think of smoking skylines in New York and Washington. And why shouldn't I? It is not so hard to imagine finding this text rather than a Qur'an in Muhammad Atta's luggage:

> The great day of YHWH is near,
>   near and hastening fast;

the sound of the day of YHWH is bitter,
　the warrior cries aloud there.
That day will be a day of wrath,
　a day of distress and anguish,
a day of ruin and devastation,
　a day of darkness and gloom,
a day of clouds and thick darkness,
　a day of trumpet blast and battle cry
against the fortified cities
　and against the lofty battlements.
I will bring such distress upon people
　that they shall walk like the blind;
　because they have sinned against YHWH,
their blood shall be poured out like dust,
　and their flesh like dung.
Neither their silver nor their gold
　will be able to save them
　on the day of YHWH's wrath;
in the fire of his passion the whole earth shall be consumed;
for a full, a terrible end
　he will make of all the inhabitants of the earth.

(Zeph. 1:14-18)

I can already hear objections from my fellow Christians. "But it is a judgment on the prophet's own people, not on other nations!" True, God's judgment in these verses is upon Judah and Jerusalem (Zeph. 1:4). Yet the passages before and after extend the warning to all the earth, both generally (Zeph. 1:2-3) and specifically (Zeph. 2). "But that was back in Old Testament times! Those kinds of sentiments no longer apply today." Well, they do to the writer of Revelation 14:5, who uses Zephaniah 3:13 to describe those who remain righteous and loyal to Jesus in times of tribulation. They do to the writer of the Hebrews, who echoes Zephaniah 1:18 in Hebrews 10:27, and to Paul, who echoes Zephaniah 1:14-15 in Romans 2:5. The God of Christian faith has not taken back these dreadful words. It is still a fearful thing to fall into his hands.

The Qur'an has similar promises for those who deny the God of Muslim faith — a category that a considerable share of Muslims think includes Christians like me.

For them will be cut out a garment of fire: over their heads will be poured out boiling water. With it will be scalded what is within their bodies, as well as their skins. In addition there will be maces of iron to punish them. Every time they wish to get away therefrom, from anguish, they will be forced back therein, and it will be said, "Taste you the penalty of burning!" (Qur'an 22:19-22; cf. 22:17)

Becoming acquainted with the Wahhabi Islam that has been taking over centers of Muslim power in the past fifty years has been a revolting and discouraging experience. In some of the most prominent mosques of the Middle East, Friday *khutba* prayers regularly end with calls for God to avenge Islam by destroying Americans, Christians, and especially Jews. This example, televised from the grand mosque at Sanaa, Yemen, is illustrative:

O God, deal with Jews and their supporters and Christians and their supporters and lackeys. O God, shake the land under their feet, instill fear in their hearts, and freeze the blood in their veins. O God, count them one by one, kill them all, and don't leave anyone.[3]

My ancestral religion of liberal Protestantism prepared me for God actually to exist, but not for God to be my enemy. One day, after reading a whole series of these Friday invocations, I decided that I would proudly go to hell rather than submit to such a tyrant. I have no interest in kneeling to the God of Wahhabi Islam, even to save my own skin. I am his moral superior.

But there's the rub: Doesn't the God of biblical faith bear a rather uncomfortable resemblance?

For me this is a new thought. My American culture sees God as a kindred spirit, a soulmate in whom fellow Americans find affirmation of life's comforts and refuge from life's troubles. "The American finds God in herself or himself," Harold Bloom claims, "but only after finding the freedom to know God by experiencing a total inward solitude."[4] This image of a fundamentally friendly God — Bloom calls it "Gnostic" — has naturally influenced my own theology. Discovering that millions of Muslims — per-

---

3. Friday, 2 August, sermon: "O God, deal with Jews and their supporters and Christians and their supporters," http://www.imra.org.il/story.php3?id=13093.

4. Harold Bloom, *The American Religion: The Emergence of the Post-Christian Nation* (New York: Simon and Schuster, 1992), p. 32.

haps ten to fifteen percent of the Muslim world by some estimates — would root for al-Qaeda's God in ways that echo passages from my own Scriptures has been one of the most spiritually shaking events of my life. It has made my familiar God seem like a stranger.

Everyone doubts, but everyone doubts differently. This is the shape my doubt took in the two years after September 11. What if God is not humanity's fond dream but its recurring nightmare? I am not worried that militant Islamists might be right; I am worried that they might be biblical. I am worried that the God of biblical faith might really be like their God rather than the sentimentalized deity of the western Church.

That would suggest a bleak future for the world. For a while, atheists assured themselves that the secularization of the west was both irreversible and irresistibly contagious, and liberals foresaw a world of peacefully coexisting religions tamed by a common humanism. But those futures are looking more and more unlikely. Samuel Huntington posits that America is going through another spiritual Great Awakening.[5] Both Islam and Christianity are returning to Europe through immigration from former colonies. Philip Jenkins's *The Next Christendom*[6] has chronicled the growth of a confident Christianity alongside resurgent Islam in the southern hemisphere. The worlds of the Bible and the Qur'an are gaining more and more inhabitants, and Jenkins foresees a violent future along the fault lines between their communities. Jihad and crusade — or at least prayers for them — look like persistent features of humanity's future. We may never be rid of this vengeful God.

A Litany of Complaints

None of this is really new. Complaints, laments, and debates over God's character have been accumulating ever since people started calling on the God of Israel. Why do evil people prosper so? How long must the oppressed wait for deliverance from their sufferings? Has God abandoned us? Is there any respite from his righteous anger? What kind of God lies behind such a state of affairs? Is he just a mirage?

5. Samuel P. Huntington, *Who We Are: The Challenges to America's National Identity* (New York: Simon & Schuster, 2004).

6. Philip Jenkins, *The Next Christendom* (New York: Oxford University Press, 2002).

God's true believers have forever been hushing up these questions or trying to dispatch them with facile answers. Their loyalty stands in ironic contrast to the Bible itself, which raises similar objections at least as starkly and insistently as the average modern skeptic. The Bible's self-criticism is particularly acute in the place one might least expect to find it: the Psalter that serves as the church's oldest and most official hymnal. Consider these opening lines from a few of its prayers:

> Be gracious to me, O YHWH, for I am languishing;
>   O YHWH, heal me, for my bones are shaking with terror.
> My soul also is struck with terror,
>   while you, O YHWH — how long?
>
> (Ps. 6:2-3)

> Why, O YHWH, do you stand far off?
>   Why do you hide yourself in times of trouble?
>
> (Ps. 10:1)

> Help, O YHWH, for there is no longer anyone who is godly;
>   the faithful have disappeared from humankind.
>
> (Ps. 12:1)

> How long, O YHWH? Will you forget me forever?
>   How long will you hide your face from me?
> How long must I bear pain in my soul,
>   and have sorrow in my heart all day long?
> How long shall my enemy be exalted over me?
>
> (Ps. 13:1-2)

> My God, my God, why have you forsaken me?
>   Why are you so far from helping me, from the words
>   of my groaning?
> O my God, I cry by day, but you do not answer;
>   and by night, but find no rest.
>
> (Ps. 22:1-2)

> O YHWH, do not rebuke me in your anger,
>   or discipline me in your wrath.

9

For your arrows have sunk into me,
    and your hand has come down on me.

(Ps. 38:1)

Vindicate me, O God, and defend my cause
    against an ungodly people;
from those who are deceitful and unjust
    deliver me!
For you are the God in whom I take refuge;
    why have you cast me off?
Why must I walk about mournfully
    because of the oppression of the enemy?

(Ps. 43:1-2)

O God, you have rejected us, broken our defenses;
    you have been angry; now restore us!
You have caused the land to quake; you have torn it open;
    repair the cracks in it, for it is tottering.
You have made your people suffer hard things;
    you have given us wine to drink that made us reel.

(Ps. 60:1-3)

Save me, O God,
    for the waters have come up to my neck.
I sink in deep mire,
    where there is no foothold;
I have come into deep waters,
    and the flood sweeps over me.
I am weary with my crying;
    my throat is parched.
My eyes grow dim with waiting for my God.

(Ps. 69:1-3)

O God, why do you cast us off forever?
Why does your anger smoke against the sheep of your pasture?

(Ps. 74:1)

I cry aloud to God,
    aloud to God, that he may hear me.

10

In the day of my trouble I seek the Lord;
    in the night my hand is stretched out without wearying;
    my soul refuses to be comforted.
I think of God, and I moan;
    I meditate, and my spirit faints.

                                                        (Ps. 77:1-3)

O God, the nations have come into your inheritance;
    they have defiled your holy temple;
    they have laid Jerusalem in ruins.
They have given the bodies of your servants
    to the birds of the air for food,
    the flesh of your faithful to the wild animals of the earth.
They have poured out their blood like water
    all around Jerusalem,
    and there was no one to bury them.
We have become a taunt to our neighbors,
    mocked and derided by those around us.
How long, O YHWH? Will you be angry forever?

                                                        (Ps. 79:1-5)

O YHWH, you God of vengeance,
    you God of vengeance, shine forth!
Rise up, O judge of the earth;
    give to the proud what they deserve!
O YHWH, how long shall the wicked,
    how long shall the wicked exult?

                                                        (Ps. 94:1-3)

Do not be silent, O God of my praise.
For wicked and deceitful mouths are opened against me,
    speaking against me with lying tongues.
They beset me with words of hate,
    and attack me without cause.
In return for my love they accuse me,
    even while I make prayer for them.
So they reward me evil for good,
    and hatred for my love.

                                                        (Ps. 109:1-5)

11

Had enough already? Then let's not go on to read Psalms 3:1; 14:1; 28:1; 36:1; 53:1; 55:1-2; 56:1-2; 59:1-2; 64:1-6; 70:1-3; 73:1-14; 83:1-8; all of 88; all of 90; 103:1-11; all of 120; all of 137; 140:1-11; all of 142; and all of 143. It seems the faithful have a chronic problem trusting the one they trust.

These cries have gone up every day for millennia. They come especially from Christians who pray the Daily Office. Anglicans cycle through the Psalms every seven weeks. Eastern Orthodox monks do it weekly. That is a lot of complaining.

Yes, but is it fair to choose only opening lines? Don't these psalms *end* happily? Not all the time — not by a long shot. Sometimes their hope sounds forced and tacked on. Sometimes it is tinged with desperation. Sometimes it is entirely absent. Consider the following *closing* lines:

On every side the wicked prowl,
> as vileness is exalted among humankind.

> > > > (Ps. 12:8)

May integrity and uprightness preserve me,
> for I wait for you.
Redeem Israel, O God,
> out of all its troubles.

> > > > (Ps. 25:21-22)

Do not forsake me, O YHWH;
> O my God, do not be far from me;
make haste to help me,
> O Lord, my salvation.

> > > > (Ps. 38:22)

Turn your gaze away from me, that I may smile again,
> before I depart and am no more.

> > > > (Ps. 39:13)

I say to God, my rock,
> "Why have you forgotten me?
Why must I walk about mournfully
> because the enemy oppresses me?"
As with a deadly wound in my body,

my adversaries taunt me,
while they say to me continually,
    "Where is your God?"
Why are you cast down, O my soul,
    and why are you disquieted within me?
Hope in God; for I shall again praise him,
    my help and my God.

(Ps. 42:9-11)

Rouse yourself! Why do you sleep, O Lord?
    Awake, do not cast us off forever!
Why do you hide your face?
    Why do you forget our affliction and oppression?
For we sink down to the dust;
    our bodies cling to the ground.
Rise up, come to our help.
    Redeem us for the sake of your steadfast love.

(Ps. 44:23-26)

Rise up, O God, plead your cause;
    remember how the impious scoff at you all day long.
Do not forget the clamor of your foes,
    the uproar of your adversaries that goes up continually.

(Ps. 74:22-23)

You have caused friend and neighbor to shun me;
    my companions are in darkness.

(Ps. 88:18)

Have mercy upon us, O YHWH, have mercy upon us,
    for we have had more than enough of contempt.
Our soul has had more than its fill
    of the scorn of those who are at ease,
    of the contempt of the proud.

(Ps. 123:3-4)

O daughter Babylon, you devastator!
    Happy shall they be who pay you back

13

what you have done to us!
Happy shall they be who take your little ones
    and dash them against the rock!

(Ps. 137:8-9)

How many American evangelical songwriters have the courage to write material like this? We are too optimistic for our own Bible. Far from not grieving the Holy Spirit, we refuse to let the Holy Spirit grieve us.

Of course, alongside these miserable passages are many more that extol God's goodness, compassion, mercy, providence, and deliverance. In my circles these are far better known and more often read. So the debate rages — even in God's own churches, even in the midst of worship, even in the pages of Scripture: What is the character of God? What does God want from us? When, if ever, will deliverance come? Is God's vengeance something we suffer, we forsake, or we demand? Are there ever answers, or only the same questions? Is YHWH really a figure in whom we should be putting our trust?

A Troubled Nonbeliever

As if the pressure from September 11 were not high enough, God sent someone into my life to intensify it. I keep an online journal, called a weblog ("blog" for short). In 2002 my writings captured the attention of a reader who e-mailed me. That message initiated a friendship with a fellow blogger whose pen name is Camassia. A self-described "troubled nonbeliever" at first, she has been reading and writing about the Christian faith, attending church, and dialoguing online with Catholics, varieties of Protestants, and assorted non-Christians.

A recurring theme in our exchanges has been the trustworthiness of God. Why call God good when he seems to refuse to save everyone he could? Do Scripture's divine killing sprees and hell's eternal apartheid of the damned reveal a cruel streak? Camassia was intellectually attracted to the Zoroastrian and Manichaean approach of positing two causes of everything — one good and the other evil — rather than one originator, governor, and redeemer of all things. With her secular upbringing and her compassionate heart, she is not necessarily loyal to theism, nor is she easily persuaded by Christians' usual claims that sin and suffering began to afflict

God's good creation through the good creatures themselves. Yet she keeps circling around Christianity. She reminds me of the pre-Christian Augustine: she wants to know the truth, and is open to believing; but first she wants to be convinced that the God of Jesus Christ warrants the total trust he demands. She knows a relationship with him is not one to take lightly. She wants her own soul as well as her loved ones to be safe, and she wants her witness to others to be genuine. She is not yet persuaded that Jesus is the best way to meet these needs, let alone the only one; she is unsure that her soul would be entirely safe with him, let alone his worshippers.

My months of blogging along with Camassia, our e-mail exchanges, our conversations and prayers after church, our participation in a weekly "Alpha" course for people interested in learning more about the Christian faith, and her friendship with me and with other Christians have always dragged us back to this place. Knowing that God exists will not solve her problem; she also wants assurance of God's good character. And as I have fumbled around making theological arguments and facilitating relationships and suggesting readings like a bewildered tour guide, I have discovered my limitations as a teacher of the Christian faith. Camassia is not like the hundreds of students I have taught at Christian college and seminary. Most of those students are believers whose convictions I am generally reinforcing in an idyllic suburban college setting. She is a skeptic — not a hardened one but a firm one — who demands an answer I have not yet managed to offer. If God became a stranger to me, God remains a stranger to her.

I have the feeling that if September 11 were not making God seem strange to me too, I would be better at introducing these two strangers. Until I refresh my familiarity with the God I already know, I will struggle to help others know him too. So, for me, for Camassia, and for any who wonder as they sing the Bible's psalms of triumph and lament, it is time to ask afresh, "Who *is* this king of glory?" (Ps. 24:10). Who indeed?

"Our Father in Heaven"

Praying Along

The psalm I have just cited is a clue to where we will find the right answer to our question. Christopher Cocksworth notes that it celebrates Israel's God in a threefold way:

God is the creator who has fashioned the whole cosmos [cf. Ps. 24:1-2]; the redeemer who has defeated all that sets itself against his purposes [24:3-6]; the indweller, who resides with his people and makes them holy [24:7-10]. . . . When YHWH, the God of Israel, is identified as the one divine creator, redeemer and indweller, this God and this God alone should be worshipped and the way of this God, and his way alone, followed.[7]

Christian faith obeys a similar logic by laying down this rule:

Every good answer to every question about God's character
appeals to God as Triune.

A sentence like that cries out for qualification. First, we were taught in school to avoid blanket claims and adjectives like "every." Surely there are exceptions to the rule, right? Second, to answer such a clear and simple question with such a mysterious and complicated doctrine guarantees that eyes will glaze over, expressions will frown in confusion, and heads will separate from hearts. The original disciples got along without a doctrine of the Trinity, so we can too, right?

Wrong, and wrong. My claim is no overstatement; it is an axiom of Christian faith. It is a theological rule the church has followed so we will not forget nor distort what we know of God in Jesus Christ, and so our knowledge of God in Jesus Christ will inform everything else we know and want to know better. Trinitarianism makes explicit the whole structure of Christian thought, which since its beginning has imitated and radicalized "the three structures of the Jewish understanding of God" in light of Jesus Christ.[8] It is neither a generalization nor a speculative exercise. It is our way to honor Christ's memory and follow in his footsteps:

All things have been handed over to me by my Father; and no one knows the Son except the Father, and no one knows the Father except the Son and anyone to whom the Son chooses to reveal him.
　　Come to me, all you that are weary and are carrying heavy burdens, and I will give you rest. Take my yoke upon you, and learn

7. Christopher Cocksworth, *Holy, Holy, Holy: Worshipping the Trinitarian God* (London: Darton, Longman and Todd, 1997), pp. 125-26.
8. Cocksworth, *Holy, Holy, Holy,* p. 125.

from me; for I am gentle and humble in heart, and you will find rest for your souls. For my yoke is easy, and my burden is light. (Matt. 11:27-30)

Look again at that passage. This is not the obscure jargon of scholasticism, nor even the dense rabbinical exegesis of Paul, nor even the enigmatic language of John (wonderful as they all are). This is a saying of Jesus, which comes from the same down-to-earth gospel that contains the Sermon on the Mount, the Trinitarian baptismal formula — and the Lord's Prayer. The doctrine of the Trinity is realistic. It lightens our burden and eases our path. It shows rest for the soul.

You see, the doctrine of the Trinity reminds us that God is not far off when we pray, "Our Father in heaven." Our worries about God are not attacks on a foe or a victim. Our complaints are not bitter invectives against a tyrant. Our praises are not ingratiating words to appease a vainglorious deity. Our petitions are not meek and tentative requests before some fearful and arbitrary power. Nor are we alone when we address our Lord. So, as we say in church, "we are bold to pray" them. Immanuel Kant dared us to know. The church does something more courageous still: it dares us to pray.

All this is because of Jesus Christ. Since he is one of us, and since he is the only Son of the Father, praying these words puts us on both common and holy ground. The Messiah has made us insiders.

Those who learn this find it a breakthrough. It is a pity that so few do. In my experience, many — especially theological conservatives — are familiar with the Lord's Prayer as something believers learned *from the Lord Jesus.* Many others — especially theological liberals — are familiar with the Lord's Prayer as something believers pray *along with our brother Jesus.* Surprisingly few know them as words believers pray *along with the Lord Jesus.*

Such "conservatives" (I am overgeneralizing, but not as much as I wish) are making the common mistake of separating the Father's relationship to Jesus from the Father's relationship to us. If the two relationships were unrelated, then we would mean something else by "our Father" than Jesus meant by "my Father." We would pray the Lord's Prayer, but the Lord would not. Christ would just be a teacher of the prayer, not an exemplar.

At first, this "conservatism" makes sense: it seems odd for a divine and sinless Christ to be praying, "forgive us our sins . . . lead us not into temptation . . . yours is the kingdom, the power, and the glory." But if that were the case, then the "conservative" Jesus would have come and gone without changing much of anything. God's relationship to us would be no more than a Creator's relationship with his creatures. Still aloof from his fellow human beings, the Son would not truly be one of us, not *Emmanuel*, not God *with us* (Matt. 1:23).

On the other hand, such "liberals" (just as risky and apt an over-generalization) are making the even more common mistake of collapsing the Father's relationship to Jesus into the Father's relationship to every creature. Jesus would be both an exemplar and a teacher of prayer — a spiritual giant among us, a pioneer who leads us into a frontier like an avatar — but he would be no more than that.

At first this "liberalism" makes sense too: It respects the profound distinction Jesus makes here and elsewhere between himself and the Father who sent him. It seems right for a human and fallible Christ to be praying, "forgive us our sins . . . lead us not into temptation . . . yours is the kingdom, the power, and the glory." However, that would make God's fatherhood something generic. "Father" would be a sentimental, personal word that really meant nothing more than the technical, impersonal title "creator." This "liberal" Jesus would be no more than a prophet offering words like those of the first psalm, or the Qur'an's opening Surah for that matter:

> In the name of God, the merciful, the compassionate. Praise be to God the cherisher and sustainer of the worlds; most gracious, most merciful, master of the Day of Judgment. You we worship, and your aid we seek. Show us the straight way, the way of those on whom you have bestowed your grace, those whose portion is not wrath, and who do not go astray.[9]

Don't get me wrong: This is a fine prayer. I have been honored to pray it on occasion. But there is no compelling reason to begin it with the words, "Our Father." If that were all Jesus meant by the Lord's Prayer, then his coming would still have left everything more or less as it was before. The Son would be far away from the "Father." He would have no basis for claiming that all things have been handed over to him, or that no one but he knows the Father, or that no one but he chooses who else knows the Father too. He would not truly be *God* with us.

---

9. From *The Meaning of the Holy Quran*, trans. ʿAbdullah Yusuf ʿAli (Brentwood, Md.: Amana, 1993).

This is old and well trodden theological ground. A whole historical vocabulary has developed to describe people who have made one or more of these "conservative" and "liberal" mistakes: Ebionites, Docetists, Arians, Apollinarians, Modalists, Eutychians, and Tritheists. The names are foreign to people outside my academic guild, but the ideas are familiar. One set of ideas distances Jesus from us. The other distances Jesus from God. Other movements like Nestorianism and Oneness Pentecostalism distance Jesus' humanity from his divinity. For all their variety, these many schools of thought produce curiously similar results. All make heaven's God far away and unknowable and leave this prayer entirely in creaturely hands.

However, *if the Lord Jesus prays his prayer along with us,* then everything is new. And in fact, the Lord Jesus *does* pray his prayer along with us. His prayer in the Garden of Gethsemane — "My Father, your will be done" (Matt. 26:41) — is the same prayer we have prayed ever since: "Your will be done on earth as it is in heaven" (6:10). The heavenly and earthly authority he received from the Father is ours too as we pray, baptize, and teach in his incomparable name (28:18-20). Our boldness to pray rests on his boldness to pray with us forever. Our standing as God's children and God's standing as our Father depend entirely upon the grace not just of "the Lord" or "God" but of *the Son* (7:21-27).

Jesus' willingness to pray along with us, not just for us, is what I need to face a world of theological bigotry, indifference, and distortion. It is what I need to face a God of jealousy, power, and holiness. It is also what I need to face my own fallen self. Jesus' solidarity with both the Father and with sinners holds together a web of connections that unites heaven and earth and eternally answers the perennial questions of our faith — including questions about God's character.

The Forgotten Father

Events over the centuries have drawn theological attention toward the Son, the Holy Spirit, and humanity. These are worthy topics! Without the Son, that web of relationships would have no form. Without the Holy Spirit, it would have no strength. Without humanity, it would lack fullness. Yet all this attention has often turned us away from the Father. This is a massive oversight, for without the Father, the web would have no substance.

Unlike so many of today's theology texts, Matthew's Gospel showers attention on the Father. The Son knows and loves the Father (Matt. 11:27). The Father knows and loves the Son he sent through the gift of the Holy Spirit (3:13-17; 12:18). The Son shows and commends the Father to the world (7:21-27; 12:18-21). The Son knows and loves the Father's people, cleansing and healing them through the Spirit (12:22-32). Out of that love he calls forth laborers who have the same Spirit (10:20) and are to show the same love (9:35-38; 10:1-25). He gives them the keys to his kingdom (16:18-29) and the same freedom from tax and tribute he has with this Father (17:24-27).

Just so, the Father loves the world into which he sent the Son, sent the Spirit, and sends the Son's Spirit-empowered disciples (5:14-16). To accept the love of a disciple is to accept the love of the Father and receive a disciple's reward (10:40-42) — and even to become the Father's own kin (12:46-50) and dwell freely in his house (17:24-27).[10]

The word most common to all these passages is *love*. Love is the web itself. It is the Father's being, the Son's form, and the Spirit's strength. By grace, the self-gift of the God who is love (cf. 1 John 4:8), love is also humanity's fullness. Pay close attention in the Sermon on the Mount to the links Jesus makes among love as the Father's perfect character, love as the motive of the Creator, love as the work of the Son, and love as the force behind his disciples' mercy on all:

> You have heard that it was said, "You shall love your neighbor [Lev. 19:18] and hate your enemy [cf. Deut. 23:4-7]." But I say to you, Love your enemies and pray for those who persecute you, so that you may be children [literally 'sons'] of your Father who is in heaven; for he makes the sun rise on the evil and on the good, and sends rain on the righteous and the unrighteous. For if you love those who love you, what reward have you? Do not even the tax collectors do the same? And if you greet only your brothers and sisters, what more are you doing than others? Do not even the Gentiles do the same? Be perfect, therefore, as your heavenly Father is perfect. (Matt. 5:43-48)

---

10. Marianne Meye Thompson, *The Promise of the Father: Jesus and God in the New Testament* (Louisville: Westminster John Knox, 2000), p. 162.

Got that? *The perfection of the Father is the caring love of enemies.* Likewise, the Son's regard for the lost, the ill, the hungry, and the insignificant mirrors the Father's providence. To receive them is to receive him (18:5), for "their angels always behold the face of my Father in heaven" and "it is not the will of my Father who is in heaven that one of these little [lost] ones should perish" (18:10, 14). The face of the Father is hospitality for the very least. The Son is the glory of the Father, not his antithesis (17:5). His heart is the Father's heart.

Neither the "conservative" nor the "liberal" Jesus is capable of playing the Son's whole role in this story. Since neither is *really* Emmanuel, neither can communicate the Father's strength to a humanity weakened and divided by sin, nor share the Father's tenderness with a humanity hardened by pride.

Where does all this leave those who worry and lament and doubt? We have seen that humanity's debates over God's character are carried into the Holy Scriptures themselves, even into the sacred worship of the Psalter. In the career of Jesus Christ, the Triune God does not take sides in that debate or dismiss it, but embraces and assimilates the entire debate. This happens most profoundly in the last week of Jesus' life. As readers of Matthew, let us watch it unfold.

In his triumphal entry into Jerusalem, Jesus approaches the city as the crowds quote from the "Egyptian Hallel" of Psalms 113 to 118, a collection that is traditionally sung at Passover. "Blessed is the one who comes in the name of the Lord!" they cry (Ps. 118:26 in Matt. 21:9). They are announcing that the time of fulfillment has arrived at last. Jesus agrees, declaring that this Passover is Israel's moment of judgment and deliverance (cf. Ps. 118:26 in Matt. 23:37–24:2). Here and at the Temple, Jesus even allows his admirers to address their hosannas not to YHWH as in the Psalter but to him, "the Son of David" (Ps. 8:3 in Matt. 21:9-11, 14-16). After all, the inspired psalms testify that the Spirit-anointed Son is David's Lord (Ps. 110:1 in Matt. 22:43). Jesus is truly God with us.

Yet we are not with God. The King realizes that rejection must precede his enthronement (Ps. 118:22-23 in Matt. 21:42-43).[11] So at his last Passover meal, he sings these psalms of victory (Matt. 26:30)[12] only after enacting

11. See below, "The Mercy of God."

12. Cf. William L. Holladay, *The Psalms through Three Thousand Years: Prayerbook of a Cloud of Witnesses* (Minneapolis: Fortress, 1993), p. 115.

his own redeeming death in bread and wine.[13] Then he heads to the Mount of Olives to accept their fulfillment. Matthew tallies the horrible cost of this victory: Jesus suffers Psalm 41's betrayal by a dear friend (Ps. 41:5-10 in Matt. 26:20-25). He takes up Psalm 42 as his lament of pilgrimage at Gethsemane (Ps. 42:4-6 in Matt. 26:38). He personifies before Caiaphas Psalm 27's hymn of trust in the face of false witnesses (Ps. 27:12 in Matt. 26:59). He endures the tortures of Psalm 22 and 69 from there to his crucifixion (Ps. 22:6-11 in Matt. 27:28-31 and 27:39-44; Ps. 22:19 in Matt. 27:35; Ps. 22:1-2 in Matt. 27:46; Ps. 69:21 in Matt. 27:34, 48). All this sets the stage for the resurrection that fulfills Psalm 110's song of coronation (Ps. 110:1-2 in Matt. 22:41-45; 26:64; and 28:18). Outside Matthew, the pattern persists: Luke records Jesus on the cross reciting Psalm 31:5. Hebrews 10:5-7 has him speaking Psalm 40:7-9, and Hebrews 2:10-12 puts in the mouth of the glorified Jesus Psalm 22's happy ending. And 2 Corinthians 4:13 arguably finds Paul hearing Psalm 116:10 as the Messiah's words.[14]

The Son is the Psalter in flesh and blood, "the true and ultimate speaker of Israel's laments and praises."[15] His birth, life, death, and resurrection take on and resolve the debate over whether and how God cares for his suffering creation. Every voice — every desperate cry, every fear, every assurance, and every exultation from every innocent and every sinner — finds its place in his story.

Every voice also finds its reply. William L. Holladay notices a profound transformation in the way Jesus uses the Psalter. "Although he made use of at least one of the psalms of lament — perhaps more — astonishingly, he does not take on any of the spirit of 'us against them' with which those psalms are filled."[16] Jesus' tone contrasts sharply with the "us against them" interpretation of the psalms and other holy texts that arose as early as the psalms themselves,[17] dominated among many of Jesus' contemporaries,[18] and resounds down to this day among cultists, jihadis, crusaders, anti-Semites, nationalists, patriots, and ethnic tribalists. Why the difference? Because Jesus is both "us" *and* "them," a sinless Son who sides with sinners,

---

13. See below, "The Victory of God."

14. For more see Richard Hays, "Christ Prays the Psalms," in *The Conversion of the Imagination* (Grand Rapids: Eerdmans, 2005), pp. 101-18.

15. Hays, "Christ Prays," p. 109.

16. Holladay, *The Psalms*, p. 121.

17. Holladay, *The Psalms*, pp. 48-49.

18. Holladay, *The Psalms*, p. 109.

a holy one who becomes a curse, an exiled son of Israel in the land of promise, an outcast enemy of the chosen people, the beloved Son of a Father who refuses to abandon the abandoned.

God's mercy to the unrighteous and undeserving does not limit or compromise God's righteousness. It defines it (Matt. 5:17-20). And since the Psalms' internal debate is resolved in Christ, it is resolved in us who belong to Christ, and ultimately in the world into which Christ and now we are sent.

Our Father! My revulsion and fear melt in the warmth of that Triune love. Jesus prays the way he taught us to pray, not in empty words but also in deeds (Matt. 7:21-27). Actions, not platitudes, characterize this God and so must characterize his followers (21:28-32). He alone is worthy, but he can make us worthy too. That, too, is what "our Father" means: The grace of God conscripts us both as receivers and givers of forgiveness.

When we pray, "our Father in heaven," we do it as his heirs. We share the pain of bearing with a world of hate, for the Son has borne it with us, and his Father with him. We celebrate the sheer favor that has adopted us out of an orphanage of alienation into the holy family of Father, Son, and Spirit. We feel the pressure of the Spirit pushing us back out to rescue others. We have the awesome responsibility of holding the keys to God's kingdom. We discover the jeopardy of mouthing these words when we fail to live them out, the judgment upon those who spurn them, the precariousness of our safety if we persist in hypocrisy, and the assurance of restoration when we repent. We learn the heart of God. Somehow none of this knowledge weakens or discourages us. Instead, this prayer begs for "the strength of his love."[19] Nothing will withstand it. Twelve legions of angels cannot compare with it (Matt. 26:49-54).

Perhaps my own confusion and weakness of faith come from my tradition's inattention to the Father. Because Matthew's Gospel concentrates so much attention on the Father, it offers resources for any who are failing to attend to him. That makes Matthew not just a guide to prayer, but an answer to prayer.

Some will find that claim hard to believe. In our culture the word "father" has connotations that do not always match those of Jesus' world, let alone characterize his relationship with the God who sent him. Many earthly fathers model the very evils Jesus came to conquer. I do, often

---

19. Tommy Walker, "There's No Greater Love than Jesus," 1996.

enough. Yet whatever we think of contemporary fatherhood, we need to be cautious about importing modern ideas naïvely into the Scriptures. What "Father" means there is not maleness and oppression, as some feminists allege, nor superiority and control, as some reactionaries counter, but — looking again at the Lord's Prayer line by line — attention, faithfulness, generosity, love, trustworthiness, mercy, self-sacrifice, restoration, inheritance, and accountability.[20] He is our Father *in heaven*. Even if we earthlings try to improve our own practices of fatherhood by looking to him (cf. 1 John 2:13-14), we must always bear in mind the limits of the analogy, for this father is like no other (Matt. 23:9).

On the other hand, lest we avoid using the term out of respect for how God surpasses our abuses of it, we must also remember that Matthew's Jesus embraces the term precisely because the Father shares his uniqueness with all the fellowship. He is *our* Father in heaven. The incarnation and atonement of the Son achieve the fatherhood of God over all his children. They bring the story of God's creation, redemption, and communion with the world to its resolution. God's newly universal fatherhood transforms Deuteronomy's "hate your enemies" into Matthew's "love your enemies." Incarnation and atonement do not change God between Deuteronomy and Matthew, of course! Love is who God has been all along. Rather, what we see earlier is the beginning of a process that is perfected in what we see later. Jesus' career ushers in the "end-times" or the resolution of the story.[21] It creates a fathered and fraternal community Christians call the church by reaching out with fraternal mercy to those who are not yet so fathered.[22]

You Got a Problem with That?

As I imagine Camassia, my blogging companion, reading this chapter, I already hear her objecting that basic issues remain unaddressed. *Why* accept Trinity as axiomatic? Isn't this supposed divine achievement dreadfully incomplete? What took so long? What about those who remain excluded from the divine fellowship? Is all this finally just a sentimental euphemism for the saving of some and the damning of others? Does it *really* fully exon-

---

20. Thompson, *The Promise of the Father*, p. 160.
21. See below, "The Reign of God."
22. Thompson, *The Promise of the Father*, p. 156.

erate God's character? Even if Jesus' interpretation of Israel's holy texts might be more hopeful and inclusive than many others, is it really more loving than her own? At the Second Council of Constantinople in 553 the church condemned teachers of universal salvation, but isn't a "heretical" humanist or a universalist who wants everyone to live abundantly still morally superior to an "orthodox" Christian who will settle for only some?

This may disturb some fellow worshippers, but I sympathize with those objections. Some of Camassia's problems with Christian life and teaching are well posed. When she crafts an argument for something that seems better to her and we believers shrug our shoulders and say "This is how it is," I understand and even share her disappointment.

While I do not share Camassia's suspicion of a God who would make our world and save it in this way, I admire her heart for the lost, and I long for it to make a lasting connection with the God whose heart it resembles. The continuing difference between her and me is not that she is the only one who sees a discrepancy between the way things are and the way she thinks they should be. I see discrepancies too. The difference is that I resolve them by trusting in God, and she does not.

Yet even here there is common ground. The Christian thing to do when things seem askew is not to reject the God of Israel as king of the universe or set ourselves against him, as skeptics do. It is not to retreat into wishful thinking, selective memory, forced biblical interpretation, or revised theology to construct more palatable positions, as some liberals do. It is not to dismiss the problem stoically or fatalistically under the guise of "faith," as some conservatives do. It is not to turn away in bitterness or pout and wish that things were better. *It is to pray.*

Does Camassia really think that healing every single human being would be more honoring to God and more appropriate to his loving character? Then let her pray for universal salvation. Let her do what Abraham did for wayward Sodom, what Moses did for the idolatrous Hebrews, what the king of Nineveh did for his clueless city, what the Canaanite woman did for unclean Gentiles, what Jesus did for his petty disciples, and what we do every day for those we love and even those we hate. Let her intercede before our heavenly Father and plead in the name of Christ and the power of the Spirit that no one would be lost. Maybe her secular eyes have seen something our religious ones have missed. Let her make her case — not to me, for that outcome is not mine to grant, let alone to teach — but to the One with the power to hear such an audacious request. "Who knows?" (Jonah 3:9). She would not be the first to discover that the One she has been seeing as her opponent is in fact her advocate. I remember another story from Matthew's collection:

> Just then a Canaanite woman from that region came out and started shouting, "Have mercy on me, Lord, Son of David; my daughter is tormented by a demon." But [Jesus] did not answer her at all. And his disciples came and urged him, saying, "Send her away, for she keeps shouting after us." He answered, "I was sent only to the lost sheep of the house of Israel." But she came and knelt before him, saying, "Lord, help me." He answered, "It is not fair to take the children's food and throw it to the dogs." She said, "Yes, Lord, yet even the dogs eat the crumbs that fall from their masters' table." Then Jesus answered her, "Woman, great is your faith! Let it be done for you as you wish." And her daughter was healed instantly. (Matt. 15:22-28)

And what about you? What is your dispute with the Almighty? The line between the greatest faith and the bitterest unbelief is nothing more than the willingness to kneel.

CHAPTER 2

The Reputation of God

Religion is an attempt to get control over the sensory world, in which we are placed, by means of the wish-world, which we have developed inside us as a result of biological and psychological necessities.

Sigmund Freud, *New Introductory Lectures of Psychoanalysis: A Philosophy of Life*

Blasphemed among the Nations

If God is really not the bloodthirsty tyrant some make him out to be, but a Father, Son, and Holy Spirit of sacrificial favor, it raises a different problem: How can God put up with all the slander? Why is God so unknown?

Consider the western intellectual tradition's last few centuries. They produced some of the most scathing attacks on God's character since the critiques of the ancient Roman pagan Celsus. For Sigmund Freud, God is an overbearing parent dreamed up by insecure human beings who want a father figure who will always be there in times of need. For Ludwig Feuerbach, God is the safe in which we lock away our human potential and consign ourselves to poverty. For Karl Marx, God is a projection of the power of owners and kings into the consciences of the poor, anesthetizing workers with promises of paradise if they go along with the system and hell if they transgress its laws of private property. Among radical feminists, God is an extension of male power that gives metaphysical backing to the oppression of women. To hard secularists, God is a philosophical habit or an evolutionary side-effect that dulls scientific curiosity and saps the personal ambition of the true masters of the universe — our own human race.[1]

The problem is not restricted to skeptics. If anything, it is worse among God's advocates, who rival Job's friends in our ignorance. In the church itself many of us invoke a god who is little more than a source of social reinforcement, personal empowerment, and self-esteem. On the Christian left, God is little more than a champion of causes that are shaped not by Christian tradition but soft secular progressivism — *justice, diversity, peace,* and so on — and U2's Bono is its resident theologian. On the right, a runaway Christian bestseller looks to a heretofore obscure passage — in 1 Chronicles of all places — as a paradigm for spiritual breakthrough: "Jabez called on the God of Israel, saying, 'Oh that you would bless me and enlarge my border, and that your hand might be with me, and that you would keep me from hurt and harm!' And God granted what he asked" (1 Chron. 4:10). In the heartland of global democratic capitalism, it is no coincidence that members of the Christian left recruit God and superstars to help them defeat the Christian right, or that a ten-dollar pocket-size devotional centering on a narrow interpretation of a single marginal verse has sold millions of copies. But what does it say about a God who lets it happen among his own worshippers? Why does the Lord allow Marx's spiritual grandchildren to write his devotionals or Jabez's prayer to surpass his own in the evangelical marketplace? Does he care?

God is everywhere in our culture. According to a decade's worth of polls from the Barna Research Group, a steady proportion of around nine in ten American adults believe in "God."[2] And we Americans use the word "God" as freely as we use it often. When offered a list of choices for describing God, 7% of individuals surveyed agreed with the definition of God as the total realization of human potential. Four percent chose to affirm God as "many gods, each with power and authority." Nine percent called God "a higher state of human consciousness." Four percent believed that "everyone is God." About two-thirds (69%) called God "the all-powerful, all-knowing creator of the universe, who rules the world today."

Even within that seven-in-ten majority of American adults who believe

---

1. Daniel L. Migliore, *Faith Seeking Understanding* (Grand Rapids: Eerdmans, 1991), pp. 56-59, 72-74.

2. Up-to-date statistics are available online at "Beliefs: Theological," http://www.barna .org/FlexPage.aspx?Page=Topic&TopicID=5.

in an omnipotent and omniscient creator and ruler of the universe, one person's God often barely resembles another's. In 2003 an amorous Jesus became a character in novelist Dan Brown's thriller *The Da Vinci Code,* and in 2004 a medieval one became a media sensation with the release of Mel Gibson's *The Passion of the Christ.* Both Brown and Gibson consider themselves Christian. Barna polls have identified considerable shares of believers who think Jesus sinned and who deny the existence of the Holy Spirit. Even after exempting Jews and Muslims, American monotheism cannot be generalized as Trinitarian. When I have polled students on the character of God at the evangelical Christian colleges and churches at which I have taught, I have always received a startling spectrum of responses.

Many read this diversity as evidence of a fickle public prone to theological revisionism, but these numbers actually reveal a rather conservative attitude. These numbers have hardly budged since Barna began polling over fifteen years ago. In the popular theology at the turn of the millennium one can see the persistent influence of America's cultural and ethnic diversity. Our cultural variety draws from our long transcendentalist tradition, the sixties, the eighties' and nineties' New Age movement, and the older and still dominant traditions of western monotheism. God is apparently content for generations to come and go without correction.

A God who is everywhere like this is also nowhere. The word "God" arises out of a whole world of theological ferment and disagreement. It is the product of revival meetings and holy wars and catechisms in church basements, of atheism and idolatry. It comes through fanaticism, discipleship, apathy, and opposition. It belongs to splintering denominations and new alternative religions and shallow ecumenism. It reflects enormous ignorance and massive misunderstanding, deliberate reimagining and conspiracy theorizing. How can God tolerate the blasphemies of all the bigots, crusaders, jihadis, terrorists, triumphalists, skeptics, boosters, and consumerists who speak for him? If it is important that God be known truly — and the Bible insists that it is — then why would God stand back while his reputation is sullied by curses from those who oppose him, by insults from those who do not conceive of him, and by prayers — by *prayers!* — that run from idolatry to blood libel, repeated daily and weekly and spread throughout the world from those who trumpet their loyalty to him? When will the real God *stand up?* When will he shut *us* up? If God is more than a shifting construction of human hopes and fears, has he really cared or bothered to make himself widely known?

Perhaps that is the answer: he hasn't bothered. For whole stretches of Israel's history God seems to fall silent. In fact, he promises to hide his face just when Israel is realizing how much they have forgotten him (Deut. 31:17-18). Perhaps God has similar reasons for his passivity today.

Deism, a way of thinking born in a Europe tired of theological division and burned out on theological speculation, took this kind of distance between God and humanity as original and permanent. If the deists are right, God has no further involvement with the world. God might be as burned out on theology as we are, and willing to leave us to our own opinions. America as a nation was designed by deists who viewed God as a creator — a first cause — but not much more, and one in seven American believers considers God to be aloof from their own lives today.[3] Yet in that case, why bother searching for the truth when this greatest truth of all no longer bothers to matter?

Speculative spirituality and deism react against each other in a vicious cycle that trains common people away from serious inquiries into God's character. Spiritual questing gives way to theological apathy when the answers fail to come or when they contradict each other. Secularism gives way to conjecture and wishful thinking when the aimlessness becomes unbearable. Even many of my zealous students learn not to ask too much about the God to whom they pray. Instead they fall back on "mystery" as a socially respectable and spiritual-sounding excuse to defer the question. Yet by deferring the question they cede the debate to those with the most fashionable or strident opinions.

Alasdair MacIntyre describes such situations as "the aftermath of a defeated tradition."[4] Our multiplicities of meanings for "God" no longer signify the kind of substantial agreement and constructive difference that makes for productive dialogue. Instead they rob the term of its actual meaning. At this point we are basically babbling.

I still proclaim the God of Christian faith. Yet all this theological noise brings fatigue to my confession. The thought of a God who puts up with a world of malignant theology makes it tough to pray, to push ahead when others are apathetic, and to smile and agree when others are enthusiastic.

---

3. "Beliefs: General Religious," available online at http://www.barna.org/FlexPage .aspx?Page=Topic&TopicID=2.

4. Alasdair MacIntyre, *Three Rival Versions of Moral Enquiry: Encyclopedia, Genealogy, and Tradition* (Notre Dame: University of Notre Dame Press, 1990), pp. 149-69.

In such times faith can feel like loyalty to a losing team or membership in a party always out of office. Hearing the Friday prayers of Islamic fascists, the pronouncements of the Know-Nothing Christian right, the watery platitudes of liberal western theists, the bald speculation on the "religion" shelves of bookstore chains, the safe formulas of theological partisans, the confident and clueless theories of secular intellectuals, and the silence of multitudes feels like being a Cubs fan watching the Yankees win yet another pennant. It sometimes makes me envy agnostics. If God does not bother to counter the flood of bigotry, indifference, and distortion, why should I? Why should anyone? And why call on God to vindicate *us* when lies and gossip threaten to bury us? Can God care about our reputations when God does not care about his own?

"God's name is blasphemed among the nations" (Isa. 52:5 in Rom. 2:24). So what?

A Glimpse of Something Extraordinary

On August 14, 2002, I wrote on my weblog about an experience I had recently had at church.

> I had an experience Sunday. The worship band at my church released a new CD. To celebrate they played a set mainly of the new music. In that set, the "holiness" and Pentecostal ways of being Christian finally made sense to me. Three songs in a row — the Doxology, Jacob Park's song "For God So Loved the World," and Bob Wilson's and Tommy Walker's "Your Throne" — gave me a glimpse of something I had never seen before with such clarity.
>
> Most Christian traditions rejoice in how different God is from his fallen world, then go on to celebrate the way Jesus became one of us and gave his disciples the gift of his holiness. All three of these claims were strong in that Sunday's music. The Holy God, through Christ's incarnation and the Holy Spirit's outpouring, yields the Holy Church.
>
> Christians take this common conviction in more than one way. The Orthodox and Catholic varieties of Augustinianism tend to take it as an unconditional assurance that the Church is free from sin and stain, even when its members and leaders do horrible

things. Its pope, bishops, sacraments, Bible, and lists of saints are signs of that assurance. The Lutheran and Calvinist varieties of Augustinianism stress God's holiness as a basis for distinguishing God from his unholy world. In the present age the Church enjoys God's holiness more as a promise and an abstract truth than as a present reality, as a thing that the Church almost *has* to fail to attain until Jesus returns. Baptist churches read God's holiness as creating communities who embody God's difference from his rebellious world. The Wesleyan variety — my church's variety — envisions the Church as enjoying God's holiness as a mandate and a goal, as something given and already demanded, as a thing that is meant to make his disciples as strange as God is, so that when Jesus returns they are not surprised and he is not disappointed.

All these varieties have good reasons for their teachings, though of course all of them cannot be right in the same way. All of them produce characteristic abuses: Catholic superstition, Orthodox triumphalism, Lutheran license, Reformed resignation, Baptist isolationism, Wesleyan pettiness and legalism, Pentecostal elitism. Though I have learned to appreciate the grammar and beauty of each school, the deep grammar of the Wesleyan holiness tradition has been slowest in coming to me — even though I earned my doctorate at a Methodist school and have attended Pentecostal or Wesleyan churches for five years. However, after singing those songs on Sunday with a room full of people who both wanted and knew the gift of holiness, I get Wesleyan Christianity in a way that textbooks have not taught me — cannot teach me. At my church we go crazy singing God's holiness and striving to appropriate it as our own. Holiness is why and how we resolve to be different in this world.

And now that I get it, I want it a lot more than I did before.

"Let Your Name Be Held Holy"

Dualism, Monism, and Holiness

There is a way out of the mire. But it is a narrow one, full of convoluted narration and treacherous dramatic turns:

The Reputation of God

*The whole story of creation culminates
in the hallowing of God's name.*

The tale begins in the paradox of a God who creates a heavens and earth that cannot help but be radically different from him. Then it adds another paradox: God finishes it all off by forming the dust of that earth into human beings and calling them, not as objects now but as fellow subjects, to be his representatives. "Be like me," God commands the soil, and it is so.

How can this be? How can beings made utterly different from God be similar to him at the same time? We are physical. We are temporal. We are descended from (or, at the very least, related to) other species that image only themselves. We carry their vestigial organs and behaviors, their survival instincts, their hunters' eyes and carnivores' teeth, their genes, their pheromones, and above all their mortality. How can we with these qualities even know an all-powerful, all-knowing, transcendent, and eternal Creator "who alone has immortality and dwells in unapproachable light, whom no human being has ever seen or can see" (1 Tim. 6:16), let alone image that Creator?

The apparent contradiction cries out for an explanation, and people have lined up to supply them. The common ones fall into two basic groups, both of which are immensely popular, and dead wrong.

Dualism, the first group, draws any of a variety of dichotomies that either set God at odds with the world or split the world and its human beings into two opposite things. Greek Platonists considered human nature to be eternal soul entombed in a material body. Gnostics such as Marcion taught that the world was an inferior emanation of the evil creator god YHWH, himself an inferior emanation of true Being, whose inhabitants needed to be rescued by angelic representatives of that originating Being of light. Manichees taught that within the human soul was a spark of light trapped in the dark world of created matter, struggling to escape and rejoin its source. In the two intellectual capitals of ancient Christianity, Apollinarians and Eutychians who denied the full humanity of Jesus as incompatible with his divinity battled Nestorians who denied that the two could be united in one person. Islamic philosophy simply asserted the contradiction of dissimilarity and similarity as *tanzih* and *tashbih,* God's distance and God's nearness. In the Middle Ages, Bogomilists in the east and Albigensians and Cathars in the west revived the basics of Manichaeism.[5] In the Reformation, Spiritualists such as Caspar Schwenkfeld and Sebastian Franck turned away from the material world and even body and soul toward the inward Spirit for any sign of God's presence.[6] Even Ulrich Zwingli of Zurich, a theological father of many evangelicals, stopped short of fully acknowledging the permanent unity of Christ's flesh and spirit.[7] Today many of my students mistakenly think the historic Christian faith teaches that in rising from the dead Jesus left his humanity behind.

In modernity the same tendency persists. Descartes divorced the human ghost from its organic machine, while Kant split the world into an inner noumenal realm and an outer phenomenal realm. As science has dissolved more and more of life into raw nature, the last refuges of human difference in our era have been ethics (now morphing into evolutionary psychology);[8] the arts (now darkened by late modern anxiety);[9] — and religion (now, thanks to sociology and psychology, becoming a dimension of social self-identification and a sector of our brains devoted to so-called "mystical experience)."[10] The trouble with dualism is that if God is absolutely otherworldly, then our physical organs of thinking and communicating are utterly incapable of making sense of him. Even "mystery" says too much. A dualist God can only retreat. And, sure enough, modern science has become one of faith's most feared enemies, leading believers to surrender to its arguments, flee to anti-intellectualism, or bisect themselves into "heart" and "mind." My beginning students indulge in modern dichotomizing when they insist that human nature is originally and unalterably sinful and needs to be defeated by "spirituality." They are genuinely shocked when I deny it.

Dualism's intolerable tension has fueled the rise of alternative monistic accounts of the world. These emphasize commonality over transcendence. They too span the globe and pervade human history, from pagan traditions in the west to Hindu traditions in the east. Sufism has brought

5. Brian Moynahan, *The Faith: A History of Christianity* (New York: Doubleday, 2002), pp. 280-85.

6. Carter Lindberg, *The European Reformations* (Malden, Mass.: Blackwell, 1996), pp. 225-27.

7. Lindberg, *The European Reformations*, pp. 189-97.

8. See below, "The Mercy of God."

9. See below, "The Victory of God."

10. See below, "The Presence of God."

them into the cosmopolitan Muslim world, and the Hegelian dialectic of worldly self-realization of Spirit has brought them into the modern Christian world. Liberal and conservative progressives imagine the modern world to have its own internal dynamic of perfection. Mormons and process theologians take God to be a product of evolution. Folk religion everywhere mixes incompatibles into popular and surprisingly resilient syntheses of nature and supernature; New Agers radicalize old-school transcendentalism into pantheism. All of these movements find an underlying unity in all things that dispenses with absolute distinctions between creator and creature.

The trouble with monism is that if God is fundamentally at home in the world, then he is no more than yet another neighbor. "Mystery" is false modesty. A monist God can only dissolve under the same reductionistic pressure of modern science and philosophy — and has.

Dualism and monism leave us with unappealing options: escaping physicality, abolishing transcendence, or cutting ourselves in half. But what else is there?

Followers of Thomas Aquinas might appeal to "analogy" as the proper way to proceed: We are similar in the context of being different. God is both like us and unlike us. Thomas's tidy Aristotelian answer has proven persuasive to Catholic philosophical theologians and many others ever since. Yet, however plausible the approach might be, it does not resolve the dichotomy but only domesticates it. It lives with it as something to take into account by thinking carefully and to manage by living accordingly. However, Luther (and the reformers who followed him) correctly perceived that something so radical as the relationship between God and the world cannot be *taken into account,* let alone *managed.* Above all, analogy fails because analogy misses the relationship between God and the world that God actually *achieves.* Its notion of mystery is basically static rather than narrative, and that puts it out of step with the faith of Israel and the Church. Whatever analogies there may be between time and eternity, change and immutability, limitation and infinity are finally beside the point.

Dualism, monism, and analogy of being might be elegant philosophical accounts of the way things are. However, the Church is not authorized to construct elegant accounts of the way things are. We are authorized only to witness to what was, is, and will be — and only as the God of Israel has showed us. So the Church tells a different story than dualism, monism, or analogy: the story of *holiness.*

Holiness is not dualism. It is not another word for transcendence or mere contrast. Holiness is not monism. It is not another word for immanence or mere comparison. Holiness is not a philosophical abstraction, nor can it be reduced to one, any more than Trinity can. The category of holiness does not attempt to solve a philosophical problem or hypothetically explain a set of phenomena. Instead — and these dry words are chosen carefully, so pay attention — *holiness celebrates the otherness of the specific relationships that have bridged difference, incompatibility, distance, and opposition.* The word arises out of these particular relationships. The meaning of the word is therefore the story of the relationships.

Holiness beyond Otherness

We began this exercise with the story of creation. If current biological speculation is correct, human beings are who we are because of a confluence of natural developments that seem to have come step by step. Our hominid ancestors' evolved intelligence gave them creativity unprecedented among God's creatures. Their adaptability came up with weapons to keep predators away. Their curiosity drove them to travel out of the middle of Africa into every other kind of environment. Their compassion helped the temporarily weak survive. Their ability to conquer fear allowed them to tame fire. Their ability to cook shortened their mealtimes and reformed their digestive systems. Their aesthetics turned their work toward beautification rather than mere utility. Their symbolic imaginations made clothing and decoration into social markers. Their tongues and brains allowed language to flower into cooperation that freed others from having to rely on brutish violence. Above all, the profound challenges of a disaster seventy thousand years ago pressed its few human survivors to new levels of capability with which they outperformed their hominid competitors from Africa to Europe to Indonesia and proceeded to dominate the earth. Like pieces of a puzzle — or refinements of a design, if you prefer — all these factors were producing a species unique among the earth's beasts. It may not yet have been in the image of God, but it was certainly becoming the kind of material on which such an image might be struck.[11]

11. See Sally McBrearty and Alison Brooks, "The Revolution that Wasn't: A New Interpretation of the Origin of Modern Human Behavior," *Journal of Human Evolution* 39:5 (No-

Nevertheless, however recognizably human these beings would have been seventy or even thirty thousand years ago, they were not yet holy. It is significant that the word "holiness" does not appear in the Old Testament's creation narratives (Gen. 1–3, Ps. 8, Ps. 104, and so on). In fact, it does not appear in Genesis at all! That is a clue that holiness is not the Creator's essential transcendence over creation or the intrinsic sacredness of the universe or even some qualities of analogous resemblance with certain creatures. It belongs not to the lexicon of beginnings, but of endings.

The first mention of holiness in the Bible refers to the ground onto which God draws Moses by turning him toward the burning bush (Exod. 3:5). There, as throughout Israel's story, the word is associated with God's delivering presence. In the Torah God's dwelling, his mountain, his tabernacle, its accoutrements, its priests, its sacrifices, the people who meet there, their camp, their sabbaths, holidays, and other peculiar ways of life, and the instructions themselves that regulate that life are all holy. Above all, the God who mightily saves his people is holy (Exod. 15:11), and the holiness of the people he saves is the logical conclusion of the salvation he brings. "I am YHWH who brought you up from the land of Egypt, to be your God; you shall be holy, for I am holy" (Lev. 11:45).

Here we must be careful to avoid a common mistake. For Israel there are things "most holy" (literally, "holy of holies") as well as "holy" (Lev. 21:22). Rabbinic Judaism inferred a hierarchy of holiness in which the Temple's Holy of Holies, then the sanctuary, then the walls of Jerusalem, then walled cities, then the Holy Land itself enjoyed descending levels of holiness. Likewise the high priest is holy, then the priests, then Levites, then Israelites, then converts, then freed slaves, and so on, at ever lower levels of sanctity.[12] To this day many Christians think in terms of similar gradations. Thus the epithet "holier than thou" and the constant negotiations among my students and their youth pastors over where to draw boundaries between permissible and impermissible classes of language, music, dancing, clothing, body-piercing, and the like. In my guild, these debates take more sophisticated forms as hierarchies of oppression and inclusion and accounts of "progressive sanctification." However, holiness is *not* a matter of degree, progress, or even relative purity. There is not a "more

vember 2000): 453-563, marvelously popularized in "Search for the Ultimate Survivor," National Geographic Channel, July 2005.

12. *Mishnah Keleim* 1:6-9.

holy" or "less holy" in the Torah. The things devoted to destruction —
idolatrous Canaanite towns, among other things — are "most holy" as well
(Lev. 27:28-29). There is clean and there is unclean; there is sanctification
and there is desecration. Paul calls the Corinthians to be not *more* holy, but
perfectly (that is, finally) holy (2 Cor. 7:1). Classical music is not more or
less holy than rock 'n' roll.

Holiness does not emanate or derive from greater holiness, nor cleanliness from cleanliness. Holiness and cleanliness follow only from divine
election (Num. 16:5; Acts 10:9). Holiness distinguishes the things that are
holy from the *different,* the *common,* and the *unclean* (cf. Lev. 10:10). These
are not identical, and they are not arranged along a spectrum. The holy
God has chosen Israel to be thrice holy: a beloved bride, a people set apart,
and a light to the nations who walk in darkness. Israel is to be holy to
YHWH (Deut. 7:6), holy to itself (Lev. 11:44-45), and holy to the world
(Exod. 15:11). These three sets of relationships across the distances between
God and humanity, between humanity and the rest of creation, and between this people and the other peoples, are what constitute Israel as other
— as Israel.

Sanctifying the Name

Chosen by the Holy One, Israel chooses idols instead. Israel ignores
YHWH, worships the creation, and imitates the oppressive peoples on its
every side. Its unholiness, its sheer dreary *sameness,* threatens to sully the
good reputation God had begun to cultivate for himself in the exodus
(Exod. 9:16, Rom. 9:17). The prophets chronicle the drama that follows.

Here we are at a turning point in the story of the relationships that
comprise holiness. It is a good time to make another crucial distinction between what holiness really is and what we often think it is.

A fashionable recent movement among historians of religion has been
to write "biographically" about a God they do not consider to be alive. They
construct a "life" — a *bios,* as it were — out of a series of perceived developments in the *notion* of God over the course of Israel's and the Church's histories. Like comic book or cartoon illustrators, they animate the figure by
flipping through snapshots at each developmental stage. Jack Miles's *God: A
Biography* is one such project. When he reaches the time of the prophets,
Miles says the God of Isaiah

is engaged in a life-or-death struggle to hold himself together in fusion that will still be dynamic or, changing the angle of vision, that the prophets are trying to put pressure on the elements of the original fusion so as to bring them once again to criticality. His character may need to explode again if it is to fuse again. Often unstable in person, the prophets are destabilizing in effect, but, without destabilization of some kind, the life of God threatens to come to a close.[13]

This is a clever postmodern way to speak critically and postcritically at the same time. In a way it is even brilliant. However, it turns God and his prophets into wholly different characters in *another* story: the cartoon story of *Religionsgeschichte* ("the history of religions") that secular modern Europeans fabricated to make sense of a living past they suddenly found lifeless, baffling, and embarrassing.

Miles's rhetoric may be extreme, but his sensibilities are widely shared even by believers nowadays. Both modernists who rely on correspondence theories of truth and postmodernists who grant the social construction of reality live self-consciously in worlds of human words. We feel responsible for both our concepts of God and the languages we use to communicate with them, and we realize that they are ever changing. Miles's way of illustrating God once soothed historians of religion who were convinced that the west was inexorably climbing up a slope of progress, but it tempts us to panic when the history of ideas veers in unwelcome directions. Rising fundamentalisms alarm progressives even more than creeping liberalism alarms traditionalists. Superheroes always master their villains but have to submit to their writers. What will God turn into next? Who is in charge of this narrative?!

Miles may be a brilliant animator. He may even have the artistic skill to reassure his readers that the visions of Osama bin Laden and Jerry Falwell are not of lasting significance — that things will return to normal in next month's issue. But he still has things precisely backwards. On his own admission he is writing a "life story" that makes just as much sense if God is dead or fictional; and that cannot be true to his material. His interpretation of the Scriptures is just as forced as Sigmund Freud's preposterous psychoanalysis of Moses, because he is pressing the biblical characters into new and foreign roles in a story not their own.

---

13. Miles, *God: A Biography* (New York: Vintage, 1995), p. 197.

Isaiah and his followers are not incubating an idea. They are not crafting a *persona* that turns into "a difficult but dynamic secular ideal."[14] Rather, they are remembering a critical moment in a relationship that maintains their own community of faith. The book of Isaiah is an epic narrative of an Israel who strays from holiness and a God who does not. Here holiness is not a fragile human concept but a firm love and powerful resolve that manifests itself in the sweep of cosmic history: "Holy, holy, holy is YHWH Almighty; the whole earth is filled with his glory" (Isa. 6:3).

Weaklings like me need to learn the lesson here: God's good reputation follows from God's holiness, not the other way around. It is not Isaiah's theological creativity but God's own steady hand that carries Israel through disaster, exile, and return. It is God's holiness, not the idea of it, that convicts Israel of its sin, renews its faith, and restores its own holiness. Holiness is the strength that sees Israel through its own failure.

In the middle of Isaiah comes one of the two Old Testament passages that point toward the first petition of the Lord's Prayer:

The tyrant shall be no more,
the scoffer shall cease to be;
and those diligent for evil shall be wiped out,
who cause people to lose their lawsuits,
laying a snare for the arbiter at the gate,
and wronging by falsehood
him who was in the right.
Assuredly, thus said YHWH to the House of Jacob,
    who redeemed Abraham:
No longer shall Jacob be ashamed,
no longer shall his face grow pale.
For when he sees his children,
the work of my hands, in his midst,
they will sanctify my name;
they will sanctify the Holy One of Jacob,
and will stand in awe of the God of Israel.
And those who err in spirit will come to understanding,
and those who grumble will accept instruction.

(Isa. 29:20-24)

14. Miles, *God: A Biography,* p. 7.

The scoffing and slandering will cease when Israel sees his children gathered and hallows God's name. The solution to blasphemy begins in these divine relationships. God's people are held together not by imagination or successful public relations, but by the powerful gift of holiness — to the Lord, among ourselves, and for the world. When we pray the Lord's Prayer, we beg to be the family of the Father who will cause us to hold his name holy.

The cast of Isaiah's prophecies includes mysterious figures who play pivotal roles in bringing Israel back into good standing with God, back to its own senses, and back to the center of world history. A boy called Emmanuel (Isa. 7), a blind servant-teacher (Isa. 42), a suffering servant (Isa. 53), and an anointed evangelist (Isa. 61) are among the best known to Christians. Yet while these people play key roles, they are not the central characters. In this epic there are only two stars: YHWH and Israel.

In Ezekiel's version of the story, there is really only one:

> It is not for your sake, O house of Israel, that I am about to act, but for the sake of my holy name. . . . *I will sanctify my great name,* which has been profaned among the nations, and which you have profaned among them; and the nations shall know that I am YHWH . . . when through you I display my holiness before their eyes. I will take you from the nations, and gather you from all the countries, and bring you into your own land. I will sprinkle clean water upon you, and you shall be clean from all your uncleannesses, and from all your idols I will cleanse you. (Ezek. 36:17-25)

Ezekiel follows that great act with a return to the Torah's language of sanctity. It now centers in an eschatological Temple in a new Jerusalem (Ezek. 40–48). God cares about his reputation after all!

The Holy One of God

Consumers of comic book religion come to the New Testament expecting a sudden plot twist. We don't get one. While the story of Jesus of Nazareth adds crucial new *detail* to the story of holiness, it does not add further chapters or characters.

Since the first prophets, Israel has been reconstituted in exile as Judaism. First-century Judaism is much more diverse than casual exposure to either the New Testament's Jews or later rabbinic Judaism suggests. Its varieties spring in large part from different visions of what it means to be a holy nation. The Essenes took holiness as a mandate to isolate themselves from the corrupt structures of Roman-occupied Israel, withdraw as a community, and await God's deliverance. Zealots took holiness as a mandate to fight as the Maccabees had for the purification of the land and its holy institutions. Priests, Sadducees, and Herodians were willing to cooperate with their unclean rulers for the greater good. John the Baptist and his circle were preparing an imminent and mysterious way forward. Pharisees — the most popular party in Jesus' day, and the party that survived the struggle and helped create rabbinic Judaism after Rome's victory in and after the Jewish War — took Torah observance as the personal responsibility of every Jew and sought to realize Ezekiel's eschatological vision of personal and communal purity even while they awaited the new Jerusalem.

All these camps might have looked back with some legitimacy to earlier characters and ages in Israel's saga: Essenes to the wilderness wanderers and exiles; Zealots to the land's original conquerors, the judges, and the Maccabees; Sadducees and Herodians to Daniel, Nehemiah, and Esther; John to Moses and Elijah; and Pharisees to the Levites and the children of Sinai. Moreover — and here lies another lesson for contemporary students of holiness — these visions also resemble the trajectories of holiness that many Christians have taken. Essenes remind us of monks and fundamentalists; Zealots of Crusaders and Puritans; Herodians of the Christian left; Sadducees of the Christian right; John of Adventists and Dispensationalists; and Pharisees of mystics, Pietists, and quiet American evangelicals who act as if holiness meant living lives that would be rated "G" if they were being filmed.

These parties have their roles in the New Testament, but its story swirls around another figure: Jesus of Nazareth. Jesus falls into none of these schools of first-century Judaism, not even John's. That is a fact that should give today's Christian sanctificationists pause! Yet Jesus does not introduce a new character of his own, either. Instead he embodies all the old characters in a new and perfect way. He is the God of Israel and the Israel of God. His holiness is at once the holiness of both. His life displays holiness to the Father, holiness among his own, and holiness for his enemies.

In the Messiah all things hold together across each of these distances. Jesus is the figure to which Isaiah's mysterious roles turn out to point

(Matt. 2:23, cf. Isa. 7:14; Matt. 12:18-21, cf. Isa. 42:1-4; Matt. 8:17 and others, cf. Isa. 53; Luke 4:18-19, cf. Isa. 61:1-2). He is the Holy One (Luke 1:35, cf. Isa. 4:3), conceived and raised in holiness, who sanctifies and is sanctified (John 6:69, cf. Judges 16:17; Acts 4:26-27, cf. Ps. 2:2), and who does not see corruption in the grave but is highly exalted (Ps. 16:10 in Acts 2:25-33 and 13:35). He bears the Name above all names (Acts 3:14-16, Phil. 2:9-11, cf. Isa. 45:23). He is the Rock in the wilderness, sustaining Israel even through the sinful strikes of its leader and affirming God's holiness (Num. 20:6-13, 1 Cor. 10:4-5). He is Israel, faithful where his people had earlier been unfaithful (Deut. 6 and 8 in Luke 4:1-13). He is David's heir, receiver of the Holy One's divine blessings (Isa. 55:3-5 LXX in Acts 13:34). He is both the psalmist who acclaims the Lord as holy and the Lord whom the Psalms acclaim. His Spirit is at once Isaiah's anointing spirit, Genesis' creator spirit, the finger of God who delivers Israel and writes its commandments, and the new Torah he fulfills in the flesh and writes on the people's hearts.

I suspect that this is why the first ones to identify Jesus' holiness in the Gospels are angels and demons. They dwell in the domain of powers and principalities of which he is the Pantocrator. Angels pronounce Jesus holy to comfort the oppressed (Luke 1:35), while demons do it in awful recognition of the conquering Lord of hosts (Mark 1:24). The same dynamic is at work as people catch on to him. Jesus' disciples name him holy out of hope (John 6:69), while his detractors acknowledge him in dread (Acts 2:22-37). The battle for eternal life has now been decisively joined.

We who associate holiness with moral superiority, clericalism, otherworldliness, exemplariness, aloofness, prudishness, and the rest will miss what is going on in these stories. Jesus' contemporaries misunderstand holiness too, for the same reason that they misread Jesus. They fail to perceive the true way of Torah, the point of the Temple, and what makes one clean and unclean because they do not understand his relationships with the Father, the Spirit, and his fellow Israelites.

Likewise, our similar misimpressions of the biblical holiness codes as overbearing, unrealistic, and picayunish — both the new holiness practices in Ezekiel and Matthew and the old ones in the Torah — lead us to imagine that it must take great strength to observe them. We then either strive to master them and fail, or we abandon them and fail again. This is because we either mistake strength as prior to holiness or holiness as prior to strength. But Israel's weakness in the face of its enemies is neither the cause nor the effect of its unholiness. Its weakness *is* its unholiness. Holiness does not follow from strength or lead to it; holiness *is* strength. *Holy, holy, holy is the Lord God Almighty; the whole earth is filled with his glory.* Likewise the Church in the west fails in the face of so many challenges because it is weak, because it is unholy and inglorious, because it has allowed itself to be seduced by gods that are no gods at all and has returned to being the same as everything around it. However — to repeat Mary's response to the news that her son will be called holy — "the Mighty One has done great things . . . holy is his name. . . . He has shown strength with his arm" (Luke 1:49-51). To the chorus of "holy, holy, holy" heaven's angels and elders add a new refrain, "worthy . . . worthy . . . worthy," because the christened Lamb's redemption has finally achieved the sanctification of the Father's name (Rev. 4:8, 4:11, 5:9, 5:12).

God does not become holy. The divine persons are holy apart from the existence of unclean, common, or distant things in the creation. Instead, in the creation Christ displays and works out the Triune God's eternal holiness — the divine persons' eternal mutual otherness. In the Lord's Prayer and on the cross the Son exalts the Father in the Spirit, calling him holy. At Jesus' conception, resurrection, and ascension the Father exalts the Son with the Spirit, calling him holy. At Pentecost the Father exalts the Spirit in the Son, calling him holy. In his warning against unforgiven sin and his high priestly prayer the Son exalts the Spirit from the Father, calling him holy. YHWH's holiness names the eternal mutual difference of the Father, the Son, and the Holy Spirit. Nothing shall separate them from each other's love.

God does become worthy, however — by virtue of conceiving and accomplishing "the plan of the mystery" (Eph. 3:9) by which others can learn and share in his holiness. When Christ allows himself to be born of woman, born under the law, and numbered with the transgressors, the rules of holiness change. The Son shares his holiness with other persons *not* divine — with creatures of dust who are now fellow creatures, who are common, and even who are unclean. The ones far away are brought near (Acts 2:38-39, cf. Joel 2:32). The "fulness of Christ" (Eph. 1:23) encloses all — God and human beings, Jew and Greek, slave and free, male and female — into collective sonship of the Father and inheritance of the Spirit. If justification[15] is the outward aspect of these relationships' righting, sanctification is the inward aspect. The incompatibilities, distances, and

---

15. See below, "The Mercy of God."

oppositions between the chosen people and other peoples, and even between the Righteous One and sinners, are hallowed into the distinctions proper to one, *holy,* catholic, apostolic Church.

The body of Christ is the instrument God has chosen to rescue his reputation in the world. When Israel sees its children gathered into his body (Isa. 29:23 MT), they will hallow God's name. Jesus promises that the Holy Spirit who dwells in God's fellowship of saints will convict the world regarding sin and justice and judgment (John 16:7-8). To all who believe, the Son has made known the Father's name, that the Father's love for the Son may be in them, and the Son too (John 17:26).

A world enslaved to mistaken, idolatrous, and even murderous theological apprehensions seems to be too great a challenge for such a frail, divided, compromised community as the Church of Jesus Christ. And it is! *That is why the Lord's Prayer is a prayer!* We disciples do not accept the hallowing of God's name as a mission we can make ourselves able to accomplish. We beg for it as a gift we can receive in faith by grace. God's reputation may be in tatters today among the nations and even among his own people, but God's reputation is eternally secure among the Father, the Son, and the Holy Spirit, and that is what really matters. These three are God's true biographers; we are merely their publicists.

So we ask joyfully, knowing that the Name is already holy and that the hard work of bridging the distances has already been done, the greatest gift already given, and the promises sealed. "There shall no more be anything accursed, but the throne of God and of the Lamb shall be in it, and his servants shall worship him; they shall see his face, *and his name shall be on their foreheads*" (Rev. 22:3-4). That arresting image should not surprise the psalmist who sings that

> YHWH is king; let the peoples tremble!
>   He sits enthroned upon the cherubim; let the earth quake!
> YHWH is great in Zion;
>   he is exalted over all the peoples.
> *Let them praise your great and awesome name.*
>   *Holy is he!*
> Mighty King, lover of justice,
>   you have established equity;
> you have executed justice
>   and righteousness in Jacob.

Extol YHWH our God;
    worship at his footstool.
    Holy is he!
Moses and Aaron were among his priests,
    Samuel also was among those who called on his name.
    They cried to YHWH, and he answered them.
He spoke to them in the pillar of cloud;
    they kept his decrees,
    and the statutes that he gave them.
O YHWH our God, you answered them;
    you were a forgiving God to them,
    but an avenger of their wrongdoings.
Extol YHWH our God,
    and worship at his holy mountain;
    for YHWH our God is holy.

(Ps. 99)

God's reputation is safe among the witnesses who really count. They have defeated every enemy. Our part is just perseverance.

CHAPTER 3

The Reign of God

Whatever makes men good Christians, makes them good citizens. Our fathers came here to enjoy their religion free and unmolested; and, at the end of two centuries, there is nothing upon which we can pronounce more confidently, nothing of which we can express a more deep and earnest conviction, than of the inestimable importance of that religion to man, both in regard to this life and that which is to come.

Daniel Webster, *Plymouth Oration*

No one is fit to be trusted with power.

Charles Percy Snow, *The Light and the Dark*

Trivial Pursuits, Lost Causes, and Utopian Fantasies

"I want you to come with me after class to pray for someone."

This request came at the beginning of class from Abby, one of my students. Abby was a religious studies major, a fine scholar, a Pentecostal, and a prophetess — one of those people whose lives are one long miracle. I gulped and agreed.

After class Abby led me to the room of another one of my students. She had been incapacitated for days with vertigo. Though it was mid-

47

afternoon, in order to enter I had to break my school's rules on opposite-sex visiting hours. Well, I reasoned, the Sabbath was made for humanity, not humanity for the Sabbath. It is not as if she could have come out to meet me, and praying through her window would have been ridiculous.

We began to pray together. I prayed for my ailing student for a couple of minutes, thanking God for her, asking God to heal her, and so on. The usual.

Abby's turn came next. As I finished and Abby took over, I began to feel faint. It couldn't be a head-rush, since I had already been standing. I wondered if it were some kind of sugar-low. After thirty seconds the dizziness had not passed; in fact, it was overwhelming. I had stopped listening to Abby praying and was wondering how I would stay on my feet. Young male faculty do not relish the prospect of keeling over in women's rooms during closed hours. I finally knelt down and waited until Abby was finished. I never lost consciousness, and as soon as we all said *amen* I quickly excused myself and sat on some steps outside to recover.

Abby followed after a few seconds with a bottle of water. Five minutes later I felt ready to get back up, and she walked me back to my office. "Do you know what happened back there?" she asked.

"I have no idea," I replied in all honesty. "Maybe I shouldn't have skipped both breakfast and lunch today."

Abby's silence was deafening.

"And what do *you* think happened back there?" I asked her.

"God was showing you what she was going through."

"Interesting!" I replied professorially, turning over her hypothesis in my head. "Maybe so!"

"No, that *is* what was happening," she insisted.

This was just Abby's style. There is no gray with her, just black and white. Abby was also as obstinate as she was insistent. Professors with our doctoral degrees *never* intimidated her. So she and I had grown used to playful but firm exchanges like this. We often butted heads in class and in conversation. I would say something, she would roll her eyes, and we would fall into our typical roles.

"What makes you so sure?" I asked her.

"It has happened to everyone who has prayed with her. You are the third one today."

Now I was the silent one!

For someone who calls himself a Pentecostal, I have very few stories like this to tell. Only rarely have things happened to me that seem truly extraordinary, truly resistant to natural explanation. They happen no more than once every few years. But they do happen.

They are happening much more often outside the west. Sustained intercessory prayer, speaking and praying in tongues, spiritual warfare, healings and exorcisms, expectations of miracles, and ecstatic spirituality are now business as usual for millions of Christians the world over. These believers take experiences like mine for granted.

Bracket all the charismatic excesses and abuses for the moment — the absurd televangelists, the credulous believers, and the historical arrogance that draws a line straight from Los Angeles back to Pentecost as if the Holy Spirit were idling in between — and grant for the sake of argument that *some* of these events are legitimate. What do they mean? Why are they so numerous in others' lives, so few in mine, and missing from many others'?

Or grant none of it, and consider instead the unspectacular works of God that the world's Christians celebrate: The presence of Christ at communion, the personal experiences of Jesus at revivals and Bible camps, the lives slowly transformed by Scripture, the sacred stillness of Christmas Eve, the kindness of friends, and the smiles and handshakes at Sunday church services. If you are a believer, reflect on the moments that have made you one, and you will face the same questions. Why, if God is working through these ways, are they so subtle and small in a world of such profound suffering and vast need? Wars rage. Plagues decimate Christian Africa. Christians and others are victims of persecution and ethnic cleansing. The western Church is falling into apostasy. And God wants me to feel sixty seconds of a student's vertigo or a sense of the sacred on Christmas Eve? What kind of priorities are those?

Not long ago I sat across from Charles H. Kraft, professor of anthropology and intercultural communication at Fuller Theological Seminary, as we prayed for a woman troubled from childhood by demons. Kraft is famous in charismatic circles for his advocacy of charismatic practices of deliverance. "There seem to be a *very* large number of satanic beings in the world," Kraft says in *Defeating Dark Angels*:

Satanic beings are involved in every kind of disruptive human activity. . . . They seem to have authority over places and territories, such as buildings, cities, and temples. Additionally, they appear to have authority over social organizations and groups, and influence sinful behavior such as homosexuality, drug addiction, lust, incest, rape, and murder. The fallen angels we call demons or evil spirits seem to be the "ground level" troops, as opposed to the "cosmic level" principalities, powers, and rulers of Ephesians 6:12. These are the ones we encounter most often during spiritual warfare.[1]

I came along to offer moral support rather than expertise. It was the first time I had been involved so directly in spiritual warfare. As we prayed, Kraft addressed the demons directly. Some were silent, while the woman "channeled" the responses Kraft elicited from others. The proceedings would have been disappointing to people who expect theatrics; no one even raised his or her voice. It was odd to hear my friend speaking about herself in the third person, but I still do not know whether the speech she conveyed that afternoon came from conscious beings, fragments of her psyche, or sheer suggestion. That is beside the point anyway. As I listened to the exchange, the same questions surfaced in me. My friend's troubles had arisen from seemingly trivial events in an otherwise normal, even privileged life. They could just as easily be events in the future lives of my own young children, events so unexceptional or enigmatic at the time that I as their father might not hear about them for years afterward. But they had grown to dominate my friend and strangle her hope. I wondered at their power, and began to panic at the thought of a world of billions whose lives looked much, much worse. If a typical childhood event can evolve into such a formidable evil power, then what about wars, plagues, genocides, natural disasters, hunger, and corruption? What are Christians supposed to do in the face of *those*? What is the connection between power from Jesus on behalf of a few people who need deliverance and hope for the whole world?

Is all this charismatic stuff too spooky for you? Then consider several of my students, both male and female, who have struggled with something more conventional: sexual temptation. (As you may know, "struggle with" is now a euphemism for "repeatedly succumb to and repent of.") These children of healthy and faithful families have been swept along in the tide of sexual experimentation and permissiveness that has nurtured hundreds of millions here in the west in habits of vice. They have come to places of victory, but not until after long and hard seasons of frustration.

1. Charles H. Kraft, *Defeating Dark Angels: Breaking Demonic Oppression in the Believer's Life* (Ventura: Regal, 1992), pp. 19-20.

The road back to chastity from the middle-aged and adolescent American sexual norm is long and anguished. Habits are easy to acquire, hard to break, and tend to resurface. If what I saw in Kraft's office is at all significant, deliverance involves dimensions of spiritual combat that few churches (charismatic or not) are equipped even to appreciate, let alone practice. My delight at witnessing and participating in a few successes is tempered by the awareness that they happened against the backdrop of an avalanche of failures.

Are sexual sins too culturally conservative for you? Then move leftward and consider the demonology of Walter Wink in *The Powers that Be*. Wink traveled in 1982 to Chile to experience demonic oppression in the form of Augusto Pinochet's military dictatorship.

> We spoke with a lawyer who represented the families of people who had been "disappeared," as they put it. We spent an excruciating evening in dialogue with a woman who had been tortured. And so it went, week after week. . . .
>
> At the end of the trip I became physically ill. I had planned to begin writing about the Powers, but I was so sick and underweight that I could scarcely function. On top of the physical ailment, I was overwhelmed by despair as well. I had gone to Latin America hoping that our experience there would help me write something that could make a difference. Instead, the evils we encountered were so monstrous, so massively supported by our own government, in some cases so anchored in a long history of tyranny, that it seemed nothing could make a difference. I had gone there to observe the Powers; I ended up their captive.[2]

Sin is personal, but it is just as profoundly structural. The world's powers conspire to form what Wink calls "the Domination System."

> It is characterized by unjust economic relations, oppressive political relations, biased race relations, and the use of violence to maintain them all. No matter what shape the dominating system of the moment might take (from the ancient Near Eastern states to the Pax

---

2. Walter Wink, *The Powers that Be: Theology for a New Millennium* (New York: Doubleday, 1998), pp. 6-7.

Romana to feudal Europe to communist state capitalism to modern market capitalism), the basic structure has persisted now for at least five thousand years, since the rise of the great conquest states of Mesopotamia around 3000 BCE.[3]

Christians oppose these temptations and domination systems by laboring for systemic reform, resistance, and revolution. Yet the constant frustration of both secular and Christian efforts to improve the world seems to be a chorus of testimony against our effectuality in the face of the Powers. Consider (to pick on the left this time) some of the legacies of Christian causes in ages past: corrupt and self-indulgent labor unions, languishing European socialism, flabby and self-parodying political correctness, a United Nations turned into a tool of criminals and dictators great and small, marginal Catholic Worker houses, declining schools of liberal theology, aging base communities of liberation theologians, deteriorating mainline denominations, and irrelevant ecumenical councils of churches. (We could compile a similar list to discourage conservatives.) After five thousand years the few fragile deliverances seem to pale in comparison with the defeats.

Invest or Withdraw?

When Christians fall into thinking of *ourselves* and *the world,* it is only a matter of time before Christian life becomes a trivial pursuit, a lost cause, or a utopian fantasy. We like to cultivate an air of outward social optimism — especially we who were raised on liberal, moderate, and conservative schools of western progress. Yet it quickly crumbles into pessimism and cynicism once we honestly consider the scale of the challenges that face the gospel and the great reversals of faith that have come in both Christianity's old heartlands and our own circles. The same questions keep coming up: Where is the power? Where is the hope? And what are we supposed to *do* in this world of these powerful institutions and authorities?

Our history of engagement reinforces a longstanding dilemma in Christian culture between two ways of relating to the world: *investment* and *withdrawal.* It goes practically unquestioned among American Christians that these are the only serious alternatives.

3. Wink, *The Powers,* pp. 39-40.

Let us examine how this dilemma works itself out by focusing on a matter of persistent importance to Americans in the past few years: patriotism. In June 2005, MSNBC reported on Roper polls between 2001 and 2005 that showed American patriotism more popular than at any time since 1991. The catalyst was the September 11 attacks, which raised religious observance, volunteerism, and patriotism dramatically. Nine months later religion and volunteerism had returned to their prior levels, but American patriotism stayed popular — among blacks, Hispanics, and whites; Democrats and Republicans; baby boomers and Gen-Xers; liberals and conservatives alike.[4] Especially in a patriotic age, in what ways do Christians relate to the world?

Divided Loyalties?
American Patriotism and Christian Identity

Investment: Involvement as Christian Identity

The first strategy for Christians to relate to the wider world is *investment*. We can express our faith through our qualified allegiance to spiritual, cultural, economic, and political powers — either to them in their current form, or to what they might become. An academic term for this strategy, at least as it applies to the realm of the expressly political, is "Constantinianism."

Classical Constantinianism describes a formal alliance between civil institutions and Christian institutions, or even a fusion of the two. In the United Kingdom, Queen Elizabeth II is both the head of state and the head of the Church. This makes Britain an ideal example of Constantinianism (and Buckingham Palace the pinnacle of women in Christian leadership). By contrast, America has a constitutional prohibition on such a relationship, so first we do not seem to be a Constantinian nation. But the First Amendment merely states that "Congress shall pass no law respecting an establishment of religion or prohibiting the free exercise thereof." The courts have interpreted that clause to allow a Pledge of Allegiance, a currency, oaths in court, and other national symbols to appeal to a "God" under whom the nation lives, in whom it trusts, and to whom it swears. The

---

4. "Poll: U.S. Patriotism Continues to Soar," July 4, 2005, http://www.msnbc.msn.com/id/8410977.

Establishment Clause has shaped American Constantinianism into a new and more subtle form.

Let me speak from experience. I inherited from my parents a respect for "God and country" that basically equated faithful service to God with faithful service to country. The purest form of this fusion in my life was the Boy Scouts, in which my whole family was involved. In fact, the Boy Scouts serves such a useful purpose in exposing the nuances of the relationships between ourselves and the world that my diagnosis will center on it. We take life most seriously when it involves our children, and the Boy Scouts is a microcosm of the way one generation teaches the next generation how to be invested in the world, in ways far beyond the formally political. To dismiss it as kids' stuff is to deny how important children are both to our national identities and to our Christian identities.

At every meeting I took the Scout Oath: "On my honor, I will do my best, *to do my duty, to God and my country,* to obey the Scout Law. To help other people at all times, to keep myself physically strong, mentally awake, and morally straight." Note well the breadth of this oath. Neither Scouting nor other Constantinian visions practice absolute allegiance to narrowly political powers. Instead, they embrace nearly every dimension of modern life. Scouting's formal mission statement takes character, citizenship, and fitness as fundamental aspects of healthy personhood. They come together or not at all. Scouting therefore goes far beyond camping and saluting the flag. It offers more than 100 merit badges, in an astonishing variety of areas. (Those that begin with "A" are Agribusiness, American Business, American Cultures, American Heritage, American Labor, Animal Science, Archaeology, Archery, Architecture, Art, Astronomy, Athletics, Atomic Energy, Auto Mechanics, and Aviation.) The Scouts are an investment vehicle for a *whole* life in the midst of the powers — cultural, economic, political, and spiritual.

There is room in the Boy Scouts of America for most every religious faith: Jewish, Hindu, Buddhist, Orthodox, Muslim, Catholic, various flavors of Protestant, Unitarian, and Mormon. The Scouts understand all these confessions to converge neatly with character, fitness, and duty to the United States. When you think about that, it is a staggering claim. But it is accepted every day in this country. (In fact, the Scouts' "God and my country" echoes the motto of the U.S. Army Chaplain Corps, "For God and Country," another juxtaposition that is accepted uncritically by most Americans, and most American Christian communities.) Furthermore, it is accepted in every nation-state in which the Scouts operate, even those that go to war against each other.

As a Christian Scout you can earn a special award, called "God and Country," in association with your church. (The God and Country program actually operates at every age level in Scouting: "God and Me" for Tiger Cubs and Cub Scouts from grades 1-3, "God and Family" for Cubs and Webelos in grades 4-5, "God and Church" for Boy Scouts in grades 6-8, "God and Life" for older Boy Scouts and Varsity Scouts, and the "God and Country" program for adult mentoring of children. Note how God's relevance broadens only as a boy matures, and note where the Church lies on the spectrum.)

Muslim Scouts have a parallel set of programs, the "Bismillah" or "In the Name of God" program and the "Allaho Akber" program. Buddhist programs train Scouts in the Four Noble Truths and the Noble Eightfold Path. Mormon Cubs can earn the "Faith in God" award, and Boy Scouts the "On My Honor" award. (Mormonism has become the most influential religious group in the BSA. Mormon wards sponsor more Scout Troops than any other organization except for public schools.)

It is easy to mistake the Scouts' religious pluralism as an expression of American-style diversity and separation between church and state. However, the overtly theistic Scout Oath makes it impossible for *atheists* to participate in Scouting. The Scouts are happy to juxtapose loyalty to America and loyalty to a God defined in all these incompatible ways — *or even a God left undefined,* who (or which?) after all is the closest match with the mysterious One invoked on America's money and in its Declaration of Independence. But Scouting cannot tolerate a loyalty to America that is independent of loyalty to any of the Known and Unknown Gods.

Scout religion is civil religion. For the Scouts, Christian identity, like other forms of acceptable religious identity, necessarily manifests itself in patriotism and a host of other forms of secular investment, and vice versa. They are not different loyalties, but one loyalty expressed in compatible ways. As the *Scout Handbook* has said since 1911, "The Boy Scouts of America maintains that no member can grow into the best kind of citizen without recognizing an obligation to God. . . . The recognition of God as the ruling and leading power in the universe and the grateful acknowledgment of His favors and blessings are necessary to the best type of citizenship and are wholesome precepts in the education of the growing members."[5] Religious observance is a necessary expression of social responsibility.

Not coincidentally, this relationship is exactly duplicated in the youth and adult branches of the Masonic Service Organization. The Order of DeMolay (for boys), International Order of the Rainbow for Girls, and International Order of Job's Daughters all demand both patriotism and religion (of the member's choice). If the Church of England was once the Conservative Party at prayer, the Scouts are the Masons around a campfire.

Masonic American Constantinianism is not only the dominant vision of civic involvement in Christian circles, but also the dominant paradigm for the American public. "The goodness of a person and of the society he or she lives in often comes down to very simple things and words found in the Scout Law," says President George W. Bush on the Scouting website. "Every society depends on trust and loyalty, on courtesy and kindness, on bravery and reverence. These are the values of Scouting, and these are the values of Americans."[6]

My father would have emphatically endorsed the president's statement. Bush's vision of neat convergence between Christian commitment and diversified investment in the powers is also the dominant vision in my own family. I am an Eagle Scout, brother of an Eagle Scout, son of an Eagle Scout, nephew of an Eagle Scout, and grandson of an Eagle Scout. It has come as something of a shock to realize that my proud family tradition of teenage Monday nights and weekend camping trips was a catechism in Masonic American Constantinianism.

But it is not only those who accept Scouting's particular vision of God and country who reveal the shape of Masonic American Constantinianism. Three camps that dispute its vision — Unitarian Universalists, Jehovah's Witnesses, and atheists — demonstrate the same point.

Divestment as Investment

Unitarians share the Scouts' Constantinian paradigm that commends investment in the world as the appropriate expression of religious faith. They

---

5. *Boy Scouts of America: The Official Handbook for Boys* (Bedford, Mass.: Applewood, 1997).

6. http://www.scouting.org/factsheets/02-559.html.

are enthusiastically participatory in American public life — in (usually liberal to radical) politics, in local, national, and global activism, in culture, and in public service. Investment and involvement have been features of Unitarian culture since its American ascendancy in the eighteenth century. Especially in the eighteenth and nineteenth centuries Unitarians were prominent in American politics (Thomas Jefferson, for instance, is an honorary and perhaps unofficial Unitarian), American education (Harvard University), and American culture (the Transcendentalists). Unitarians and Scouts seem made for each other. And for decades the two cooperated harmoniously.

However, the late 1960s brought a countercultural twist to the notion of patriotism that became vastly influential, and since then the Culture Wars have split the country ideologically between "conservative" and "liberal." One mode of patriotism became associated with the culture and family structures of the generations born before 1945; with aspects of the Democratic Party of Roosevelt and Truman and the Republican Party of Goldwater, then Nixon, then Reagan; with support for the Cold War; with opposition or indifference to affirmative action; with economic deregulation, free trade, and low taxation, and high growth; and so on. Another mode of patriotism became associated with sixties youth culture and nonnuclear family structures; with the Democratic Party of McGovern, then Mondale; with opposition to the Vietnam War; with national pacifism and disarmament; with support for affirmative action and the extension of antidiscrimination measures to other than ethnic groups in the service of "diversity"; with government intervention in the economy and trade; with environmentalism and new social practices and organizations; and so on. (Some institutions, such as big business, labor, Roman Catholics, and some ethnic communities, were left trying to straddle the divide.)

It is important to recognize that *both* of these political cultures were essentially patriotic, even when they thought of themselves (and each other) as subversive. Both sides have often seen public activism as the measure of social and individual identity — including religious identity.

Consider the first traumatic days after September 11, 2001. During the September 13 episode of *The 700 Club*, Jerry Falwell offered a receptive Pat Robertson his interpretation of the attacks of two days earlier:

> I really believe that the pagans, and the abortionists, and the feminists, and the gays and lesbians who are actively trying to make that an alternative lifestyle, the ACLU, People for the American Way —

all of them who have tried to secularize America — I point the finger in their face and say, "You helped this happen."[7]

This claim, which called down wrath from the center and left and (public) disavowal from the right, and which forced retractions from both televangelists over the next several days, is both patriotic and subversive — an affirmation of American public life only as a call for its thorough reformation.

Fourteen days after the attacks, Barbara Kingsolver responded in the *San Francisco Chronicle* from the other side of the Culture Wars, alleging that

> patriotism threatens free speech with death. It is infuriated by thoughtful hesitation, constructive criticism of our leaders and pleas for peace. It despises people of foreign birth who've spent years learning our culture and contributing their talents to our economy. It has specifically blamed homosexuals, feminists and the American Civil Liberties Union. In other words, the American flag stands for intimidation, censorship, violence, bigotry, sexism, homophobia, and shoving the Constitution through a paper shredder?[8]

No one accused Kingsolver of being a patriot (though many accused her of taking leave of her rationality). But reading further yields a different picture:

> . . . my patriotic duty is to recapture my flag from the men now waving it in the name of jingoism and censorship. . . . I would like to stand up for my flag and wave it over a few things I believe in, including but not limited to the protection of dissenting points of view. After 225 years, I vote to retire the rocket's red glare and the bullet wound as obsolete symbols of Old Glory. We desperately need a new iconography of patriotism.

This is anti-patriotism as a form of patriotism, an affirmation of America only as a call for its transformation. Barbara Kingsolver and Jerry Falwell are feathers in the left and right wings of the same eagle.

7. Transcript available online at http://www.beliefnet.com/story/87/story_8770_1.html.
8. Available online at http://www.sfgate.com/cgibin/article.cgi?file=/chronicle/archive/2001/09/25/ED34658.DTL.

The split between Unitarians and Scouts occurred because the two organizations took different sides in the Culture Wars. Unitarian Universalists are radically inclusivist, allowing people to join their church whether they believe in one God, many, or none at all. (In fact, in forcibly inserting every religious tradition they like into their cosmological scheme, they are as imperialistic as the Masons.) Furthermore, Unitarians have taken a strong position against discrimination in all forms, including discrimination on the basis of sexual practice. Meanwhile, Scouting has slowly moved from its place in the American mainline to occupy mainly the conservative side of the Culture Wars, without cutting its ties to the organizations in the American mainline that have moved to the liberal side.

As a result, Unitarian commitments to God and country now conflict with Scouting's commitments to God and country. Unitarians have a strained relationship with Scouting today not because either is unpatriotic, but because their positions on homosexuality conflict. One group discriminates against homosexuals, the other rejects discrimination against homosexuals. The God of exclusion battles the God of inclusion in the American public square. (Unitarian Universalist Association churches still give out "Religion in Life" awards to Unitarian Scouts, but now over the BSA's own objections.)

The Scouts have won the Supreme Court battle over this one, but they are bound to lose the war, because their strategy of defining God in terms of American public life plays entirely on the Unitarians' terms. The fact that homosexuality, not the absurdity of Mormons and Hindus and Buddhists and Unitarians all swearing duty to "God," sparks the greatest cultural battle in Scouting history shows that the Culture Wars are not a war between Christian faith and secular humanism, but a skirmish between two varieties of Constantinianism. Much anti-patriotism, at least most of what makes it into the papers and onto the evening news, is really just shadow patriotism. The left's divestment from the Scouts is a consequence and form of its investment in the culture.

This is how the relationship of patriotism and Christian identity is usually debated in America. Should we invest or divest in the name of patriotism? Should we be American Revolutionaries or French Revolutionaries?

"Neither," answer Jehovah's Witnesses. And that brings us to the opposite of Christian investment in the world: withdrawal.

Withdrawal: Involvement or Christian Identity

One popular alternative to both wings of Masonic American Constantinianism considers Christian and civil loyalty to be incompatible. God and Caesar are inevitable competitors. Devotion to one is apostasy from the other. The logical course of action for believers with integrity is separation.

Jehovah's Witnesses see symbols of American civil religion much as early Christians saw images of the Roman emperor. So Witnesses practice *withdrawal* from civic involvements they consider incompatible with following Jehovah. This is not because America is worse than other governments, but because all worldly governments are instituted by Satan. Scouting's loyalty oaths and salutes to the flag make participation strictly forbidden. Rather than taking part in American or French revolutions, Jehovah's Witnesses wait for apocalyptic deliverance.

Where Mormons are Constantinians and Unitarians are shadow Constantinians, Witnesses are "counter-Constantinians." Against the sunny patriotism of Mormons and the Moral Majority and the restless patriotism of Unitarians, Jehovah's Witnesses are the true anti-patriots. They offer no contribution whatsoever to American governmental authority. (Organizations like the American Civil Liberties Union have found the Witnesses helpful in exposing contradictions between Americans' theoretical religious freedoms and the actual constraints placed upon Americans by institutions such as flag salutes, public oaths, compulsory public and military service, and so on. However, Witnesses have not *set out* to protect these freedoms.)

Yet as the Unitarians and Scouts look like opposites but turn out to be estranged brothers, so the Jehovah's Witnesses that reject both turn out to have more in common with them than we might think. In passively withdrawing from the public sphere, Witnesses leave its claims unchallenged. Regardless of whether Mormons, Unitarians, and Witnesses invest in the modern nation-state, all of them accept its hegemony in American public life. All respect the rules that democratic society places on them, and all agree to contribute or not to contribute according to those rules.

Compartmentalization: Involvement and Christian Identity

A third objection to the Scouts' vision comes from atheists and agnostics. Both are prohibited from leadership as adults and from membership as chil-

60

dren. Many are supportive American citizens who would like to participate in everything about Scouts except the civil religion, but the Scout Oath excludes them. They argue that the "God" of the Boy Scouts is irrelevant to the organization's mission and inconsistent with its character as a quasi-public institution. The Scouts' insistence on belief, they argue, is "un-American." While the Scouts contend that religion is a personal matter with public consequences, agnostics argue that religion is a personal matter with private consequences, and thus unimportant to both citizenship and Scouting.

The agnostics who would decouple Scouting's religion from Scouting's patriotism suggest a third way to relate ourselves and the world. We should talk not of patriotism *as* Christian identity, or of patriotism *against* Christian identity, but simply of patriotism *alongside* Christian identity. I call this position "para-Constantinianism." Patriotism and religious identity are two different things. Each operates alongside the other in its own sphere. I may be a Scout who happens to be agnostic; you may be a Scout who happens to be a believer. That an American or a Scout can "happen to be" a Christian and that a Christian can "happen to be" an American or a Scout expresses mutual indifference between political practice and religious practice. This allows Christians to invest and withdraw at the same time. Politics and religion pass each other in the night — or at least they should, for modernity construes the border between them as the border between public and private, between fact and value, between objectivity and subjectivity, between science and faith, between obligation and conscience.

Fundamentalists and evangelicals are the agnostics' para-Constantinian fellow travelers. Fundamentalists spent fifty years in the American cultural wilderness. They retreated from wider American society after the Scopes trial and, with a few exceptions like Billy Graham, re-emerged only in the seventies. Meanwhile, evangelicals developed a host of organizations that paralleled mainstream American institutions: specifically evangelical denominations, schools and colleges, bookstore chains, media outlets — and versions of Scouting. They retreated from their nineteenth-century Reformed and Wesleyan styles of American Constantinianism that used state assistance in waging their campaigns against evils like slavery and alcohol abuse, into a twentieth-century para-Constantinianism that viewed the American establishment with relative indifference.

Unlike Jehovah's Witnesses, evangelical organizations have not been especially *hostile* to civic involvement, patriotism, and even nationalism. Especially since Jimmy Carter's election in 1976, evangelicals have participated in elected office. Evangelicals tend to be enthusiastic participants in the U.S. military. However, these involvements have generally been seen as secondary to the real mission of evangelicalism, which is overt promulgation of the good news itself. Former President Jimmy Carter is a parable of this hierarchy of loyalties. In the first decade after he retired from the presidency, he returned to teaching Sunday school, and worked tirelessly on behalf of Habitat for Humanity, giving the impression that he saw this as a promotion. (His current shift to liberal political advocacy follows the evangelical left's subsequent move away from overt evangelism and mission toward a revived social gospel.)

The feeling is mutual. Scouting has traditionally been reluctant to allow awards from evangelical groups, not because it sees them as threatening, but because it does not see these groups as "traditional." (This attitude gets especially ugly when the unrecognized traditions are historic African-American denominations, such as the AME Zion Church, which have plenty of good reasons to dispute Scouting's "traditional" vision of patriotism as Christian identity.) Moreover, evangelicals who were already unhappy with liberal Protestantism were happy to create their own evangelical versions of Scouting such as Pioneer Clubs, Royal Ambassadors, and the Christian Service Brigade. These ersatz Scouts have evangelical statements of faith to ensure that the institutional identity and mission of these organizations stay distinctively evangelical. The websites of all three of these youth organizations make no appeals to patriotic loyalty as intrinsic to their own missions. They are focused on things besides "duty to country."

An exception that proves the rule is the "Royal Rangers" program of the Assemblies of God. Like the others, it takes over much of Scouting while leaving out the Scouts' religious pluralism. Yet the Royal Rangers allow para-Constantinianism to split them down the middle. The Royal Rangers say three "pledges of allegiance": To the American flag, the so-called "Christian flag" ("I pledge allegiance to the Christian flag and to the Savior for Whose Kingdom it stands; one brotherhood, uniting all true Christians in service and in love"), and the Holy Bible ("I pledge allegiance to the Bible, God's Holy Word. I will make it a lamp unto my feet and a light unto my path, and will hide its words in my heart that I may not sin against God"). These loyalties are distinguished as neatly as I imagine Royal Rangers' lives are compartmentalized between the sacred and the secular. The Royal Rangers website pictures two rangers, one holding the American flag and the other holding the Christian flag. (The American flag is higher.)

Evangelicalism today is somewhat different from its earlier forms. The last hundred years saw evangelicalism's mood swing wildly away from Constantinianism and back. First evangelicals moved from postmillennial optimism to premillennial pessimism, and from social activism to fundamentalist — sometimes even Jehovah's Witness-style — abandonment from American public life. Then, as its institutions formed and matured, it moved to a parallel, Pentecostal-style duplication of American public life. As it began to move within reach of the centers of American power, it then took on a participatory, Mormon-like argument with American public life and introduced an interior bifurcation between life's sacred and secular aspects. Nowadays evangelicals are becoming ever more integrated and assimilated into American public life. George W. Bush personifies the present synthesis of evangelical and patriotic identity. We are the new Episcopalians, the new mainline, and it shows.

Christian Conundrum

I hope this analysis does not come across as a smug ivory-tower dismissal of everyone outside. I am sympathetic to every one of these visions. My Scout sash and uniform still sit in my closet. I am grateful for Scouting's role in my life and newly excited about its potential to mature my three boys, the oldest two of whom have just joined. In fact I now rave about the program. I love my deceased mainline father, who was a Scoutmaster; my traditionalist Episcopalian mother, who as a latter-day culture warrior now supports the Scouts more vociferously than ever; my postmodern Episcopalian sister, who admires Barbara Kingsolver; and my modern Unitarian brother, who teaches world religions in his pluralist Sunday school. I also feel nostalgia for my youthful days as a naïve Boy Scout, then a Hal Lindsey–era premillennial conspiracy theorist, then a Pat Robertson admirer and Christian activist, then an apolitical evangelist. Either I or someone in my nuclear family has occupied every one of these visions of the relationship between ourselves and the world. Nevertheless, something leaves me dissatisfied with all of them. Something drives me back to the drawing board, back upon the Christian tradition, to revisit the question.

Furthermore, my dissatisfaction seems mirrored by the restlessness of my fellow evangelicals as we have careened from one extreme position to another in our quest for Christian faithfulness in our powerful, threatening, promising world. We find nowhere to rest because all of these relationships leave the powers' dominance in the sphere of patriotism unquestioned. Both investment and withdrawal work around the Domination System rather than taking it on in the name of Jesus Christ. They focus on swimming with or against the cultural tide. Our various forms of investment and withdrawal merely underwrite Christian dilution, burnout, and defeatism in response to the system's persecutions. Investment turns Christians into conformists and worldly significance into cultural assimilation — salt that has lost its saltiness. Withdrawal leaves Christians impotent, irrelevant, and invisible — light hidden under a bushel. (Persecution is the setting of the "salt and light" passage in the Sermon on the Mount, as the context makes clear. That our churches have rarely noticed that is further testimony of how thoroughly we have blinded ourselves.)

What is the alternative? Prophesying the Kingdom and preparing for the consequences, as Jesus did (Matt. 5:10-12). Perhaps that missing something, that source of dissatisfaction, is the Holy Spirit.

"Your Kingdom Come"

Dilution, burnout, and defeatism are literally a world away from the language of the Lord's Prayer. Old systematic theologies speak not of the Church conformist, the Church reformist, or the Church impotent, but of the Church militant and the Church triumphant. This is not just fancy language for living believers and dead believers. It alludes to an entirely different way of looking at ourselves and the world — from the perspective of the Kingdom or reign of God.

When we turn away wearily from the world of powers and principalities to pray "let your reign come" with the Messiah, we discover that we have had it precisely backwards. The real question is not whether we are invested in the world, but whether the world is invested in God's reign. The key to transcending the categories of the world and ourselves that pose insoluble dilemmas of investment or withdrawal is investment in God's future for the world.

Christian power is not cultural power, cultural powerlessness,
nor countercultural power. It is eschatological power.

Eschatological power, end-times power, is not the power to which the present age has become accustomed. Sometimes eschatological power looks weak, as it did on the cross (1 Cor. 1:21-25) and in the fear and trembling of the Apostle Paul (1 Cor. 2:3). Other times it looks strong — as it did in Jesus' itinerant ministry of signs and wonders (Matt. 11:12, 12:28) and in the resurrection that Paul preaches (1 Cor. 15:50). Sometimes it appears negligible, other times compelling (Luke 13:18-19). These resemblances, however, are incidental. Because eschatological power comes from above the world of principalities and powers, it is not defined in terms of anything but the God whose purpose is accomplished through it. It is neither this-worldly nor otherworldly, but eternal. The world cannot construct it or destroy it, for it is imperishable (1 Cor. 15:50). By the will of God it arrives or leaves, spreads or withdraws, suffers or conquers, includes us or excludes us. The Kingdom is a given. It stands on its own.

The Lord's Prayer, in its marvelous grace, attests that we do not. Christians do not control, build, or determine God's Kingdom. Yet, by the mystery of God's openness to his own creation, we can and do truly interact with it. We are not passive before the Kingdom any more than Christ is. We can invite it, enter it, dwell in it, celebrate it, proclaim it — and we can also deny it, reject it, and leave it. Nor are we passive before the world, any more than Christ is. We can go into it with his gospel, his Spirit, and his signs — and we can also assimilate into it, hide from its persecutions, and lose our souls in gaining it.

The Lord's Prayer makes the fundamental question not how Christians should be involved in the world, but how Christians should be involved in the Kingdom. Praying it cultivates a perspective in which the Kingdom is central, not marginal. Eschatology is a presupposition for those who pray in its Spirit, not an afterthought. "Do not be anxious about your life, what you shall eat or what you shall drink, nor about your body, what you shall put on," the Lord tells shortly after leading us in his prayer. "But seek first his kingdom and his righteousness, and all these things shall be yours as well" (Matt. 6:25, 33).

Eternity Misunderstood

Christian life is eschatological life (Acts 2:17, 1 Cor. 10:11) — eternal life (1 John 5:13). However, just as misunderstandings about the identity of Jesus Christ obscure the character of the Father, so misunderstandings about eternity obscure the nature of the end times. Each misconception makes this petition of the Lord's Prayer a call for the absurd and confuses those who pray it.

The most popular eschatological mistake in our day is worldly *progress*. The future is a world empire, a New Israel, a worker's paradise, a Thousand Year Reich, a global market, a global village, a United Nations, a nöosphere, a technological wonderland, an ecological Eden, or a universal caliphate. Here we meet again just what we have been trying to escape: a world that demands investment on its own terms. All these utopias are intensified (and often estranged) descendants of the Christian Constantinianism we already examined at length. As Constantinianism envisions Christian political power as a postmillennial realization of Christ's earthly reign,[9] so each of these false Messiahs pictures itself as the end of history as we know it, as the world's arrival at eternity — and through its own efforts rather than the cross.[10]

> Mine eyes have seen the glory of the coming of the Lord,
> He is trampling out the vintage where the grapes of wrath are stored,
> He has loosed the fateful lightning of His terrible swift sword,
> His truth is marching on.[11]

If eternity lies within the world's own reach, why bother to pray for the Kingdom to come? God helps those who help themselves! In a world of progress, prayer becomes inspiration, encouragement, and introspection — a formality before an action already decided. A culture that takes matters into its own hands prays to a God of its own making, and before long only to itself.[12]

Another common misconception sees eternity as *timelessness*. Here Platonism, which opposes the material world of corruption and change to the immutable "God" who is its source, is still making its ancient influence felt. In C. S. Lewis's classic *The Great Divorce*, the narrator says:

9. Rodney Clapp, *A Peculiar People: The Church as Culture in a Post-Christian Society* (Downers Grove: IVP, 1996), pp. 23-24.

10. Lesslie Newbigin, *The Gospel in a Pluralist Society* (Grand Rapids: Eerdmans, 1989), pp. 152-53.

11. Julia Ward Howe, "The Battle Hymn of the Republic."

12. See below, "The Presence of God."

Suddenly all was changed. I saw a great assembly of gigantic forms all motionless, all in deepest silence, standing forever about a little silver table and looking upon it. And on the table there were little figures like chessmen who went to and fro doing this and that. And I knew that each chessman was the *idolum* or puppet representative of some one of the great presences that stood by. And the acts and motions of each chessman were a moving portrait, a mimicry or pantomime, which delineated the inmost nature of his giant master. And these chessmen are men and women as they appear to themselves and to one another in this world. And the silver table is Time. And those who stand and watch are the immortal souls of those same men and women.[13]

Lewis pleaded in his introduction that his readers not take his "imaginative supposal" as "even a guess or a speculation at what may actually await us" (p. 8), but such images — whether from his pen or his fellow Christian Platonist Augustine's — have been too vivid to resist. "When the Last Day comes and goes, and time will be no more, I'll be praising you," my church sometimes sings. "A thousand years from now, before your throne of grace and power, I'll be praising you." The lines are literally nonsensical. We can sing without time? Time will end in exactly one thousand years? Will the worshiping Church be frozen in amber and the song silenced like a recording locked away in a safe? If the Kingdom were timeless, the world would have nothing to do but fade away, fossilize, or run along keeping its distance. The *coming* of the Kingdom would make no sense.

A third misconception is that eternity is *another dimension* in which one can skate through time up and down and sideways like a time traveler. Edwin A. Abbott, a nineteenth-century clergyman, describes such a world in *Flatland: A Romance of Many Dimensions*. This geometrical fantasy is the monologue of a Square who lives in a two-dimensional realm. One day a Sphere mysteriously visits him and leads him, as Beatrice leads Dante, up into Spaceland then down into Lineland and Pointland. When he moves to break the law and "evangelize the whole of Flatland" to "the Gospel of Three Dimensions,"[14] he is imprisoned and writes these memoirs. He closes them on a note of desperation proper to a Victorian English clergyman:

13. C. S. Lewis, *The Great Divorce* (New York: Macmillan, 1946), p. 126.

14. Edwin A. Abbott, *Flatland: A Romance of Many Dimensions* (New York: Dover, 1992), p. 77.

The millennial Revelation has been made to me for nothing. Prometheus up in Spaceland was bound for bringing down fire to mortals, but I — poor Flatland Prometheus — lie here in prison for bringing nothing to my countrymen. Yet I exist in the hope that these memoirs, in some manner, I know not how, may find their way to the minds of humanity in Some Dimension, and may stir up a race of rebels who shall refuse to be confined to limited Dimensionality. . . . It is part of the martyrdom which I endure for the cause of the Truth that there are seasons of mental weakness, when Cubes and Spheres flit away into the background of scarce-possible existences; when the Land of Three Dimensions seems almost as visionary as the Land of One or None; nay, when even this hard wall that bars me from my freedom, these very tablets on which I am writing, and all the substantial realities of Flatland itself, appear no better than the offspring of a diseased imagination, or the baseless fabric of a dream.[15]

Flatland gets an enthusiastic reception among some modern evangelicals, who see in its mathematical analogy a handy solution to the problems of divine transcendence, foreknowledge, and incarnation. There is only one problem: Israel does not conceive of heaven as a higher dimension in which our narrative universe is enclosed like a scroll. The Kingdom does not come in an angel's millennial visitation to reawaken us to worlds beyond, nor through a material cross-section called Jesus of a hyper-being called God. Christ is the Alpha and the Omega, the whole Word made whole flesh, and his Kingdom shall have no end. Second Peter 3:8's "with the Lord one day is as a thousand years, and a thousand years as one day" is about patience, not transcendence. Heaven as hyperspace is a fascinating intellectual project, but it is not the good news.

Finally, it is possible to get the basic eschatological framework right but the details tragically wrong. What is true of comedy is equally true of eschatology: even with great material, timing is still everything. Jews, Muslims, and even many Christians are still waiting for the end-times to begin. Since at least the thirteenth century Jesus' refusal to arrive as predicted has not deterred eschatological prophets from drawing real and fictional scenarios of the Last Day. Adventists are descendants of Millerites who origi-

---

15. Abbott, *Flatland,* p. 82.

nally miscalculated the date of Christ's second coming as October 22, 1843. Jehovah's Witnesses have proclaimed human existence to have ended imperceptibly in 1975.

To review the wrong turns: Eternity-as-progress turns the coming of the Kingdom into the world's *emergence* at the climax of the present age. Eternity-as-timelessness twists the Kingdom's coming into immortal souls' *going* into transcendence. Eternity-as-hypertime reduces it to ongoing sacramental or evangelical *traffic* with parallel realms. Eternity-as-predictive-timeline imagines a scenario of coming that *fails to come.* Each of these mirages is powerful. Each holds people in its thrall, at least for a while, until some other picture replaces it, or until boredom or revulsion drives some away from eschatology altogether and back to the old world with its dilemmas. "A picture held us captive," Ludwig Wittgenstein says of the modern idea that propositions depict the world beyond. His diagnosis applies just as well to each of these notions of eternity. "We could not get outside it, for it lay in our language and language seemed to repeat it to us inexorably."[16]

What defuses these popular abstractions of eternity and frees us from our slavery to them is the Kingdom that *has actually come near.* Jesus' advents are the definitive content of the Kingdom of God. They alone show us the way out of the maze of eternities.

The Kingdom as the Good News

"The kingdom of God is not food and drink but righteousness and peace and joy in the Holy Spirit" (Rom. 14:17). This sentence is one of only a few references to the Kingdom of God in Paul's letters. Paul uses it as if to encapsulate the whole flow of his letter to the Romans: the righteousness of Christ for the benefit of sinners (Rom. 1–4) yields peace with God and each other (Rom. 5–14), which overflows in lives of joy (Rom. 15–16).

Today "Kingdom of God" (*basileia tou theou* in the original Greek) is a dead metaphor that people use without hearing its overtones. Consider a few livelier translations: *God's regime* has taken power. The *dominion of the God of Israel* has approached. The *theocracy* has arrived. The *YHWH Ad-*

---

16. Ludwig Wittgenstein, *Philosophical Investigations,* 2d ed. (Malden, Mass.: Blackwell, 1958), vol. I, pp. 115, 148.

ministration has made Jesus Davidson dictator-for-life, and Chief of Staff Peter Jonason would like to see you now.

Paul announces this new order as "the good news of God" (Rom. 1:1) "concerning his Son" (Rom. 1:3, 1:9). His message is not just "information" as we understand the term nowadays, but "the power of God for salvation" (Rom. 1:16). "The kingdom of God does not consist in talk," Paul tells some of his chattering competitors, "but in power" (1 Cor. 4:20). Its power is the Spirit's own (1 Thess. 1:5, 10). The apostle's story is God's eschatological regime taking power in a man's life.

Mark's Gospel puts the same linkage on Jesus' own lips at the outset of his career: "The moment has finally come, and the YHWH Administration has approached; change your ways and trust that the news is good" (Mark 1:1, 9-15). All three other Gospels follow behind him in their own ways (Matt. 4:12-17, 23; Luke 4:14-15, 43; John 4–5). To keep things manageable, let us focus on Matthew.

What an odd sort of power we find there! This dominion belongs to the spiritually poor and to those mistreated for doing good (Matt. 5:3, 10). It is nonviolent and suffers persecution (5:38-48, 10:16-33), yet wields a sword and advances violently (10:34-39, 11:12). It is unlike anything people have ever heard or seen (7:28, 9:33), yet resembles all kinds of everyday things: salt, yeast, fishing nets, and buried treasure. It performs unprecedented acts, then defends them with common sense. It seems totally new but already at home in the world, rejected but triumphant, negligible but momentous.

This distinguishes God's authentic dominion from the eschatological mirages we normally see. Jesus is none of the mistakes we have surveyed. He is not the adolescence of the world; he is not the event horizon from time to timelessness; he is not the portal between time and eternity. Rather, Jesus is the frontier of the new meeting the old (cf. 13:51-52).

By grace, Jesus' disciples are too. In Matthew 10 Jesus sends out his apostles to the lost sheep of the house of Israel. He predicts works of power (Matt. 10:8a), hospitality (10:8b-12a), and rejection (10:12b-15) on the way. As rewards for his disciples' faithfulness he promises gifts of prophecy (10:18-20) and righteousness (10:32). This sobering apostolic scenario plays out in the next two chapters (Matt. 11:1). John in prison, the crowds that had gone out for his baptism, the Jewish cities to which Jesus preaches, and the Pharisees have all fallen out of step with the times. They are like wallflowers at a dance (11:2-19) or political parties voted out of power. Their skewed eschatologies have misled them and even turned their piety into a pretense for evil (12:1-4). Jesus' disciples contrast absolutely. As trained officials in the YHWH Administration, they understand the difference between new and old, and know when is the right time to bring out each (13:51-52).

Regime Change

Like all changes in government, this one must inevitably become a contest of powers. Yet like a losing politician or a washed-up celebrity, in the course of these two chapters Jesus moves from a crowded open space (perhaps a marketplace) to a field, then to a synagogue, and finally to a house at the seaside. The scope of his operation narrows accordingly. In every place his power is met with curiosity, wonder, loyalty, and opposition — against a vast backdrop of indifference (11:20-24). The YHWH Administration should be a sensation, not a sideshow! The revolution should be scaling up, not down. What is going on?

All is according to plan, Jesus says. Then in a series of parables of the Kingdom he backs up that astounding claim.

Any farmer knows that waste, harsh weather, and weeds are unavoidable contingencies in agriculture (13:18-22). They need not threaten a good harvest (13:23). So inaction in the face of adversity should not be taken as neglect or naïveté. It may even be the best approach (13:24-30, 36-43). The perfect is the enemy of the good: no utopian farmer who demanded that every seed yield grain, spent his hours pulling up every weed, and demanded instant results would stay in business. The engineering aphorism — "better, faster, cheaper: pick any two" — is here overturned. Better, faster, cheaper: pick one. The YHWH Administration is slow, expensive, and wonderful.

As for practically going underground with the good news, Jesus' message has been hidden since the foundation of the world (13:35), and it remains hidden even now. However, where once it was hidden away, now it is hidden differently: in soil where it grows into an eschatological tree (13:31-32), in flour that it leavens (13:33), in a field where it can be discovered, reburied, and obtained (13:44), in an inventory where it must be sought out and purchased at great expense (13:45-46), and in an underwater net that works out of sight (13:47-50). Hiding is explicit in two of these images and obscurity is implicit in the others. In our age the YHWH Administration's PR strategy seems bizarre. It is neither investment nor withdrawal. It seemed strange in Jesus' day too. What monarch reigns incognito? Yet the Kingdom is not purposefully marginal or aloof from its context, as counter- and para-Constantinians might think. All these similes depend on interaction — with the soil, the lump, the field, the shop, the sea — to make sense. This is a deliberate strategy of engagement.

As for the Kingdom's tiny scale, Jesus refuses the classic Constantinian confusion of size with power. A minuscule seed in a field, a pinch of yeast, a treasure chest in a field, one pearl, a net in a sea — none of these impresses except by its smallness. Yet each is powerful — in some cases, more powerful than the large thing it inhabits. That explains the astonishment that follows these teachings in Jesus' hometown synagogue. "Where did this one get his wisdom and wonders?" (13:54). He is only one man, and from an undistinguished family! Jesus' neighbors discount his significance because they overlook his connection with the Father and the Spirit. Their God is too big.

Moreover, in this Administration small things signify big things. As a little signature unleashes vast executive power and a tiny key opens enormous gates, so symbolic actions here lead to momentous actions elsewhere. "I will give you the keys of the kingdom of heaven, and whatever you bind on earth has been bound in heaven, and whatever you loose on earth has been loosed in heaven" (16:19).

Small things also reveal big things. What ruler would tolerate hypocrisy among his officials? So forgiving fellow citizens shows trust in the Father's grace (18:21-35). Welcoming the humble and caring for them shows trust in the Father's own welcome and does his will that none should perish (18:1-20, 19:13-15). Releasing one's own wealth into the regime's blind trust invests in its far greater resources (19:16-29). The YHWH Administration demands lives of total consistency.

Finally, small things are a prelude to big things. "To those who have, more will be given, and they will have an abundance," Jesus says. "But from those who have nothing, even what they have will be taken away" (13:12). This is not just remedial prophecy (cf. Isa. 6:9-13); it is remedial wisdom (Proverbs 1:29-33)! No decent ruler trusts state secrets to strangers, let alone to fools and enemies (Matt. 10:10-11). First, he finds out who can be trusted. Jesus scatters signs of deliverance before the crowds, and sorts his audiences according to their response. Antagonists get refutation and intentional confusion (12:24-45), while followers receive a security clearance, inside information (13:18-23), and the promise of heavenly authority (16:16-20).

Jesus repeats himself in the parable of the talents (25:29) to describe the final cut between the fruitful and the unfruitful: "To those who have, more will be given, and they will have an abundance; but from those who have nothing, even what they have will be taken away." What chief executive rewards incompetents with cabinet positions? Ruling is serious business! No, one starts out over only "a little" (and a talent was the equivalent of about half a million dollars, so "little" is relative), and only those who have proven themselves gain executive authority. The loser gets the sack, while the master in the parable sets the servants who double his capital "over much" (25:21, 23).

Over much *what?* Clouds and harps? Hardly. In Luke's version, these faithful servants become the mayors of many cities (Luke 19:17, 19). Is this just an incidental detail in the parable, or does evangelical fidelity in the present age actually yield political power in the next?

It seems so. The faithful and wise servant who is ready for his master's arrival is set over all the master's possessions (Matt. 24:47). The ready maidens celebrate the feast (25:10). The sheep inherit the kingdom (25:34). All of these describe activity following the day of judgment (Matt. 24–25).[17] Judgment Day is commonly treated as the last significant event in human history, but these stories suggest the opposite. In every case the work increases after the final cut is made. The talents are as much a test as anything, for the master has much over which the servants are not presently set. Perhaps the eschatological YHWH Administration thinks small because the really big events follow the eschaton.

Think about it. Why would discipleship stress the cultivation of virtues, habits, and practices that had nothing to do with life in the new creation? Where is the glory in demanding costly discipleship as mere admission into a paradise of Platonic idleness, let alone Muslim sensuality? What use is eternal passivity to a humanity created for work (Gen. 1–2)? The sab-

17. By the way, we cannot read these parables as endorsements of premillennial Dispensationalism. There is no Millennium in Matthew, and the judgment in these scenes is final, at least for the ones being judged. Likewise, being taken or left in Matt. 24:36-44 is not a "rapture" that lifts up the righteous *before* judgment but a flood *of* judgment that washes away the wicked and leaves behind the heirs. However, we can be certain that the current tasks of discipleship are a mere prelude to future tasks.

bath was made for humanity, not humanity for the sabbath (Mark 2:27). The faithful stewards in these stories enter into the master's *joy*, not his rest (Matt. 25:21, 23). The saints "shall reign for ever and ever" in the New Jerusalem (Rev. 22:5). "Reigning" does not mean retiring.

As an analogy, consider my profession's strange institution of tenure. The first years of one's teaching career are a time of probation. The object of tenure is not to make junior faculty work like dogs, burn them out, then reward them with academic social security while they kick back. When that happens, it is an abuse of tenure and a display of the teacher's bad faith. Yet that is just what we often imagine life in the new creation will be! No, tenure is properly a season of proving oneself that leads to being vested with full power. Tenure endows a proven professor with full academic freedom. It opens doors to administrative power. In sum, it *entrusts,* in the confident expectation that the trust will not be betrayed. "To sit at my right hand or at my left is not mine to grant," Jesus says, "but it is for those for whom it has been prepared by my Father" (20:23). Jesus and his disciples are not being exploited or hazed, but readied.

Christian symbolism is similarly eschatological. Both charismatic and sacramental signs are significant only if they are symbols of things that last. If faith, hope, and love really survive the knowledge, prophecy, and tongues that now respectively mediate them (1 Cor. 13), then they will still take tangible forms. If baptism and healing anticipate resurrection and Eucharist and marriage anticipate the wedding banquet, then ordination and spiritual gifts anticipate something too. As vast as the Church's power already is — power to forgive sins, to bind and loose, to witness before the world's great ones, to speak for God himself — it is a shadow of the power to come.

Perhaps *this* is why the YHWH Administration seems so concerned with a young woman's vertigo or a young man's chastity while nations lurch from one war to the next. What commander would send soldiers into battle without training? What ruler would appoint a judge who had not passed a bar exam? A nation at war and suffering injustice needs the patience to train its public servants if things are ever to improve. When a regime refuses to panic and subordinate the important to the urgent, its boot camps and law schools become signs of victories and justice to come. For God's kingdom, the Church is to be that kind of sign. "Nation will rise against nation, and kingdom against kingdom, and there will be famines and earthquakes in various places: all this is but the beginning of the birth pangs. Then they will deliver you up to tribulation, and put you to death; and you will be hated by all nations for my name's sake" (Matt. 24:8-9). "This gospel of the kingdom will be preached throughout the whole world, as a testimony to all nations; and then the end will come" (24:14). Steadfastness in the face of persecution reassures everyone that the YHWH Administration is determined and able to see the whole creation through her long, traumatic labor.

At the center of all this stands Jesus' crucifixion. Jesus follows his third prediction of it with one of his clearest interpretations of his regime's engagement with the world:

> You know that the rulers of the Gentiles lord it over them, and their great ones exercise authority over them. It shall not be so among you; but whoever would be great among you must be your servant, and whoever would be first among you must be your slave; even as the Son of Man came not to be served but to serve, and to give his life as a ransom for many. (Matt. 20:25-28)

This event too is a small thing from the world's perspective — just another execution — but it signifies, reveals, invites, and accomplishes events at the heart of God and the center of history.

"The hour has approached, and the Son of Man is betrayed into the hands of sinners" (26:45). At Calvary the world's great ones and the Kingdom's lay their respective claims: in the Jewish authorities' refusal to receive the Son of the Father (21:33-41), the Father's exaltation of the Son above them (21:42-45), Pilate's expedience (27:24), the disciples' greed and fear (20:20-24; 26:31-35, 69-75), and the Son's faithfulness to the Father and his disciples at all cost (20:25-28).[18] Jesus refuses to alter the course he has pursued from the beginning (26:39), and so becomes the definitive embodiment of the kingdom ethic he has proclaimed in the Sermon on the Mount. After all others have given up praying the Lord's Prayer, Jesus remains steadfast. He continues to invite and await his Father's Kingdom. Jesus allows the divinely ordained powers, both Jewish and Gentile, to judge and reject him and the theocracy he represents (26:25, 26:63-64a, 27:11). He does so out of trust in the sown seed to sprout and the buried treasure to last. He will wait patiently for the One who ordained those powers to vin-

---

18. See below, "The Mercy of God."

dicate him in the face of their injustices and insurgencies (26:29-32, 26:64b-66, 27:46).

The crucifixion is Jesus' tenure review, and the Father passes him. "Hereafter you will see the Son of Man seated at the right hand of Power, and coming on the clouds of heaven" (26:64), he says at his trial. "*All* authority in heaven and on earth has been given to me" (28:18), he says at his first worship service. He is neither invested in the world nor withdrawn from it; *he is its Lord.* The world is entrusted to him.

Why Patience Is a Virtue

Christians quickly saw Jesus' resurrection and glorification as pointing to a new stage for humanity (cf. 1 Cor. 15).[19] The walk from the first things to the last things has been far longer than either the first Hebrews or the first Christians thought. If evolutionary anthropologists are right that humanity is more a journey than an essence — and signs are pointing that way[20] — then who knows what is coming next? Who can fathom the responsibilities and capacities the next age might hold for us? Jesus' disciples are still on our tenure tracks (Matt. 7:21-27). Much is already entrusted to us, and a greater trust awaits. Our current arrangement between the times is a time for preparation that calls for extraordinary patience.

The Church has failed to exercise patience in two common ways that tie into the first section of this chapter. I know them both from experience.

First, dissatisfaction with the shape of the Church's authority has tempted disciples to retrench into their old Constantinian habits[21] and turn mission into what Stanley Hauerwas and Will Willimon call "activism."[22] The activist Church enters the world to take it by force. "Our kingdom come!" Activism acknowledges the Son's incarnation but not his ascension, his resurrection but not his crucifixion. Overreaching like this is a special temptation for the emerging churches of the southern

19. N. T. Wright, *The Resurrection of the Son of God* (Minneapolis: Fortress, 2003).

20. For an accessible introduction see Spencer Wells, *The Journey of Man* (New York: Random House, 2002).

21. Rodney Clapp, *A Peculiar People: The Church as Culture in a Post-Christian Society* (Downers Grove, Ill.: InterVarsity, 1996), pp. 19-21.

22. Stanley Hauerwas and William H. Willimon, *Resident Aliens: Life in the Christian Colony* (Nashville: Abingdon, 1989), pp. 44-45.

hemisphere whose most common contexts are persecution and new social dominance.[23]

Second, complacency with the Church's apparent limits has tempted disciples either to capitulate to the present order and accept subordination as "religions," "spirituality," and value systems, or to retreat into insular and even private realms beyond the world's apparent reach[24] This turns mission into what Hauerwas and Willimon call "conversionism."[25] The conversionist Church enters the world only to pluck "souls" out of it. "Your kingdom take us away!" Underreaching like this is a classic stance of spiritualists who acknowledge the Son's ascension but not his incarnation, his crucifixion but not his resurrection.

Dissatisfaction and complacency refuse to accept the story of Jesus Christ as our story. As a result we soon find ourselves impotent, hopeless, and in trouble with the regime.

To return to the apostle with whom we began this section, our impatience resembles that of Paul's fellow Israelites. They have sought to establish a righteousness of their own and rebelled against the one that actually comes from God through trust (Rom. 10:3-4). As a result they find themselves in the very position Moses warns Israel about in Deuteronomy 30, intimidated by the challenges that face them in the Promised Land and oppressed by God's demands on them. In their frustration they imagine God remains in the heavens, and thus aloof, or they fear that God is far away from them (beyond the sea in Egypt?), and thus powerless. The first fantasy turns Israel's calling into a utopian fantasy, while the second nightmare turns it into a lost cause. Israel cannot help but fail to obtain what it seeks, and so for the moment it has become hardened, marginal, and trivial (Rom. 11:7).

Glossing the prophetic passage in Deuteronomy with his usual intrepid genius, Paul advocates a proper strategy in response:

> Do not say in your heart, "Who will ascend into heaven?" (that is, to bring Christ down) or "Who will descend into the abyss?" (that is, to bring Christ up from the dead). . . . "The word is near you, on

---

23. Philip Jenkins, *The Next Christendom: The Coming of Global Christianity* (New York: Oxford, 2002), pp. 163-90.

24. Clapp, *Peculiar People*, pp. 18-19, 21.

25. Hauerwas and Willimon, *Resident Aliens*, p. 45.

your lips and in your heart" — that is, the word of faith which we preach. If you confessed with your lips that Jesus is Lord and believed in your heart that God raised him from the dead, you would be saved. For one trusts with the heart unto justification and confesses with the lips unto salvation. (Rom. 10:6-10)

Our Constantinian ambitions tempt us to pull down heaven, while our counter-Constantinian timidity and para-Constantinian separatism tempt us to flee to it. All are forms of unbelief. God is not out of our reach; Christ is Lord! We are not out of God's reach; Christ is risen! The Father's will *has been done* on earth. The Kingdom *has approached.*

Thus proper belief keeps praying, "your Kingdom come." It stays focused on the master's orders as long as he is away. Disciples *confess* the God who has come to justify and save his world whether their boldness is met with agreement or opposition. They do not worry about investing in the world or withdrawing from it, but *go into it* with apostolic patience to announce the approaching of God's reign.

Preaching that God's dominion has approached and praying for it to come seem inconsistent, but they are two necessary aspects of mission. Praying accepts God's invitation in Jesus Christ to rule. Preaching extends that invitation to those who have not received or accepted the offer. What sense does one make without the other? Only in this way are the tensions in these biblical texts resolved. In Matthew 28 the Lord's Prayer is answered in Christ's resurrection, the disciples' worship, and their great commission. In Deuteronomy 30–32 Israel's entry into the land provokes even Gentiles, from Rahab onward (cf. Josh. 1:9-14, Matt. 1:5), to rejoice along with God's people (32:43). In Romans 12–15 the righteousness of Christ unites Jews and Gentiles in a common life of sacrifice, purity, and fellowship in the midst of the powers that echoes Christ's deference to the Father (Rom. 15:5-6) and fulfills Deuteronomy's promise to confirm God's faithfulness to Israel and his good plans for every nation.

We usually ask the wrong questions. The question Christ poses to the world is whether it is invested in God's reign. The question he poses to his disciples is whether they have the patience to keep posing it.

CHAPTER 4

The Presence of God

I do not belittle the American master story; it has meant life and hope to millions of families including my own. At least on one point, though, it contrasts sharply with the biblical master story just reviewed: In the story Americans tell themselves, every great problem from independence to slavery to totalitarian threats is finally resolved by the ultima ratio *of war. . . . In surprising contrast, the biblical master story pivots upon a slave people who ran away "in urgent haste" (Deut. 16:3), upon a Savior who enters the capital city riding on a donkey and who is called the Prince of Peace; today it demands a living witness to that peace.*

James Wm. McClendon, Jr., *Witness*

Will the Son of Man Find Faith on Earth When He Comes?

"Jesus proclaimed the Kingdom of God," Alfred Loisy famously complained, "but what came was the Church." Library shelves are filled with accounts of how the Church, like Israel in Canaan, was dissolved into the world it came to save. The typical storyline traces Christianity's gradual assimilation into the culture of the Roman Empire: Christians traded Jewish-style elders for Roman-style monarchical bishops. They traded local communities for a formal network of apostolic districts centered in Rome where Caesar's roads already converged. They traded theological diversity for creedal uniformity, universal participation for a professional clergy, and countercultural power for cultural power. In sum, they arrived — or fell away — and entered a Constantinian way of life that Christians have never really been able to exit, with the exceptions of a few marginal curiosities (monks, the Amish, Jehovah's Witnesses, and so on).

American Christians traditionally fit our church histories into this Eurocentric picture, making American Christianity either a restoration of the true apostolic Church or a further betrayal. But should we? The United States was as much an alternative to Europe as it was an heir. Moreover, in the centuries since the Revolutionary War it has become something much more distinctly *American,* if still more European than African or Asian and more English than continental in character. This may not be obvious on the university campuses that Tom Wolfe rightly calls "little colonies of Europe" where the continental traditions still dominate, but it is evident enough elsewhere.

An alternative profile of American Christianity from a truly American perspective can draw on Walter Russell Mead's path-breaking analysis, *Special Providence: American Foreign Policy and How It Changed the World.*[1] Mead seeks to overturn a dominant paradigm for understanding American foreign policy. That account begins with the myth that America's original vision was isolationist, innocent of the intrigues of international politics and the "entangling alliances" they entail, and thus naïve and incompetent against colonial and post-colonial European approaches. To this myth it adds the corresponding myth that America abandoned its earlier innocence in favor of continental-style *Realpolitik* in order to make headway as a great power in the world that World War I created.

Does that sound familiar? It should. It is the same old story, with Bismarck as Constantine.

Against Eurocentric foreign policy traditions, Mead appeals to a body of evidence that the American republic had an aggressive, bellicose, complex, and sophisticated foreign policy tradition from its beginnings, and that there is more continuity than discontinuity over the twenty-one decades that transformed it from an agrarian British colony to the greatest power in the

---

1. New York: Routledge, 2001. This chapter draws freely from Mead's analysis of American foreign policy, which has influenced and been influenced by American Christianity. In this insightful account, Mead traces four main schools of foreign policy in American history: the Hamiltonian, Wilsonian, Jeffersonian, and Jacksonian.

history of the world.[2] America is a cultural force in its own right rather than just a derivative of Europe. That means the pattern in the chaos of American Christianity may not be resistance against and then seduction by imperial power after all, but something more distinctly American.

Mead traces four main schools of American self-understanding and foreign policy that have spanned America's history. Businesslike Hamiltonians champion American integration into international affairs on the terms that best serve American interests and particularly American commerce. Diplomatic Wilsonians propagate American ideals across the world — democracy, human rights, and so on — and unapologetically seek to influence other states' domestic affairs in order to advance them. Protective Jeffersonians fear the threat foreign entanglements pose to fragile democracy at home, making them diplomatically cautious and sometimes even isolationist. Populist Jacksonians defend American honor and life when provoked, are proud of military strength, and are unembarrassed about their lower regard for the well-being of America's rivals and enemies.

All these American visions originally drew from its Christians' notions of life and mission. In turn, the concerns of these four camps not only resemble currents in contemporary American Christianity, but powerfully shape them. The Constantinian agendas of the oldest and most established churches have a distinctly Hamiltonian ring. Wilsonian internationalism haunts the mainline bodies that have turned mission into interreligious dialogue or imperialism and politically correct or incorrect activism. Jeffersonian worries reinforce the vast self-protective subcultures of fundamentalism and the elite networks of postliberalism. Jacksonian patriotism animates folk Christians of every ethnicity, social class, and denominational tradition. An extended look at each of these four American visions reveals a deep, and disquieting, logic to American faith.

Businesslike Hamiltonians

For the *Hamiltonian* school, named after Alexander Hamilton, a primary responsibility of the federal government is to use wise financial and trade policies to ensure national prosperity in an uncertain and inhospitable

---

2. Mead, *Special Providence,* pp. xvi-xvii. Subsequent references to this work are indicated by parenthetical page citations in the text. Direct quotations are footnoted.

world. When looking abroad, Hamiltonians are interested above all in promoting the economic interests of their constituents, because the heart of political strength is economic prosperity. Peaceful seas are a military priority; favorable terms for trade are a diplomatic priority; a stable system of finance and currency exchange is a monetary priority.

Because communal self-interest is their goal, Hamiltonians pursue it pragmatically. When Britain dominated the world, Hamiltonians sought to minimize the threats it imposed and exploit it to its best advantage (114-19). Hamiltonians picked the British Empire clean of its assets when it collapsed after World War II and assumed its caretaker roles without replicating its imperial structure (125-28). When conditions were favorable in the nineteenth century, Hamiltonians fought for protectionism at home and open ports abroad. When the interwar economy made this unfeasible they shifted to favoring free trade (109-10).

This is neither mere self-interest nor the zero-sum vision of the world that dominated in continental Europe, in which one power only wins if others lose. It is a hard but optimistic sensibility in which "business is the highest form of philanthropy" and "commerce is the fastest road to world peace."[3] One teaches the hungry to fish, and a poor catch can be just as powerful a lesson as a good one.

There is a strong Hamiltonian strain in American Christianity. Most American Christians think the adage that "God helps those who help themselves" comes from the Bible, not the Unitarian Benjamin Franklin (who helped himself to Aesop's aphorism). Churches encourage parishioners to get out of debt, to live below our means, to save for the future, to pursue self-improvement and invest in our children's education — in sum, to thrive in the fallen world by negotiating it on favorable terms. In fact, many Christian traditions have done this so successfully and for so long that their worldly achievements have crowded out other aspects of their character.

American Christianity is persistently Hamiltonian in dedicating most of its resources to the chief benefit of its own constituents. Churches and Christian media are networking hubs for business, real estate, legal and financial services, contracting, medicine, therapy, cosmetics, mass media, books, music, and even health food. Christians found schools and colleges for our own children, then direct "charitable" fundraisers and capital cam-

3. Mead, *Special Providence*, pp. 127-28.

paigns to turn them into educational powerhouses. Churches have become multi-million-dollar entertainment centers — offering baroque musicianship and eloquent rhetoric for the upper crust and dynamic worship experiences and relevant practical wisdom for the rest of us. In an economy that tears community apart, churches have structured themselves into large- and small-group gatherings that offer convenient and safe fellowship, friendship, and romance.

Many of these activities are formally undertaken in order to advance the gospel, but without vigilant supervision the activity itself often eclipses the original mission. Is this because the ulterior mission from the outset is not really the gospel, but the interests of the group? *The Prayer of Jabez* by Bruce Wilkinson[4] hit a nerve and sold millions for an embarrassing reason: Christians in America have been praying for God to enlarge their land ever since Jamestown. The Hamiltonian Church is Hamiltonian America at prayer, making philanthropy for its own inner circles the highest form of business.

Christians in America are devoted entrepreneurial pragmatists. The Industrial Revolution overturned agrarian America, bringing severe dislocation along with almost constant growth. In response, Protestant evangelicals pioneered a staggering range of social reforms and liturgical adaptations. Franklin D. Roosevelt epitomized this approach when he described his method of ending the Great Depression: we will try something, and if it does not work then we will try something else. Entrepreneurial pragmatists responded to the Industrial Revolution with schools, the YMCA, the Salvation Army, the Temperance movement, Bible societies, labor unions, prison ministries, soup kitchens and shelters, revivalist camps, lecture circuits, and slide shows (those distant ancestors of our stadium rock concerts, blockbuster summer films, and PowerPoint sermons). These organizational, ministerial, and liturgical innovations created what James F. White calls a new "frontier tradition" of Christianity that purportedly focused on revival but also centered on *adaptation*. Wesleyans excel in entrepreneurial pragmatism, perhaps in part because their founder was a child of the Enlightenment. Lutherans, Calvinists, and Anglicans have tended to grimace at first but quietly follow suit once the innovations become more mainstream and especially when their own social survival seems at stake.

---

4. Bruce Wilkinson, *The Prayer of Jabez: Breaking Through to the Blessed Life* (Sisters, Ore.: Multnomah, 2000).

Evangelicals' efforts both remade industrial societies and industrialized Christianity. Both transformations were revolutionary. They were also, in part, Hamiltonian business as usual. Tactics that proved impractical or ineffective could be abandoned as boldly as they had been adopted, because the underlying mission had not changed. Every adjustment to the opportunities and cruelties of industrial modernity sought to preserve and extend the life and reach of Christian communities on favorable terms. Entrepreneurial pragmatism's underlying conviction is that the health of Christian communities is a function not merely of ideological or social purity but also of "relevance," meaning cultural commerce. There is optimism under this unremitting resolve, optimism grounded in a conviction that for all its sinfulness "this is my Father's world." "Beneath the Hamiltonian pinstripes beats the heart of a romantic dreamer," Mead says. The Hamiltonian Christian's dream is to glorify the Father who shines in all that's fair by thriving as the Hebrews thrived in Egypt and as Israel prospered in the midst of its enemies.

The trouble with the Hamiltonian prosperity gospel is that the thriving can overshadow the glorifying. James Tunstead Burtchaell's *The Dying of the Light*[5] chronicles the seemingly inevitable loss of Christian identity among the institutions of higher education that American denominations founded in centuries past. Economic and competitive pressure slowly diluted the original missions of schools across the denominational spectrum (even those from the more Jeffersonian Dissenters). These capitulations to the wider culture have provoked each new generation to found a new set of organizations with emphatically Christian mission statements. Yet despite every effort, these too seem to drift away from their moorings. Is this because an underlying strategy — not the only one, but a constant one — is really a Hamiltonian vision that straddles the process of secularization? Most Christian schools are founded not just to strengthen orthodoxy but to give their constituents' children a head start in life. Parents want them to become cultured, to marry well, to become marketable and financially independent, and to preserve if not gain social status. Schools have *not* drifted from this charge any more than America has drifted from mercantilism to free trade or from defending itself against Great Britain to assuming Britain's old role as the policeman of world trade. The Hamiltonian light still shines! Only the particulars have changed, according to circumstances. One

5. Grand Rapids: Eerdmans, 1998.

of those particulars seems to be the specifically Christian character of the prosperity.

Hamiltonian communities mutate pragmatically into what they have been all along: vehicles of enlightened self-interest. Hamiltonians are more sponsors of their own regime than subjects of YHWH's. King Solomon is a better patron saint for them than Emperor Constantine.

Missionary Wilsonians

Mead traces two converging ancestries behind the *Wilsonian* school of foreign policy, named for Woodrow Wilson, president of the United States during World War I and an exemplar of this way of thinking. First, English Nonconformism produced powerful reform movements in Britain and America. These spawned a self-understanding in which equality, democracy, toleration, and peace were ideal not just for England's children but for the whole world. Second, the missionary movement drove thousands from across America's Protestant denominations to the far corners of the earth. Missions made the United States a medium, instrument, beneficiary, and object of intentional cross-cultural transformation. These flowered in a conviction that "the United States has the right and the duty to change the rest of the world's behavior."[6] Call it mission, muscle, moralism, or simply meddling; the fact is that the Wilsonian school of foreign policy is a consistent and popular American foreign policy.

This policy bypassed the usual channels of official diplomacy and journalism and brought world consciousness into the sanctuary of every typical church in America and into many village commons around the world (139). It spread from the sanctuary to the State Department and even back to Europe to jostle today with old style *Realpolitik* as a foreign policy of every state west of the former Soviet Union (138). Wilsonian visions of both Christian and non-Christian varieties have driven democratization, human rights, literacy, economic development, public health advances, world peace, and of course evangelism from Latin America to the Middle East, Africa, South and East Asia, and the Pacific islands.

Today Wilsonian visions are more likely to be left-of-center and secularist (143) and their institutions are more likely to be NGOs and interna-

6. Mead, *Special Providence,* p. 138.

tional bodies than mission boards (146). Moreover, repentance for past sins produces the Wilsonian alter egos of relativism and multiculturalism as often as renewal and revivalism (155). Wilsonians insist on changing the whole world, or at least writing its master narrative, in ways conveniently hospitable to themselves.

Since Wilsonianism is indebted to the missionary movement, the Wilsonian flavor of American Christianity is obvious. It is also admirable. Millions of disciples have given sacrificially. Multitudes invested their whole lives in tasks that promised risk, obscurity, and poverty. Wilsonians put first the things that were least in the world's eyes: indigenous peoples hidden in jungles and isolated islands, societies whose morals revolted western sensibilities, those whose race, class, gender, or circumstance made them powerless and invisible, and even outlaws and enemies of their own causes. Much of what people of most every confession take for granted to be right with the world is due to their prophetic and apostolic vision.

Nevertheless, Wilsonian Christianity's less attractive qualities have made both liberal and conservative Christians squeamish about studying it too closely and reluctant to admit its staying powers (140-41). So, far from merely belaboring the obvious (Wilsonian cultural insensitivity, condescension, and imperialism), looking Wilsonian Christianity in the mirror reveals features we have learned to overlook.

One unappetizing feature is Wilsonians' habitual dependence on American power won by other means. Yesterday's Wilsonian reformers did not shrink from using federal and state power to advance their agendas. Today their liberal and conservative descendants rely on judicial activism, legislation, and executive orders to right America's wrongs. The same is true abroad. Missionaries, relief workers, and social revolutionaries have all depended on the resources, protections, and initiatives of their powerful governments (147): safe travel, a lot of money to pay for it, advanced western medicine, congregational literacy, sophisticated linguistics for accurate Bible translation, and diplomatic muscle to fend off and remedy persecution. This is as true in the age of the Internet as in the age of the steamboat. Wilsonian checks are backed by Hamiltonian bank balances.

The dependency goes in both directions. Like good-cop-bad-cop interrogators, Wilsonians and Hamiltonians make a formidable combination that wins more concessions from opponents than either could do on its own. Together they have undermined classical colonialism and promoted global capitalism and democracy with breathtaking success (149,

162-65). Since both camps consider these conditions favorable to their own purposes, the two often find common cause (167-68). A revolving door connects the Wilsonian Church and Hamiltonian America. Missionaries took responsibility for the pastoral care and moral policing of expatriates in diplomatic and business occupations (144-45), and in the 1940s missionary kids became valuable assets and as many as half the "foreign culture experts" the American government and American-headquartered world businesses relied on during and after World War II (154). While Jacksonians dominate the rank-and-file of America's armed forces, Wilsonians also populate their numbers, fusing (and confusing) the aims of American defense, personal betterment, global democracy, and world evangelization. Mead likens large mission boards to early multinational corporations (143) — and sure enough, after decades of Mormon world missions Utah is a cosmopolitan center of world business relationships (154) and a bastion of patriotism, and the Mormon Church and its members hold stakes in a veritable mountain of global assets. Many Wilsonians indeed recover in this age a hundredfold what they had left behind.

If Hamiltonian power underwrites Wilsonian charity, Wilsonian mission also runs cover for Hamiltonian self-interest (171-72). Multinational corporations fund huge advertising campaigns trumpeting the pocket change they throw at charitable causes. States and counties close libraries symbolically in order to force bond funds and tax measures that mainly go into the pockets of public-sector employees and constituents. Likewise, in many American churches paltry missions and relief budgets receive glowing publicity while Hamiltonian projects receive the lion's share of church funds. Other churches dedicate themselves more sacrificially to liberal or conservative Wilsonian ends; yet truly rare is the church or denomination that forgoes traditional priorities and makes mission its cultural, political, or even financial ordering principle.

These tactics are not purely cynical. Hamiltonian causes *do* enable Wilsonian efforts. Moreover, they fuel a missional self-understanding that keeps the world a formal congregational priority, trains churches away from becoming wholly complacent with their own betterment, and strengthens the traditions of hospitality in which churches offer their impressive resources to strangers. Many of America's churches may be glorified Rotary clubs, but at least they are not country clubs.

Nevertheless, these qualities promote a powerful self-deception that haunts both the right and left wings of Wilsonian Christianity, just as it haunts their neoconservative and liberal activist counterparts in the wider culture. Wilsonian policy often appears idealistic, but it is in fact ideological, and there is a profound difference. Wilsonians regularly sacrifice means to ideological ends — for instance, raising state support for abolition, temperance, civil rights, and clean air, as well as redefining gender roles and undermining social distinctions when these stand in the way of their accomplishments (152). And their pragmatism is consistently selective: Wilsonian Christians on the right have been reluctant to mend the divisions among churches that compromise their witness and sap their strength, while Wilsonian Christians on the left have been more hospitable to progressives of other religious traditions than to traditionalists in their own. I suspect that this is because the ideology that inspires Wilsonian schemes of local and global transformation is not so much the good news of Jesus Christ as that other gospel, modern liberalism. And as ideology often masks self-interest, so underneath the Wilsonian ideology lurks the identity and self-interest of the ones who profess it. As Mead says of political Wilsonians,

> Europeans, Indians, Chinese, Africans, and Latin Americans have . . . noticed something about this tradition that tends to escape notice in the "Anglo-Saxon" world: that the espousal of [Wilsonians'] high ideals has not prevented the successive rise of two English-speaking empires to global hegemony. The Anglo-Saxon conscience may be sensitive and easily excited, they say, yet it is also flexible, and generally manages to concentrate its outrage on those aspects of the world's evils that threaten to thwart some interesting project of an Anglo-Saxon state. The Anglo-Saxons may be as innocent as doves, note our neighbors and critics, but that has singularly not interfered with our ability to be as cunning as serpents.[7]

Like all philosophies, ideologies grow in the cultural soil of particular peoples, tempting us to take our own experience as universal. When a studio full of American pop singers gathered in 1985 to raise money for Ethiopian famine relief by singing "We Are the World," they really thought they were! The same mindset blinds otherwise faithful and healthy churches. My favorite church pours the money its music ministry raises into mis-

7. Mead, *Special Providence*, p. 137.

sions that center in musical tours bringing contemporary Christian praise and worship revivalism to stadiums, prisons, orphanages, and ghettos in Asia, Africa, and Latin America. A consortium of evangelical churches in the Los Angeles area recently partnered with an African American church in Watts to hold an evangelistic street fair there. Along with the usual food and music it featured haircuts, makeovers, and other services that echoed earlier missionary assumptions about what the world outside the west needed for its redemption. In both cases the faith is genuine, the intentions are admirable, and the assistance is real. Yet even as the "missionaries" are consistently struck by their audiences' greater zeal for Jesus Christ, they persist in calling their visits missions. What are they offering that their audiences do not already have, except for American culture?

A church I once visited decorated its sanctuary with the flags of the nations in which it supported missionaries. One nation was missing: the United States. When I mentioned the omission to some churchgoers after the service, one replied (and the others agreed) that the church supported no missionaries in America. When another member pointed out that this was not really true — that much of the church's "outreach" was missionary in character — the other shifted her explanation: the American flag was disqualified because authentic mission is *cross-cultural*. On one level, of course, America is so culturally diverse that this statement is plainly false. Yet at a deeper level it is absolutely true. If political and technological culture rather than Christian confession is what defines the mission field, America is already planted and harvested. (Happily, the American flag later quietly took its place alongside the others.)

It was not until recently that American missionaries realized the need for missions in the old imperial centers of post-Christian Europe or the English-speaking worlds with which they felt a cultural familiarity. In secularist circles and even in Christian ones, it still strikes us as odd that relief work or missions should be directed to a former imperial center. Sending missionaries to Spain seems almost as strange as sending the Peace Corps there, while Mexico and the Philippines seem natural destinations for both, even though their Christianity (both Protestant and Catholic) is much stronger.

One suspects that an animating principle of Wilsonian Christianity is not making the world more like Christ — or at least not merely that — but also making the world more like *us*.

As this has dawned on people, as it increasingly has since the days when the so-called Masters of Suspicion (Marx, Nietzsche, Freud, and so forth) renarrated the west, a Wilsonian backlash has set in. Mead traces multiculturalism and relativism to the unexpected long-term impact of western missions. Cross-cultural contact opened Christian America to cross-pollination — funding, among other things, nineteenth-century transcendentalism (156) and creating lasting romantic western impressions of non-western cultural traditions. The trajectory of the World Council of Churches from its origins in the vital world missionary movement to its present doldrums in interreligious dialogue parallels a transformation in evangelical youth culture. Today college students hardly ever enter long-term missions. Instead, in my evangelical circles at any rate, they enroll in short-term summer- or spring-break missions that center in service rather than evangelism. The point is to grow spiritually from the "sacrifice," to benefit from the superior qualities of the indigenous churches they are visiting, and to build a building or two (regardless of the dirt-cheap labor costs and overwhelming unemployment where they are going). The exception to this rule is postcolonial victims like South Africa and Palestine, which remain fashionable destinations for longer term missions.

These shifts are not the collapses or reversals of the Wilsonian vision they seem to be. Underneath the drastic changes lies a robust and tenacious conviction. Liberalism originally conceived of persons as sovereign subjects who negotiate their own futures under a common Creator. In this scheme some things are proper to the individual (will, perspectives, and values), while other things are proper to the whole (natural law, objectivity, and facts). Self-determination, democracy, free trade, the rule of law, property, and the like are the conventional expressions of this vision in the Anglo-American tradition, and colonial rule, monarchy, mercantilism, autocracy, collectivism, and the like are its traditional enemies. Liberalism narrates past, present, and future history as the world's progressive self-realization in a new eschatological order of liberty, equality, and fraternity.[8]

Liberalism's fundamental categories have shifted rather than given way. Once truth was safeguarded in the objective world, secularism discovered the Creator was dispensable to the scheme. Liberty, equality, and fraternity were natural rather than supernatural qualities, and attainable with or without outside help. "Preach the gospel; use words if necessary," said St.

8. Lesslie Newbigin, *Signs amid the Rubble: The Purposes of God in Human History,* ed. Geoffrey Wainwright (Grand Rapids: Eerdmans, 2003), pp. 3-18.

Francis. Neo-Wilsonianism has found words — at least words about God — less and less necessary, and preachers more and more embarrassing.

Other shifts have still left the basic scheme intact. Retaining equality but abandoning individualism reframes the goal as intercultural and inter-religious harmony and multicultural affirmation. Reified "cultures" or "religions" rather than reified individuals will coexist in a new, tolerant social order. The only enemies of this gospel are the "fundamentalist" holdouts who refuse to heed the altar call.

In other respects, though, liberalism's dream has dissipated even while its categories remain in place. Both the radical left and the apocalyptic right still operate in a modern frame but oppose modernity's typical vision of progress. Sometimes they substitute their own eschatologies — Stalinism, Fascism, and Dispensationalism. Other times they abandon eschatology altogether for bitter nihilism.[9] Today missionaries are the anti-heroes of Barbara Kingsolver's *The Poisonwood Bible*.[10] The world is not being self-realized under a benevolent if rather deistic God, but being handed over to a satanic power. America is the Enemy; the Church is the oppressor; the United Nations and the World Council of Churches are the Antichrist. If Wilsonianism's eternal temptation is self-love, then anti-Wilsonianism's eternal temptation is self-hatred.

Common to these apparent opposites — proselytism, globalization, multiculturalism, and antiglobalism — is the centrality of the self. Regardless of whether we like what we see, we refuse to turn away from our mirror.

Evangelism is a key tactic for classic Wilsonians, late Wilsonians, and post-Wilsonians alike. Though modern relativism pushes objectivity out of reach and enthrones subjectivity, it remains arrogantly self-assured of the universality of its appraisal and strangely missionary about spreading the bad news.[11] Its message is contradictory, but its self-assertiveness is consistent: *we* embody the knowledge that *you* need to embody too. Relativism is liberalism on the rebound: You can be whatever you like, as long as you are like us rather than them.

If early and late Hamiltonian Christianity makes the Church a vehicle of enlightened self-interest, early and late Wilsonian Christianity makes it

9. Lesslie Newbigin, *Proper Confidence: Faith, Doubt, and Certainty in Christian Discipleship* (Grand Rapids: Eerdmans, 1995), pp. 29-44.

10. New York: HarperCollins, 1999.

11. Lesslie Newbigin, *The Gospel in a Pluralist Society* (Grand Rapids: Eerdmans, 1989).

a vehicle of liberal self-realization and reproduction. On their good days, Wilsonians are still ambassadors and emissaries of the Kingdom, but on their bad days they are autocrats posing as someone else's subjects. Like Adam and Eve, who being made like God nevertheless sought to be like God in the only way forbidden to them, so the Wilsonian drive to achieve makes their patron saint not Constantine so much as King Saul, whose spiritual confidence led him to second-guess God's own commands (1 Sam. 15), and who never gave up even after God had given up on him.

Protective Jeffersonians

Unlike these first two schools, *Jeffersonian* foreign policy likes to play defense. To Jeffersonians, who take their name from President Thomas Jefferson, the American political culture with its democracy, civil liberties, and social arrangements is "uniquely precious but achingly vulnerable." Foreign policy must therefore respect that not commerce but liberty is "infinitely precious, and almost as infinitely fragile."[12] With roots in the English and Scottish dissenters who achieved a miraculous respite in the New World from Europe's hopeless class divisions, warring monarchies, and Catholic legacy, Jeffersonians seek above all to protect and deepen what they have won from the corrosive effects of power both at home and abroad. Pessimists at heart, they see a world not of Hamiltonian opportunity nor Wilsonian progress, but of trials and temptations to lose one's soul. Empires and moral crusades alike must be resisted, especially the wars that ratchet up federal power. Likewise, Jeffersonians practice constant vigilance and wage domestic battles against new and old priesthoods, aristocracies, conspiracies, and other concentrations of power.

For Jeffersonians, small (enough) is beautiful. In American history, Jeffersonians still balanced state powers and appended a Bill of Rights to the Hamiltonian Constitution after the more Jeffersonian and centrifugal Confederation failed. They demilitarized post–Civil War America to almost antebellum levels (202). Jeffersonian expansions such as the Louisiana Purchase and policies such as the Monroe Doctrine safeguarded the U.S. against European ventures in its neighborhood, but Jeffersonians opposed the annexation of Texas, let alone the acquisition of territories in the far-

12. Mead, *Special Providence*, p. 183.

away Pacific (184). They also pruned diplomatic budgets relentlessly and fought governmental secrecy that left citizens out of the intelligence loop.

Today's Jeffersonians built the meritocratic engineer-culture of Silicon Valley;[13] mock the ossifying aristocracy of the East Coast; and inhabit either the libertarian "right" and worry at the size of the Federal Register or inhabit the countercultural "left" and consider the Vietnam War paradigmatic, and fight off feelings of helplessness at usually being on the losing side of policymaking since the eve of World War II.

Fundamentalists and their descendants are Jeffersonian not only in sharing Jeffersonianism's ideological heritage but especially in absorbing its cultural sensibilities. Jeffersonian fundamentalists home school their children, nurture their vast but decentralized network of alternative media and institutions for passing on traditions and airing dirty laundry, and build congregational and nondenominational churches and cell groups. They weave anti-Catholic and conspiracy theories and apocalyptic paranoid fantasies in which their fragile communities vanish or earn martyrs' rewards, fund cult-watch organizations that police each other's fidelity to Protestant orthodoxy, and separate from any institution — even one of their own making — that threatens their purity. To weather contemporary storms they tie themselves to the masts of yesterday's confessions, theological systems, apologetics, and cultural adaptations. These tendencies can look individualistic, Gnostic, consumeristic, and modernistic from other perspectives, and those dimensions are sometimes present; but the tendencies are still fueled and ordered by a deeper logic whose coherence and political vision is Jeffersonian.

For these traits fundamentalists, like other Jeffersonians, are pilloried by Hamiltonian and Wilsonian Christians and non-Christians as isolationist, anti-intellectual, unsophisticated, naïve, and even stupid. The characterization is deeply unfair, as anyone knows who is acquainted with fundamentalism's robust intellectual history and demographic shape. Mead's kind words for Jeffersonians — brilliant, loyal, innovative, reformist, and rigorously critical — apply to Jeffersonian Christians as well. They have maintained and even extended their theological traditions remarkably well against awesome cultural and intellectual pressures. Their tenacious appreciation for traditions such as supernaturalism, substitutionary

13. "Two Young Men Who Went West," in Tom Wolfe, *Hooking Up* (New York: Picador, 2000), pp. 17-65.

atonement, and sexual self-discipline that others would just as soon leave behind has helped keep Christianity intact in America, confounding once-universal assumptions that secularization is inevitable in the west. I myself am a Christian in part because Jeffersonian Christians shared the good news with me in a potent, coherent, and plausible form that the liberal churches of my youth had either forgotten or did not bother to teach me.

Yet Jeffersonian sensibilities can also lead to disaster. As Jeffersonian nonresistance to Fascism leading up to World War II devastated and marginalized the Jeffersonian school until Vietnam (208), so fundamentalist self-isolation in the 1920s inaugurated a fifty-year retreat from mainline Christian denominations, which in turn slipped into unopposed modernism, Niebuhrian realism, social integration, and secular activism. Likewise, Jeffersonian reluctance to overpower slavery and segregation dealt a winning hand to Hamiltonian and Wilsonian abolitionists and civil rights advocates, who pursued their goals through a stronger and more centralized state, just as Christian Jeffersonians ceded moral ground to activist Christians who were more passionate about reversing the Church's sorry records on racial and gender oppression. At times the Jeffersonian paradigm blinds and paralyzes its advocates in the face of danger.

One disaster begets another. When Jeffersonian Christianity fails, its constituents can turn rapidly into ruthless utilitarians. As isolationist Americans turned into total warriors against Japan in World War II, so Southern Baptists have sacrificed their own ecclesiological principles and transformed themselves into a centralized denomination in order to root out liberalism and advance the fundamentalist agenda. *Roe v. Wade* and other developments in wider American society turned the fundamentalists of the sixties into the Christian right of the seventies and beyond. Today the Republican Party woos social conservatives with so-called faith-based initiatives, and American evangelicals look to governmental power where it might help them get their way. Conservatives are as Niebuhrian today as liberals were fifty years ago. Meet the new boss, same as the old boss.

Yet what exactly is being sacrificed? Here too, the apparent inconsistency can be resolved by noting a deeper consistency among Jeffersonians. Foreign policy Jeffersonians consider war a last resort, not so much because war is wrong or terrible but primarily because war is socially distorting. They may cry, "Give me liberty or give me death," but in the crunch they will accept a diminished liberty that allows them to see another day. Life, not liberty or the pursuit of happiness, is at the top of their list of inalienable rights. The Jeffersonian order is always a pragmatic balancing act. It abhors aristocracy, but owns slaves. It keeps its peace with the same lethal power it used to win independence from England. It will free-ride on the dirty work of others, as America let the British Empire bear the costs of *Pax Britannia* (199-204). The Jeffersonian vision is at least as prudent as it is principled, for at its heart is survival, not faithfulness to another. It fights the wars it deems necessary rather than go to the cross.

This trait makes it useful even for its rivals. Mead notes that Jeffersonianism is a handy temporary ideology for Hamiltonian and Wilsonian activists to embrace when their adventures fail. Vietnam and Watergate gave an immense boost to Jeffersonian fortunes after decades in eclipse (until Iran and the disastrous Carter presidency buried them again). The party out of power in Washington consistently wraps itself in Jeffersonian republican principles while it plots its return to dominance. Republicans discovered the virtues of a strong legislature for reining in the imperial presidency when they killed Bill Clinton's health care reform plan and won back control of Congress; Democrats discovered the perils of nation-building not in the Balkans but in Afghanistan and Iraq; liberals rushed to declare the conservatives' war on drugs a failure even as they refused to concede defeat in their own war on poverty — and vice versa. Jeffersonianism is at least as convenient for covering one's flanks as for saving one's soul.

Yesterday's triumphalists are today's prophets. Thirty years ago James Cone ignited a "black theology" that took a racial variant on liberation theology as the black church's core spirituality. The movement stagnated and has come to little outside politically correct circles, and Cone's recent reflection on the movement casts himself as a prophet unloved in his own country.[14] Postliberal Christians really began discovering new respect for the Anabaptist tradition and what John Howard Yoder called "the politics of Jesus" and "the Original Revolution" once ministers from the Christian right rather than from their own ranks started leading congressional prayer breakfasts. The Jesus Seminar propagates the contemporary myth of a pure primitive Christianity swept away by the Catholic establishment (third-century Gnostics? second-century catholics? first-century Pauline feminists? the "Q" community? Jesus the wandering cynic?) with an obsti-

---

14. James H. Cone, *God of the Oppressed*, rev. ed. (Maryknoll, N.Y.: Orbis, 1997), pp. ix-xviii; see also "Black Theology and the Black Church" in James H. Cone, *For My People: Black Theology and the Black Church* (Maryknoll, N.Y.: Orbis, 1984), pp. 99-121.

nacy familiar to evangelicals. The myth of Christian innocence resembles the romantic myth of American innocence. The old Christian mainline is the new fundamentalism — lamenting the selling out of American Christianity from its deteriorating theological bastions, turning *The Da Vinci Code* into a liberal *Left Behind,* envisioning itself in Babylonian exile, indulging in Jeffersonian pessimism, lashing out at the new evangelical mainline, and dreaming of another day.

Jeffersonians would have as their patron saint Samuel, who warned against the trappings of monarchy, but the dark side of Jeffersonian Christianity will accept a Herodian throne or Essene wilderness rather than submit to a Roman prison, let alone a cross. A truer mascot is King Hezekiah, who prayed for God's deliverance only after stripping the temple to pay off Assyria failed, and whose diplomatic ambition and incompetence brought the very same ruin from Babylon instead (2 Kings 19).

Tribal Jacksonians

Mead's final school of foreign policy is *Jacksonian,* named in honor of populist president Andrew Jackson, who harnessed the political power of the lower and middle American classes to craft a foreign and domestic politics shaped by their collective self-interest and codes of honor. Southern political dynasties, northern political machines, Midwestern farm communities, westerners suspicious of the federal government, ethnic voting blocs, suburban lobbies for middle-class welfare, military and sports cultures, and even inner-city gangs follow Jacksonian dynamics.

Jacksonians are not missionaries, but their gospel spreads anyway. Mead characterizes the school as the folk ideology of the United States, rooted in the culture of America's original British colonizers, especially the Scotch-Irish who settled its frontiers (227). These had long ago become hardened in their opposition to English power, fighting it physically rather than intellectually as Jeffersonians did. Their warrior culture took root in the United States, renewed itself every generation through frontier, civil, international, and world war (227), and assimilated ethnic immigrants into its ways, if not always its circles, with astounding success (229). Its core values descend from the honor codes of the American frontier: self-reliance (with a side order of entitlement to the deserving) rather than inheritance, welfare, or affirmative action; respect for rights and dignity rather than condescension or humiliation; prosperity through equality of opportunity and self-improvement rather than aristocracy or equality of result; independence for youth and reverence (and political muscle) for elders; individualism governed by deference to the tribe; freedom of conscience and self-expression (taking economic form as consumerism rather than thrift) rather than theological and economic discipline; honesty to one's own community; loyalty to family; sexual decency (tolerating premarital sexual activity but not homosexuality or adultery); and courage and militarism rather than negotiation or pacifism (231-35). These values delineate its communities. To be outside one is to be outside the other, and to be outside is to forgo the group's respect, protection, and even toleration — as elites, Catholics, ideologues, prison inmates, slaves, indigenous Americans, and foreign powers have all learned from often brutal experience (236-37). Honorable insiders are respected; dishonorable insiders are disciplined or expelled; outsiders are ignored; trespassers are shot. On this last point, Mead's numbers are devastating: in its wars both great and small, America has killed more foreign civilians for each military casualty of its own than even Nazis did on their eastern front (218-20). The nation is an extension of the Jacksonian family (245), and Jacksonians do all they can to win the wars their country starts.

The tribe's combination of carrots and sticks explains the Jacksonian ethic's popularity and its ability to spread. The early history of the Muslim world offers an instructive parallel, when the tribe of Quraysh — the first to convert to Islam — embarked upon its astoundingly successful conquest of the southern Mediterranean. It made a formidable combination of tribal social cohesion, military discipline, financial and political bounty, ideological confidence, a sense of theological destiny — and a willingness to accept other tribes into its ranks and share the plunder of conquest according to a system in which the earliest tribes to join got the biggest cuts. Submitters were treated generously, opponents ruthlessly. The resemblances between sixth- and seventh-century Arabia and nineteenth-century Middle America help explain why there are so many Pakistanis of Indian heritage with the surname "Qurayshi" and Americans of Mayan descent named "Edward." These are tribes it is better to join than to cross. These are the social engines that power civilizations and drive empires.

Jacksonians have shifted their party registrations (lately from Democrat to Republican beginning with Richard Nixon and accelerating between Ronald Reagan and George W. Bush), but not their political tune. They tend to be social libertarians to moderates, trade protectionists, and foreign policy hawks; they believe government exists for the well-being of the common people, and any means of promoting that well-being, including apparent ideological inconsistency and a reasonable level of corruption, are permissible within the honor code's limits (238-39). Conversely, failure to attend to constituents' interests — whether by failing to return tax dollars to their congressional districts or by sending constituents' children off to fight other people's wars — is politically unforgivable. Sky-high military budgets, yes; United Nations dues, no. War for oil, if necessary; for oil companies, let alone the House of Saud, no.

Jacksonians are more convinced of original sin than of prevenient grace. Wilsonians trying to usher in the Millennium have their heads in the clouds. Hamiltonians trying to get rich are probably doing it at the expense of the middle class. Jeffersonian pessimists are dangerous wimps.

Jacksonian culture and constituencies have staggering influence at home and abroad. American sports teams and figures are heroes in the States and worldwide. Pop, country, and rap music are worldwide musical phenomena. Crime dramas, mass-market sitcoms, and "reality television" rule the television at night, soap operas and talk shows in the daytime. (The Work family keeps its children on a Jeffersonian television diet — PBS kids' shows almost exclusively — but indulges in a guilty suburban-Jacksonian binge after bedtime: *Law and Order; Survivor; What Not to Wear* and *While You Were Out* on TLC; eighties and nineties retrospectives on VH1; *Wife Swap;* the odd *Blind Date;* and that Jeffersonian concession to the masses, *Frontier House* on PBS.) The princes of syndicated radio are Howard Stern and Rush Limbaugh. Action movies dominate box offices and video shelves and export Jacksonian militarism to the world. These are the stories we tell ourselves and the billions who want to follow along. A Jacksonian Iraqi put it famously in 2003, according to *The New York Times:*

> In the giddy spirit of the day, nothing could quite top the wish list bellowed out by one man in the throng of people greeting American troops from the 101st Airborne Division who marched into town today. What, the man was asked, did he hope to see now that the Baath Party had been driven from power in his town? What would the Americans bring? "Democracy," the man said, his voice

rising to lift each word to greater prominence. "Whisky. And sexy!" Around him, the crowd roared its approval.[15]

Almost all Christianity in the world is folk Christianity, whether purists like it or not. American Christianity is Jacksonian by second nature, if not first nature, and every indication is that it will continue to be. The twentieth century's liberal mainline Protestant subculture was in good measure Jacksonian: It authorized the New Deal and later the Great Society to save the middle class and honor its elderly. It countenanced the intentional targeting of civilians in both theaters of World War II, a targeting that culminated at Hiroshima and Nagasaki. One of its most popular figures was the positive thinker and self-improver Norman Vincent Peale. It accepted segregation in both the North and the South until Martin Luther King appealed to its instincts and convinced it to widen its tribal boundaries (237). John F. Kennedy helped convince Jacksonian America that Catholics could be faithful to the tribe as well — and American Catholics have become firmly Jacksonian when it comes to heeding Rome on matters such as marriage, finance, and sex. (The Catholic Church's recent sexual abuse scandals have only accelerated Catholic distrust of elites who seem far away, out of touch, and preoccupied with their own welfare.)

When the Democratic Party turned left and alienated its Jacksonians, it alienated many of its churchgoers too. The loss was more the Democrats' than the Jacksonians'. The only Democratic presidents since Kennedy have been southerners who, in varying degrees, embodied populist politics. With liberal Christianity in decline since the sixties, today conservative evangelicalism has the demographic edge, church attendance is a reliable predictor of Republican Party affiliation, and Middle America is still getting its programs and tax breaks.

Conservative Jacksonian Christians have diluted the qualities of their many ancestors — Wesleyan missionary initiative and social reformism, Reformed theological orthodoxy, Baptist soul competency, fundamentalist stubbornness, Pentecostal spiritualism, Dispensational pessimism, and Catholic identity — into a bland nondenominational mixture that is as appealing to the average American as it is theologically unchallenging. To-

---

15. Jim Dwyer, "A Bridgehead, and a Thirsty Welcome," *The New York Times,* April 4, 2003; available online at http://www.nytimes.com/2003/04/03/international/worldspecial/03AIRB.html.

day's evangelicals mingle almost effortlessly with the others in the Jacksonian tribe. Their spending habits and voting patterns are about the same. They digest many of the same ideas (though sometimes repackaged as "Christian" books or channeled through the Trinity Broadcasting Network instead of Fox News). They marry and divorce in similar though not identical ways. They are as litigious as the rest of America.

There is no reason to minimize the considerable strengths of Jacksonian Christianity. Its honor code draws from Christian convictions as well as other ones, bearing something of a resemblance to the honor codes of medieval Europe in which folk Christianity ran almost as deep as it ever has. It is more intellectual (if selectively so), and far more intelligent, than its detractors admit. Its inclusiveness is a powerful force for grass-roots ecumenism, racial reconciliation, and even feminism (260-61).

The Jacksonian Church also acts in ways that recognize the serious challenges to Christian faith both within and without the Christian community. Its dualistic cosmology does not wish away the power of the enemies of the faith, but respects the power of evil in the world. Thus Jacksonian Christians fight spiritual wars as determinedly as temporal ones. Charismatic Jacksonians do not just stockpile weapons of the Spirit; they use them. Many are dedicated "prayer warriors." Furthermore, as Mead notes, folk America's relative openness and capacity for self-improvement — qualities that American elites often fail (or refuse) to perceive — means that Jacksonian Christianity can be powerfully self-critical, especially when the criticisms are backed by the Holy Scriptures it holds dear. Finally, Jacksonians deserve respect just because they comprise most of Jesus Christ's American brothers and sisters. Snobbish Hamiltonian, Wilsonian, and Jeffersonian Christians who deplore their influence forget that their king and his court had Galilean accents. God uses the foolish of the world to humble the wise.

Nevertheless, conservative Jacksonian Christianity deserves its share of criticism. At the heart of the problem is the priority it gives to the tribe rather than to Christ. This school marginalizes key features of the ancient faith — the doctrine of the Trinity, fidelity to the Church, mission and hospitality to outsiders, service to the poor, and aversion to violence — and centralizes concerns that had been more marginal, such as creationism, pretribulationist eschatology (which sits uneasily beside American hyperpower), ethnic favoritism, property rights including gun ownership, and legal and psychological support for the nuclear family. Some of these obviously maintain community interests, while others mark community boundaries.

A strange thing happens to the key conviction of Protestant Christianity, the doctrine of justification by grace through faith, in Jacksonian contexts. The Prodigal Son becomes an archetype of discipline in basically Pharisaic communities. The Jacksonian Christian lives by her tribe's honor code. It is when she breaks *that* code rather than, say, the Bible's moral standards that the community of faith demands contrition and repentance and offers forgiveness and restoration. Sexual offenders need to repent, as well as disloyal children, blasphemers, abusive parents, liars, thieves, swindlers, backstabbers, and substance abusers. However, Christian businessmen do not need to repent of lives driven by greed. Overachievers do not need to repent of consuming competitiveness. Conspicuous consumers do not need to repent of how they handle their prosperity as long as it has not endangered their children. Soldiers do not need to repent of fighting unjust wars, let alone just ones. Politicians do not need to repent of working the system (so long as they have done it legally). Wage earners do not need to repent of exploiting the tax code or America's retirement system (though welfare parents might). Heretics do not need to repent of their theological mistakes. Parents and children do not need to repent of putting their families before their church commitments. Teens do not need to repent of their popularity or longings for it. When some of them do, fellow congregants react with amusement, puzzlement, discomfort, or resentment: we have a zealot in our ranks!

Moreover, Jacksonians are not expected to shape their lives according to radical demands of the gospel that challenge Jacksonian convictions. In fact, they can be discouraged from it. After all, embodying countercultural convictions as if they apply to every disciple violates the honor code. It is judgmental. It disrespects one's equals, not least one's elders. It implies the violation of others' freedom of conscience. It overturns expectations. It weakens tribal solidarity. It is, frankly, too Christlike. Fidelity to Jacksonian convictions — some of them, anyway — and Christian practices of repentance, grace, justification, and restoration arbitrate one's standing not in the Kingdom, but in the tribe.

This perpetuates a folk Christianity that rewards social conformity, punishes radical obedience, distorts the faith through peer pressure, and is suspicious and dismissive of outsiders. Many of my students come from such backgrounds. They bring their folk Christianity with them to college, and have difficulty even understanding the classic doctrine of justification, let alone living by it. The message of Galatians can hit even a senior majoring in theology like a hurricane. Jacksonian groupthink inoculates them against classical theology and drives disobedient tribe members, recovering Pharisees, and outsiders away from the Church.

Jacksonian Christology resembles the cry of the crowds on Palm Sunday and even Good Friday as much as the voice from heaven at Jesus' baptism or Jesus' cry of dereliction from the cross. It thrives on collective and personal self-assertion, self-expression, self-esteem, self-reliance, self-help, self-protection, self-defense, and self-justification. It lives with and even loves what it sees in the mirror. Its kindred spirits are the judges of Israel, who did whatever was right in their own eyes, but let its patron saint be King David — charismatic warrior, militarist until the end, uninhibited worshipper, sexual dynamo, indulgent parent, murderer, man of honor, and son of God.

Love Thyself

These are harsh words about my country and my Christian brothers and sisters, perhaps undeservingly so. They are also a departure from my usual optimistic style. In many other contexts I would be more inclined to narrate American Christianity in a more grateful and charitable way. But this is a work of prayer, and it is better to pray like a publican than like a Pharisee. I resonate with aspects of each of these schools. Every one of them has had such a powerful influence on me that even after this analysis I cannot imagine a truly post-Hamiltonian, post-Wilsonian, post-Jeffersonian, post-Jacksonian life for myself, let alone for the American Church. Mead is right to respect their combined power and flexibility in bringing the United States to the apex of world power, and a parallel analysis of their Christian circles would have to conclude the same thing of the American Church, which almost alone in the developed world has bucked the trend towards secularization. Each resonates with a figure in Israel's checkered but holy royal history. Yet each of these political visions centers on the self — self-advancement, self-realization, self-protection, and self-assertion.

No wonder the Church disappoints those who seek first the Kingdom of God. Loisy's dissatisfaction was already mutual: the world awaited a

Messiah, but the one who came was Jesus Christ. It is not polite to admit that neither party has found the other entirely satisfactory, but it is true. We — we peoples of the world, but also we Christians much of the time — have spent the last two thousand years doing what we had been doing before: trying to turn the world God gave us into the world we want, the people we were made to be into the people we would rather be, and God from the Lord we have into the Lord we prefer. This is the pattern in the chaos of American Christianity. Constantine is not the villain; we are.

A result of our extended theological makeover is that many of the problems already raised in the previous chapters — of God's character, of God's reputation, of the scope of God's work — persist in circles that know of and even worship Jesus Christ. Is God's "Fatherhood" oppressive patriarchalism? Does "holiness" set us above the world? Is Christianity a way of blessing who we already are so that we don't have to change? Is the Christian God cruel? Indifferent? Irrelevant? Nonexistent? Where "God" is a vehicle of the self, the answer to all of these questions is Yes.

If such idols can fill even our churches, then is there any escape from the self-deception?

Yes. Against the most impressive achievements and the most depressing failures of American Christians stand words that point the way out of the American theological hall of mirrors: "Your will be done on earth as it is in heaven."

"Your Will Be Done on Earth as It Is in Heaven"

We have persistently used the Father's gifts to pursue our own ends, yet the Father has remained determined that human beings represent him on earth. Investing such power in us even in the face of our failure and resistance has had terrible consequences (Rom. 1:28-32). As a tiny rudder steers a huge vessel, so the sheer leverage of human agency makes us formidable agents of creation — and destruction. But all these failures, Eden's and Israel's and America's and every other, are undone — because

the will of the Father is none other than the Holy Spirit.

The world's redemption is fragile and precarious because it depends on human will and power. Yet the world's redemption is sure because it also depends on a Determination of divine origin, divine nature, and divine destination.

The Spirit is the wind from God, the Father's will to create the heavens and the earth (Gen. 1:2, Ps. 33:6). The Spirit is the breath of God, the Father's will to share life with creatures from the inanimate earth (Gen. 2:7, Ps. 104:30). The Spirit is the finger of God, the Father's will to deliver Israel and author its Torah (Exod. 8:19, 31:18; Luke 11:20). The Spirit is the anointing of God, the Father's will to bring justice to all nations through his beloved servant-son (Isa. 42:1-4 in Matt. 12:18-21). The Spirit is the Counselor of God, the Father's will to dwell among his chosen people and guide them to their eternal destination (Joel 2:28-32 in Acts 2, 1 Cor. 16:19-20, John 16:13).

The gospel is the story of God's assuming our human stewardship over the aching creation and making it anew. As God once breathed his Spirit and "the first man Adam became a living soul" (Gen. 2:7 in 1 Cor. 15:45a), so God breathed anew and "the last Adam [became] a life-giving spirit" (1 Cor. 15:45b). Begotten of the Father, incarnate of the Virgin Mary by the Holy Spirit (Matt. 1:18-20), and with the Spirit's anointing (3:16), leading (4:1), presence (12:18), and power (12:28), the Son pursued the Father's will on earth (7:21), realized it flawlessly (26:39, 42), and forever has authority above and below (28:18). After all this, what else could the Church call Israel's God but Father *and* Son *and* Holy Spirit? As Trinity offers the only truly Christian way to understand God's character, so Trinity offers the only truly Christian way to describe the realization of God's cosmic intentions.

All the ages, cultures, traditions, communities, and families of the earth take part in the interplay of wills that hides in the mystery of the Father, begins in creation, suffers in sin, begins anew in Israel, becomes flesh in the Son, rests on him and flows from him, and extends through his Church ultimately to the whole world as the heavenly and earthly locus of his eternal Spirit.[16] All this grace is a deliberate overflowing of the creator's eternal being.

The Father wills to beget the Son, and the Son thus wills to be begotten of the Father. We have seen it in the Father willing that the only begotten Son will be made human, and the Son thus willing to inherit all things from the fecund Father. The Holy Spirit is the fullness of that eternal will.

16. Robert W. Jenson, *Systematic Theology,* vol. 1: *The Triune God* (New York: Oxford, 1997).

As the Temple of the Holy Spirit, the Church receives the Spirit as living water (John 7:37-39), inherits the Spirit as the Father's promise (Luke 24:49), and fulfills God's will by living powerfully and faithfully in the Spirit's fellowship — as in heaven, so also on earth.

Likewise, the Father determines to breathe the life-giving Spirit, and the Spirit thus determines to proceed from the living Father. We have seen it in the Father's determination to send the Spirit in the fullness of time as the giver of new life, and the Spirit's determination in response to reanimate humanity as life-giving spirit (1 Cor. 15:45). The Son is the fullness of that eternally begotten wisdom. As the body of Christ, by grace the Church dies and rises with the Son, follows him to obey the Father's will at every cost and for every benefit, and shares in his powerful prophethood, priesthood, and kingship as the world's redeemer and new creator.

Finally, the Son depends on a source for breathing the Spirit, and the Spirit depends on a source for begetting the Son. We have seen it in the incarnate Son's dependence on a loving source from whom to receive the anointing and indwelling Spirit and the Spirit's dependence on that source for conceiving, empowering, and raising the welcoming Son. The Father is the fullness of that eternal source. As the beloved children of the Father, the Church enjoys both the freedom of depending on one who is utterly dependable and the maturity of mutual servanthood, love of neighbors, and fruitfulness.

Christians are notoriously impatient with Trinitarian language. Even my own eyes glaze over as the strange nouns and verbs pile up. But they are simply organizing the details of biblical passages, Church stories, and personal experiences that fill in their meaning. "Every operation which extends from God to the Creation, and is named according to our variable conceptions of it, has its origin from the Father, and proceeds through the Son, and is perfected in the Holy Spirit."[17] Trinitarian language is our index to God's autobiography. It neither shrouds the persons of the Trinity in further mystery nor imprisons them in technical terms. The Spirit is not a *mere* will, let alone a human will; the Father's will is the infinite depth of the Holy Spirit in all he actually shows himself to be in the story of all things that centers on Jesus.

Any understatement here thins Trinitarian doctrine into heresy. Jesus

---

17. Gregory of Nyssa, *On 'Not Three Gods,'* in Philip Schaff, ed., *Nicene and Post-Nicene Fathers,* Second Series (Peabody, Mass.: Hendrickson, 1994), 5:334.

does not receive just the Holy Spirit's *life* or *power* or *presence* or *authority* or *gifts* or *fruit* as the answer to his prayers. Rather, Jesus receives the Holy Spirit himself: "when Jesus also had been baptized and was praying, the heaven was opened, and the Holy Spirit descended upon him" (Luke 3:21-22). Likewise, Jesus does not promise the Holy Spirit's *life* or *power* or *presence* or *authority* or *gifts* or *fruit* to his Church, but the Spirit himself (Acts 1:8a). God promises that God will give God. Jesus follows the Lord's Prayer with the following assurance: "If you then, who are evil, know how to give good gifts to your children, how much more *will the heavenly Father give the Holy Spirit* to those who ask him!" (Luke 11:13). When we pray the Father's will to be realized on earth, God's answer is nothing less than the third person of the Trinity.

Christian Fellowship as Reconciled Wills

Christ in the Spirit images the Father clearly: "we have beheld his glory, glory as of the only begotten" (John 1:14). The selfish American dreams beginning this chapter are the confused imaginings of subjects who image the Triune God poorly. Our human spirits also will — but they will to ignore, obscure, twist, and resist the Father's will and to advance ourselves, realize ourselves, protect ourselves, and assert ourselves. That foolish willing has a spiritual character, but it is not a holy one. It is that of "the spirit presently working in the people of disobedience" (Eph. 2:2), an empty will-to-power that recoils from the giver of life. Likewise, we determine to exercise our will and prevail against every challenge. That futile self-determination has a filial character: we are sons of our father the devil (John 8:42-44), defying the heavenly Father who then appears remote and tyrannical. Finally, we fall back on ourselves for self-determination and self-justification. That futile independence is a lordship that prefers the paternity of ill will, violence, lust, theft, and lies (Matt. 15:18-19) to service over all that the Father has. With these demonic vestiges of the Trinity we make ourselves the objects of our own worship and fail to understand why our piety does not free us.[18]

Understatement has no place here either. It does not help to lighten the awfulness of human rebellion with comforting abstractions like dam-

18. Jean-Luc Marion, *God without Being*, trans. Thomas A. Carlson (Chicago: University of Chicago Press, 1991).

nation as "the absence of God." Not to image God is in the end to image nothing. As the Son's pursuit of the Father's will brings the fullness of the Spirit, so self-assertion brings the ultimate emptiness of cultural and personal decline, self-defense the loss of our soul, self-determination our perpetual slavery, and independence the inheritance of outer darkness — the expulsion from Eden writ large.

Does the Lord's Prayer hold a solution to American selfishness? How could the antithetical realms of the Kingdom and the Republic ever reconcile?

Many Christians conceive of divine action as some kind of a trade-off between "predestination" (by which they really mean fate) and "free will" (by which they really mean self-determination). However, God's will and ours do not meet in a simple hierarchy where divine will simply determines or overpowers human will — nor are they a simple partnership of mutual dependence, let alone mutual independence. The prayer itself is wonderfully subtle: rather than employing the language of *doing* one's will that is common in the Old Testament (e.g., Ps. 145:19), it hints at a deeper mystery: "your will be *realized*." God wills people to will, and vice versa. The Father sends his Son and his Spirit from heaven to free human wills bound by sin and turn them around (Phil. 2:13, 1 Tim. 2:4, 2 Pet. 3:9).[19] People from Moses to Jesus and his followers pray to heaven in the Spirit and prophesy to other people as well as back to God, freeing God to act in ways that depend upon human cooperation (Matt. 23:38, John 17).

This leads into overly contested theological territory. "Monergists" like Luther and Calvin absolutely privilege the divine will even in the lives of human beings. "Synergists" like James Arminius and John Wesley stress that divine intention and action foster faithful and fruitful human willing and working. Paying more attention to the Triunity of God's will could break the theological logjam between these camps. Monergism does risk reducing prayer to affirmation (as if we prayed "you will let us do your will") and synergism does risk reducing prayer to consent ("we will let you do your will"). However, both these positions can honor the prayer's subtlety and mystery. Both look to a common beginning — divine initiative — and a common outcome — divine-human cooperation.

"Your Kingdom come" and "your will be realized" nuance each other in the familiar Hebrew parallel style that runs throughout the prayer. They

---

19. See below, "The Mercy of God."

contrast as well as cooperate. The Father wills with the Spirit, and sooner or later, one way or another, humanity concurs through the Son. In him God brings the world out of sinful rebellion and into true agency in realizing the Father's will (Matt. 10:32, 7:21, 12:50). These two petitions are discrete moments in one act of atonement. The former petition *summons* the Holy Spirit, while the latter *receives* the Holy Spirit. The former invites God's regime to advance along its frontier; the latter invites God to stay and make the earth a new heartland. The former confronts and liberates, the latter instructs and heals. The former recalls the exodus from Egypt and conquest of Canaan, the latter the instruction at Sinai and orderly life in the wilderness and the land.

Between that summons and that reception must lie the awful intersection of divine and rebel wills in which "it is finished," in which the heavenly theocracy and earthly autocracies pursue their ultimate ends, expose their true natures, and by grace reconcile.

For specifics on their interplay, look to the Gospels. There the Spirit's reception is startlingly uneven. Jesus' mother embodies the hope of Israel when she accepts the angel's declaration that the Spirit will overshadow her, making her son the Father's heir and David's successor: "Let it be to me according to your word" (Luke 1:38). Yet Jesus' family and community, including Mary, also embody widespread failure to appreciate the Spirit's work (Luke 2:35, 8:19-21, 4:14-29). John the Baptist embodies an Israel anticipating and heralding the Spirit's deliverance (1:15, 3:16-17), yet overtaken by events when the time finally comes (3:21-22, 7:19-29), and not abandoned even then (Acts 19:1-7). Jesus' Jewish and Roman opponents embody a world that rebels against the regime of God not only sporadically but structurally, weaving resistance to the Holy Spirit into the fabric of its ways of life and even its devotion to God (Acts 7:51). When the apostle Judas Iscariot receives Satan as Passover approaches, he embodies the hopeless ones who serve wills other than the Spirit (Luke 22:3). Jesus' other disciples embody the opposite trend that stumbles from perplexity with the Spirit to familiarity, from distance to intimacy, and from intimidation to authority (Luke 11:13, 12:11-12, Acts 2:4, 2:38, 5:32, 8:14-24, etc.). At the nexus of heaven and earth, of course, is Jesus the Anointed One, bearing both the dove of God's peace and the wounds of our resistance, awaited and rejected, filled with God and forsaken, determined to realize the Father's will to the end even while wanting some other way (22:42).

All these contrary trends persist in the Church as Luke's Gospel transitions to Acts and the New Testament transitions from Gospels to Epistles. Paul the Pharisee, "captive of the Spirit" who seeks the Father's will on his own journey to Jerusalem (Acts 20:22, 21:14), embodies the many successes. Ananias and Sapphira (5:1-11) and Simon the Magician (8:18-24) embody the many failures. The interplay of wills continues as the Son's witnesses bear the Holy Spirit in Jerusalem, Judea, Samaria, and to the ends of the earth (1:8). Everywhere there is power and life, puzzlement and joy, refusal and acceptance, rejection and submission, persecution and wonder-working, tragedy and victory. Charismatic Christians call it spiritual warfare.

That is the truest way to characterize America's Christian communities. We are neither restorations of a pristine apostolic era nor heirs of a later Constantinian fall. We are the New Testament Church in all its shame and its glory, somehow never entirely betraying the mission of our anointed and ascended King.

The New Testament letters offer more on our continuing struggle to receive the one we summon. The picture is particularly well developed in the letter to the Ephesians. Christ has joined heaven and earth, realizing the Father's will in both realms; so joining Christ enlists us into his cosmic campaign and trains us to fight at both fronts. The Church is humanity being restored to its former place as the world's ambassadors of God as well as receiving new pneumatic authority in the heavenly places (Eph. 3:10). Being members of God's earthly household means being heavenly citizens too (Eph. 2:19). We exercise our heavenly authority when we pray before the Father in Christ through the Spirit (Eph. 3:14-19).

Spiritual warfare requires spiritual *materiel,* and the Spirit is the Church's armory. The Almighty Spirit of Holiness "empowers in the Lord and in the might of his strength" (Eph. 6:10) with instruments of righteousness for fighting against spiritualities of wickedness in the heavens (6:12). Among these are truth, righteousness, good news of peace, faith, salvation, and the word of God (6:14-17). The Spirit teaches the Church to use them properly with training in prayer and proclamation, to use them wisely by cultivating virtues such as perseverance (6:18-19), and to use them faithfully by maintaining discipline in fellowship (6:19-24).

The language that closes Ephesians — obedience, service, might, principalities, powers, warfare, peacemaking, ambassadorship — is the language of foreign and domestic policy. The letter's contrast between the old self and the new (4:22-24) finds us where the first section left us. A Church that absorbs and adopts American foreign policies has become seduced by empty words (5:6). It has forgotten the Father's will (5:17). It has ignored the Holy Spirit (5:18) and grieves him (4:30). It forgets its own spiritual nature and contends against flesh and blood (6:12). No wonder its problems seem overwhelming (4:17-19)! But to receive whom we summon in prayer is to gain all that Christ himself used to win his battle and more. If the world's rebellion is structural sin, life in Christ is structural obedience that counters it, frees the captives, and develops them to maturity.

"I therefore, the prisoner in the Lord, beg you to lead a life worthy of the calling to which you have been called" (4:1). The way of Jesus the son of David and Paul the citizen of Rome has always been a struggle. But it offers us a way of being American, *truly* American, that releases us from servitude to our corporate or personal selves and empowers us to be fellow reconcilers with the Messiah's fellow prophets and apostles. God's promises remain true in spite of all our centuries of unfaithfulness. The full answer to the prayers of the American Church is the Holy Spirit, not only summoned but received.

Interlude

So the Father has become our Father, his name is being held holy in the creation, his theocracy has come near and invited us in, and the Spirit has been poured out to dwell among us as he intended. Now what?

Recall our analogy of prayer as the heart of Christian life. It does no good to circulate blood without refreshing it, or to refresh it without circulating it. So the Lord's Prayer, like the human heart, has two halves. One side sends our life to God, to the respiratory source of life, to cleanse it of the waste and poisons it has accumulated. At the same time, another auricle and ventricle bring God's life to us, to the corporeal location of creaturely life, for the energy and nourishment on which it depends. As all things are in the Word and through him, even the Spirit and the body, so this prayer crosses every threshold in every direction — between even creator and creature, holy and sinful, heaven and earth. Life is what results.

Connections across thresholds are what spirituality and prayer are all about. Yet as the ancients misunderstood the way blood flows through the human body, so we have often confused ourselves about how life flows between the parties in prayer. Galen, the ancient Greek physician, thought blood ebbed and flowed like the tides. Similarly, from antiquity the ascent of the soul to the divine has been a goal of religions and spiritualities both eastern and western. *We* go from *here* to *there* (if "there" is even an appropriate word). The Lord's Prayer, like the whole of the good news, rejects this itinerary. To ascend into heaven or descend into the abyss (Rom. 10:6-7) are impossible, ridiculous tasks.

Besides, those journeys would be superfluous! The descending and ascending that matter have already happened. The Lord is risen (Rom. 10:9,

Luke 24:34). The Holy Spirit has already brought the Father's Son down from heaven to humility, obedience, and suffering and brought him up to eternal life, exaltation, and authority (Phil. 2:5-11). The Father's holy name is on our lips; his kingdom has approached in his Son; his will has been realized on earth in the Spirit. "From him and through him and to him are all things. To him be glory for ever" (Rom. 11:34-36).

Like the first tablet of the Decalogue, the first half of the Lord's Prayer presupposes and invites descent. The Father and Son have poured out the breath of life and renewed the creation (Ps. 104:30). Like the second tablet, the prayer's second half presupposes and invites ascent. The Father and Spirit have returned the Son's body to life and to heaven (1 Tim. 3:16). Our project is now shifting from one half of the heart to the other, from the pneumatic to the somatic, from the life of the Spirit to the life of the bride, from the first commandments to the last, from glorifying God in our spirit to glorifying God in our body (cf. 1 Cor. 6:20, Majority Text).

In *The Jesus Creed*, Scot McKnight describes the Lord's Prayer as an updated Jewish *Kaddish* (prayer of sanctification), amended by Jesus himself.[1] The original Kaddish reads:

> Magnified and sanctified be his great name in the world he created according to his will. May he establish his kingdom during your life and during your days, and during the life of all the house of Israel, speedily and in the near future. Amen.

In his typical way, Jesus reinterprets this prayer around his own ministry. God is *our Father.* His Kingdom *has approached.* His will is *realized on earth,* not just restricted to Israel or reflected in the world. The Spirit's coming transforms Israel's praying (Rom. 8:26-27) just as surely as it turns John's baptism into Jesus' anointing, Israel's anointed offices into the Threefold Office, the Passover into his Supper, and Israel's Scriptures into the Old Testament. The time of Jesus is the climax of God's purpose, the unveiling of his eternal mystery, and the hinge of all history.

In Christ all these become signs and foundations of the new regime. God's full manifestation occasions the new creation of all things. Baptism

---

1. Scot McKnight, *The Jesus Creed: Loving God, Loving Others* (Brewster, Mass.: Paraclete, 2004), pp. 14-21.

becomes the inauguration of new life together. Eucharist becomes the principal sign of holy fellowship. The Old Testament's fulfillment opens up space for new Scripture and the apostles' authority and the Spirit's outpouring fill it with the New Testament.[2] Likewise, Christ can author a new Kaddish that builds upon the old. As its second half shifts focus from the God of community to the community of God and from his Kingdom to his righteousness (Matt. 6:33), so the remaining petitions of the Lord's Prayer center on "us": give us, forgive us, lead us, deliver us.

It is axiomatic in traditional theology that the Spirit's role is to point us to Christ. However, it is equally true (and should be equally axiomatic) that the Spirit's role is also to point us to each other and ourselves. What we learn as we move through the Lord's Prayer is that the one does not compete with the other. McKnight offers four lessons this prayer continually teaches him: to approach God as *Abba*, what God really wants, to think of others, and what everyone needs.[3] These obviously follow the course of the prayer. Yet the first half of the book already makes all four points, and the next half will too. God's fatherhood is as apparent in the final petition as deliverance from evil is in the first. The commandments cohere because one Christ fulfills them all. Because the descending and ascending have already been done and the home of God is now among human beings (Rev. 21:3), we do not need to move our gaze to shift focus from God to ourselves and back.

There is, however, a palpable shift in scale from the first half to the second. The prayer moves us from kingdom, heaven, and earth to meals, neighbors, and temptations. After pages and pages on global and national matters — on pulmonary arteries and veins, so to speak — it is tempting to think we are moving on to capillaries. Yet everything is connected to everything else. The first half's concerns are also personal as the second half's are also cosmic. God's fatherhood answers a friend's distrust; God's deliverance answers a culture's precipitous decline. All things are God's, and both falling empires and falling swallows are matters of the Father's attention — as well as ours.

2. Telford Work, *Living and Active: Scripture in the Economy of Salvation* (Grand Rapids: Eerdmans, 2002).

3. McKnight, *The Jesus Creed*, pp. 19-20.

PART II

THE SECOND TABLET

CHAPTER 5

The Providence of God

We are dealing here with an idol, the idol of the free market, and idols do not respond to moral persuasion. They are cast out only by the living God, and it is only the power of the gospel in the last analysis which can dethrone idols and which can create the possibility of a free society.

Lesslie Newbigin, "Gospel and Culture,"
Salvador de Bahia, Brazil, December 1996

The Culture of Money

"Where your treasure is, there will your heart be" (Matt. 6:21). Money has long bewildered me as a Christian. I do not think this is *simply* because of greed. Rather, money is tied into our lives so intimately that it comes to embody us. A book from me about money would deserve a long acknowledgments page, because of all the teachers I have had. But I am not sure to whom I could dedicate it.

First, the acknowledgments:

Money as Heritage

Money is a habit we learn, especially from our families
My father taught me to think of money as something to earn and keep

rather than just get and spend. Under his tutelage I was hired for odd office jobs every summer, winter, and spring vacation from seventh grade through college. Every year he made sure that the legal limit of my earned income went into an Individual Retirement Account. Our Republican family abhorred both taxes and middle-class welfare. The ethic was to pay our own way and help others do the same. We did not indulge in dodgy tax shelters or seek financial aid for college. My father never displayed even a hint of snobbery towards those with less, nor a hint of envy towards those with more.

My mother paid for our clothes and fast food, teaching her children what it means to be provided for. We were forbidden to work except during vacations, lest we be distracted from the schoolwork and extracurricular activities that were supposed to make for fulfilling childhoods and take us to the colleges of our choice.

We were comfortable and had a nice house, but we never lived extravagantly. My father was surely one of the few small newspaper publishers who made himself late for work jumpstarting day after day a dying 1969 Country Squire station wagon. We *always* bought American — the station wagon's successor was an early Chevy Suburban, long before they were either trendy or well made. We saved and invested our money, or used it to travel as a family, or quietly gave it away.

Both of my parents had grown up in the Great Depression in comfortable but still tight circumstances, and they never forgot its lessons. My father made sure all of us could set type, because "no matter where you go, you'll be able to get a job typesetting for the local paper." He offered this bit of wisdom about three years before personal computers wiped out the typesetting trade, but we got the message. Our family held onto a small family farm in Iowa and some agricultural land in godforsaken central Nevada just in case a new depression forced us to go there to survive. Had my grandparents invested in California real estate instead, we would now be fantastically wealthy. But what good would beachfront property have been in a famine?

Our financial caution came in handy for my mother when my father died unexpectedly at 58. Sure enough, the decades of prudence saw her through the crisis. Likewise, our grandparents' earlier sacrifices and the savings we had grown helped us kids compete with the baby boomers who turned residential real estate into a constantly receding horizon of affordability.

Like any child I enjoyed spending money, but I always wanted to save more than spend. I like to think of my cheapness as a vital expression of my Scottish-American heritage, and I seem to have inherited a double share of it. For me self-denial is *spending* money. I would rather invest it in our children, grow it for down the road, or even give it away to a worthy cause than "waste" it.

As I age and my habits harden, these convictions only strengthen. Our culture considers our financial situation honorable if unexciting. The family is still paying its own way. Our children get music lessons but we have no gardener, let alone a housekeeper. Our children wish we would buy them the toys that "all" their friends have. Our family of six lives in a nice three-bedroom house and drives two beat-up 1990s Hondas. Kim is embarrassed by our dented cars (both of whose scrapes are — ahem — my doing), but why throw away hundreds of dollars repairing cosmetic damage? Spending money on a bargain is fun, but it feels better to contribute to our retirement and thus our kids' head-starts or to tax-deductible charities. Squandering it, especially on taxes, feels worst of all.

I am grateful for the financial sensibilities and assistance my family gave me. I can feel myself urging both my children and my students to make the same choices and adopt the same priorities, raising them in the traditions in which I was brought up and hoping for similar results. That is how habits become traditions — by being passed on.

Money as Metaphysics

I also learned from wealth's theorists. A brilliant high school teacher hooked me on economics and made the so-called dismal science a lifelong delight. We learned of the invisible hand from Adam Smith, of the injustice of rent from David Ricardo, of the inevitability of poverty from Thomas Malthus, of conspicuous consumption from Thorstein Veblen, of eschatological socialism from Henri de Saint-Simons and Charles Fourier, of the labor theory of value from Karl Marx, of structural oversupply from John Maynard Keynes, and of the market's subtle power to compensate for these weaknesses from the libertarian Chicago school.[1] (Naturally, we ig-

---

1. Robert L. Heilbroner, *The Worldly Philosophers*, 5th ed. (New York: Simon and Schuster, 1980).

nored everything before the Enlightenment.) College taught me the discipline's more sober technical side through endless equations and intersecting supply and demand curves, a tour of American economic history, and unsuccessful attempts at indoctrination from several campus Marxists. An almost accidental reading of George Gilder's *Wealth and Poverty*[2] in my last year of college awakened and converted me to the conservative American vision of triumphalist capitalism. As a newly born-again Christian I devoured evangelical scholarship, and as a new conservative I devoured the burgeoning literature of right-wing political economics, in the era in which the two seemed perfect for one another.

Am I boring you? Sorry. But these are acknowledgments, after all, and while a book's acknowledgments are rarely the most fascinating part, they can be among the most revealing.

Anyway, after a few years the demands of a full-time seminary curriculum, part-time jobs in other fields, and a new marriage pushed political economy to the background, but it remains one of the disciplines I love. I am a product of a long, rich, modern economic tradition. If I learned how to handle money from my biological ancestors, I learned how to ponder it from ideological visionaries.

Money as Culture

We all have communal ancestors too, and my economic training did them less justice. My economics courses taught me Smith's invisible hand and Marx's dialectical materialism as *ideas* that basically stand on their own and apply to everyone like laws of physics. Yet money is not just what theorists say it is; money is what the peoples of the world make it. Economic activity and economic thought come from somewhere — from communities sustained by traditions that tell their own stories.

Consider the table on page 121 from Thomas J. Stanley and William D. Danko's popular bestseller, *The Millionaire Next Door*, of the top ten ancestry groups of American millionaires.[3] Stanley and Danko show that the disparity in wealth among these ethnicities cannot be explained entirely in terms of historical dominance or power, typical careers, inheritance, or

2. New York: Bantam, 1982.
3. New York: Simon and Schuster, 1996, p. 17.

Ancestry	Percent of Ancestry Group that Are Millionaire Households
Russian	22.0
Scottish	20.8
Hungarian	15.1
English	7.7
Dutch	7.2
French	5.5
Irish	4.9
Italian	4.0
German	3.3
Native American	2.0

even income level. A decisive factor is economic *tradition:* the behaviors involved in acquiring, spending, and saving money as these cultures tell their stories with their stuff. Russians are commonly manager-owners of businesses, while Hungarians tend to be more entrepreneurially inclined and Scots tend to be savers, multigenerational investors, and frugal even when wealthy. By contrast the original English advantage has dissipated and other European ethnicities have consistently underperformed.

Something consistently missing from my intellectual diet was a robust appreciation of these cultural dimensions of economics — especially as they extend backward from long before the Scottish Enlightenment or the European Enlightenment to the folk wisdom of the people who settled the world we take for granted. Oh, we tipped our hats to Max Weber and his Protestant work ethic, but the widely accepted limits of his analysis and the uncomfortable role religion played in it kept us from taking it too seriously. (With good reason, it turns out: Stanley's and Danko's chart shows that theology is by no means the most important variable. The Reformed Scottish and Dutch are very different from one another, as are the Catholic Hungarians and Italians.)

We Americans are still basically telling our founding cultures' stories. David Hackett Fischer's massive *Albion's Seed: Four British Folkways in America*[4] is to American culture what Walter Russell Mead's *Special Providence,* the book whose insights we considered in the last chapter, is to American foreign policy. Fischer traces the transmission of four ways of

4. New York: Oxford, 1989.

life from their roots in different parts of England to their new homes in America, where they still order Americans' lives.

Each folkway began in a different cultural region of Reformation Britain, traveled to America in the seventeenth and eighteenth centuries, grew, spread, and assimilated others into the blurred and faded patchwork of the contemporary United States. A wave of Puritans brought their congregational polity and ordered liberty from East Anglia and created Puritan Massachusetts. Another wave brought Anglican hierarchy and classbound honor from southwestern England to Virginia. Later an exodus of Quakers transplanted the spiritualistic, egalitarian, and ascetic world of the Midlands into the Delaware Valley. In the last decades before American independence a wave of Presbyterian "Scotch-Irish" planted the fierce, economically polarized culture of North Britain's borderlands on the western American frontier.

Totalizing ideologies (race, class, gender, etc.) reign in today's academic circles, but Fischer resists these generalized mythologies in favor of cultural specifics:

> The people in Puritan Massachusetts were in fact highly puritanical. They were not traditional peasants, modern capitalists, village communists, modern individualists, Renaissance humanists, Victorian moralists, neo-Freudian narcissists or prototypical professors of English literature. They were a people of their time and place who had an exceptionally strong sense of themselves, and a soaring spiritual purpose which has been lost beneath many layers of revisionist scholarship.[5]

There is no need for clever theorists to layer their generalized mythologies on top of the narratives of the Puritans or their American neighbors. Each of these four groups speaks for itself. Its heritage reflects the convictions of its ancestors' side in the urgent religious debate that permeated seventeenth-century England (795). Establishment Anglicans dominated Virginia; evangelical Presbyterians populated the backcountry frontier; federalistic Congregationalists founded Massachusetts and Connecticut; even more independent Separatists founded Plymouth Colony; "charismatic" believers'

---

5. Fischer, *Albion's Seed*, p. 786. Subsequent references to this work are indicated by parenthetical page citations in the text. Direct quotations are footnoted.

	Massachusetts	Virginia	Delaware Valley	Backcountry
Rank system	truncated	hierarchical	egalitarian	segmented
Deference	moderate	high	low	mixed
Equality (GINI ratio, 0-1)	.4-.6	.6-.75	.3-.5	.7-.9
Inheritance	double partible	primogeniture	single partible	mixed
Average land grant	90-120 acres	674 acres	250 acres	N/A

Baptists founded Rhode Island; and spiritualistic Quakers founded West Jersey, Pennsylvania, and Delaware (796). All of these had addressed the theological concerns of their generation in the contexts of the regional folk heritages that preceded them. They brought their answers with them to the New World (803), adjusted them to the new conditions in the colonies (805-7), engineered a new multicultural republic on their basis (823-32), and spread them as America expanded to the west (813-14).

This folk history is relevant in that each of these cultures told its story with its material possessions. All groups held the era's Protestant English convictions about law and property. However, money worked very differently in each area, as indicated in the table above.

The Puritan economy of New England was neither communistic nor capitalistic, but "an old fashioned system of agricultural production, domestic industry and commercial exchange that bore the impress of East Anglian customs and Calvinist beliefs. At its heart was a Puritan ethic that persisted for many generations,"[6] a relatively fair distribution of land and wealth that still respected Puritan hierarchies of social status, and an inheritance system combining East Anglian custom with Deuteronomy 21:16's rule that all children inherit, but the firstborn double (167-73).

In Virginia, where piety was measured in liturgical devotion more than moral uprightness, land was granted to friends of the crown, estates were conserved through primogeniture, and "wealth was regarded not primarily as a form of capital or a factor of production, but as something to be used for display and consumed for pleasure." Consequently the same

6. Fischer, *Albion's Seed*, p. 158.

structural inequality and habits of overspending and indebtedness of southwest England's gentry also characterized Virginia's (167-68, 374-82).

Industrious Quakers came from generally modest, hardworking English origins. They were "worldly ascetics" who worked, saved, and invested rather than borrowing, spending, or hoarding, and who became pioneers of American industrial capitalism (555-60). They granted land and bequeathed inheritance in a manner that fused the customs of England's North Midlands and their own disciplined spiritual egalitarianism. When their industry created economic success at odds with their own spiritual aspirations, it drove them to unequalled philanthropy (566-73).

Presbyterian North Britain's absentee landlord economy was replicated in America's southern highlands, victimizing the same landless poor who crossed the Atlantic to escape it and creating one of America's most stubbornly unequal societies. Among both the rich and the migratory poor of Appalachia, wealth correlated with power and social status (and poverty with suspicion of elites) more tightly than in any of the other three folk cultures. Yet pride and honor were available for all who would fight for them (747-56).

These groups, though dominant, were of course not the only American settlers. Other and later immigration patterns brought the stories and financial ways of other peoples into the mix. However, these four have dominated to this day. Ethnic immigrants, whether African or Irish or Jewish, have tended to adopt the folkways of the regions in which they arrived. The groups that first settled areas created cultures that have lasted centuries.

Fischer's chronicle of early American folkways shows that what I and everyone else think of money can never be reduced to an abstraction like "supply and demand" or "ownership of the means of production." Not all of us inherit possessions, but all of us inherit what our possessions mean.

We also inherit the old cultural and religious feuds embedded in those traditions. It is probably not a coincidence that my loyally Presbyterian Scottish family's economic values have been persistently Quaker. After all, Henry Work and his brothers, who originally came to America from northern Scotland around 1690, settled in Pennsylvania. Things could have been very different for us:

By horseback, Henry [Work] and his brother(s) went to Vermont to look at land owned by the Witherspoon who was sometime President of Princeton but didn't buy. . . . [T]he brothers also went to

North Carolina but were still not satisfied. They then settled in Lancaster County, Pa.[7]

My disdain towards New England liberalism may just be a function of their taste in real estate!

This brief tour of American folk history shows how ludicrous it is to reduce people's differences to "class" or any other single variable. The shared identities we gain from neighbors, business partners, schoolmates, and life mates as well as those we inherit from our biological ancestors exert compelling force on every new generation. Whether it is irresistible or just rarely resisted, tradition seems to overpower or co-opt nearly everything else — whether race, lineage, gender, philosophical currents, industrialization, formal politics, war, or world dominance.

The strongest and most invisible hand is not a market but a people. Money is nearly ubiquitous in our ways of life. I know its surface dynamics well, but its depth grammar is far more opaque to me, and far more powerful. I understand the "substitution effect" in modern economics: if beef is too expensive at the market I will buy chicken instead, and if interest rates rise then bonds become more attractive relative to stocks. What mystifies me is the "ancestor effect": I won't buy squid at any price, and whatever the interest rate I still favor stocks over bonds, as did my parents. What Wittgenstein said of language is true also of incentives: "Explanation comes to an end somewhere."[8] The mysterious depth, awesome tenacity, and dizzying complexity of our folk cultures tempts me to economic fatalism. Supply and demand can be plotted as intersecting curves, but the places and shapes of those curves are enigmas.

So much for the acknowledgments. What about the dedication?

Money as Discipleship

One other tutor in economics has been the gospel stories in which what we do with our stuff is a matter of sudden and eternal judgment (Matt. 25:13).

7. Von Gail Hamilton, *Work Family History: Twelve Generations of Works in America, 1690-1969* (Park City, Utah: Publishers Press, 1969), p. 25.

8. Ludwig Wittgenstein, *Philosophical Investigations*, 2nd ed. (Malden, Mass.: Blackwell, 1958), p. 3.

For risking or burying the king's talents we are rewarded or punished (25:14-30). For having mercy on the Son of Man's brothers and sisters or turning them away we are accepted or rejected (25:31-46). These two parables are but tips of an iceberg of radical economic expectations Jesus has for his subjects.

Some of Jesus' expectations make sense to me, but others just seem weird, wrong, and unworkable. Every time I have taught the ethics of Jesus using John Howard Yoder's brilliant study *The Politics of Jesus*,[9] I have seen the same frustration slowly arise in my students' eyes. We understand the significance of Jesus' actions in their historical context. We want to be faithful subjects of the Kingdom Yoder is portraying. We want to follow Jesus as Savior and Lord. Yet we don't know how. What do we do with *our* savings, our wages, the price of our educations, our loans, our careers, our social responsibilities, our children's futures, our spouses' security, our retirement funds, our co-workers' welfare, and especially our voices? Do we answer our parishioners' requests for how to handle this or that financial dilemma with parables lifted from the Gospels? We know our cultural distances from Jesus will not excuse us from his ethical standard. Yet because we live differently, money means different things in twenty-first-century California than it did in first-century Israel. The cultural distances paralyze us. We set aside what makes no sense, and do pretty much what we would have done anyway.

It is not just that we need to translate the Gospels into our cultural settings. The fundamental problem is that the Gospels emerge out of ways of life that cannot be fully translated into the languages of people with our ways of life. While some aspects of the good news cross into a given culture easily and others only with great interpretive effort, there are still other aspects so alien that they seem to stop short at the border. Getting them across is not a matter of mere translation. It is as if they become inapplicable, absurd, inevitably misunderstood. The new culture — in this case, the subcultures of a mixed capitalistic economy that did not exist in the first century — silences them.

Money falls into all these degrees of translatability. We know that fear and greed are spiritual problems, and no nuanced cultural analysis will excuse us. Yet it is not *only* fear, greed, and pride that make me reluctant to throw a lavish party for outcasts or to obey Jesus' command to the rich

9. Rev. ed., Grand Rapids: Eerdmans, 1994.

young man (and to all disciples in Luke 12:33) and sell all I have as alms to the poor. It is also wisdom. In significant ways, those actions seem foolish. In fact, they seem unfaithful. They have struck me this way since before I had any means to celebrate or anything to sell, so I don't think I am just rationalizing. To turn Mark Twain on his head, it is the parts of the Bible I *don't* understand that bother me.

I understand the dangers of all worldly power, including financial power. I see the point of celebrations and almsgiving in first-century Israel. I know what they signify about the coming Kingdom. I know the sacrifice and hospitality they demand are incumbent on me and every other disciple. But I also see that they had meanings and challenged sensibilities that differ from those of my day. So I keep running into them year after year, as texts whose difficulties are not diminishing either with experience or with the life changes that have come over two decades of faith. Meanwhile, the day of reckoning for how well I have heeded them approaches.

Money as Testimony

On December 26, 2004, a tsunami killed hundreds of thousands from Southeast Asia to Africa and left millions homeless. The event left me numb; the melee of responses and counterarguments left me paralyzed. Cash was urgently needed; cash would create a cycle of dependency and distort the local economy; cash would condescend to developing nations; cash threatened the local economic elites who were just looking after their own market share. Tourism is a better long-term response than direct relief because it rights the economy; tourism worsens the problem; tourism is a poor economic model for a developing country. The United States is stingy; its military is the best immediate agent for direct relief; it is propagandizing and weakening local governments; its helpfulness is winning hearts and minds in the War on Terror's south Asian theater. The United Nations is the rightful coordinator of relief efforts; the United Nations is incompetent, irrelevant, and bureaucratic.

All these contentions had an unmistakable air of confident colonialism and chastened postcolonialism. Almost wholly missing in the discussion at our Christian college, and decidedly secondary when it was mentioned at all, was the specifically Christian shape of south Asia's need or our appropriate response. We tended to support Christian relief organizations rather than secular ones, but otherwise our responses looked just like the responses everywhere else in the west, and they looked very little like the responses to others' material needs in the New Testament Church. We responded out of our own stubborn financial cultures, which we assumed must be suitable expressions of the good news.

Our reactions neatly reflected the conflicted sensibilities of the emerging class David Brooks calls "bourgeois bohemians," or "Bobos." This group displaced America's old WASP aristocracy beginning in the sixties and found itself uneasily enjoying the very social power it had only recently disparaged. In the nineties it synthesized into a new educated class the bourgeois culture of shopkeepers and the bohemian counterculture of romantics that had arisen in the eighteenth century and had viewed one another with disdain and contempt ever since.[10] These two subcultures so effectively co-opted each other that today Bobo corporations preach revolution, Bobo consumers drive formerly oxymoronic "sport utility vehicles" or sporty Swedish station wagons to the local organic market, Bobo intellectuals write bestsellers and jostle for appearances on TV talk shows, Bobo radicals invest in "ethical" mutual funds, Bobo moneymakers spend a fortune on their kitchens, and Bobo hedonists guzzle lattes rather than martinis and recoil at secondhand smoke. Members of the Bobo establishment

> are prosperous without seeming greedy; they have pleased their elders without seeming conformist; they have risen toward the top without too obviously looking down on those below; they have achieved success without committing certain socially sanctioned affronts to the ideal of social equality; they have constructed a prosperous lifestyle while avoiding the old clichés of conspicuous consumption (it's OK to hew to the new clichés).[11]

Bobos learned to get along not by overturning the old antithesis but absorbing it. The Scholastic Aptitude Test emptied top-tier schools of New England WASP deadwood and welcomed both meritocratic children raised on the old ethic of frugal industry and meritocratic children raised on the newer ethic of cultural sedition and intellectual engineering. The

10. David Brooks, *Bobos in Paradise: The New Upper Class and How They Got There* (New York: Simon and Schuster, 2000), p. 43.

11. Brooks, *Bobos*, p. 45.

two groups became freshman roommates and sex partners, graduated, and settled down together as America's latest "alpha class."[12] The current culture war between American elites is little more than the occasional internecine turf battle between the more bohemian and the more bourgeois ends of their synthesis.

An old divinity school saying predicts that "as long as Catholics marry Methodists there will always be an Episcopal Church." America simply exchanged an old set of Episcopalians for a new one.

Westmont College, where I teach, is at the margins of Bobo culture. Our wing is its "low church" that prefers sermons to incense. Yet when the tsunami struck we were true to the type. We felt terrible. We said some prayers. We raised a little money for relief. We wore $5 colored bracelets to display our compassion. We scolded ourselves for the negative consequences of both our nation's actions and its inactions. And then we went back to class and hit the books. We interpreted the calamity not as heralds of Jesus Christ but as Bobos in training.

I do not find my family's financial traditions, our financial situation, the financial culture of America's new alpha class, or Westmont's economic ethos in the pages of the New Testament. Instead I encounter a baffling economic culture to which we already are supposed to belong. How can *that* bizarre apocalyptic world also be mine? How would my stuff ever tell *that* story?

The final volume of James Wm. McClendon Jr.'s systematic theology, *Witness*,[13] diagnoses the conundrum. McClendon sees cultures in terms of the kinds of soil in Jesus' parable of the sower. Some cultural soil is fertile for the good news. It receives the word and produces a rich harvest. Other kinds of soil are less hospitable. Some is so hard that nothing grows at all. My frustration may be a symptom of the shallowness and rockiness of America's cultural soils. How hard it is for Pennsylvanians and professionals to inherit the Kingdom of God!

But who then can be saved? McClendon is not helping me resist the pull of economic fatalism. My financial culture just might be the wrong type of soil. That will be hard news to break to the kids.

Are we destined to be slaves to cultural inertia? Do mysterious economic forces in our past hold us captive in this world and in the next?

12. Brooks, *Bobos*, p. 177.
13. Nashville: Abingdon, 2001.

That can't be! It would mean a new dividing wall separating the chosen peoples of the world from the rest of us. Yet what if this is the lesson of Jesus' parables?

Well, what if it is? With God all things are possible.

"Give Us Today Our Daily Bread"

Wealth as Providence

Just what is wealth? Even just in contemporary America people have an astonishing variety of answers and authorities. Wealth is reward (Calvin). Wealth is property (Locke). Wealth is virtue (Weber). Wealth is selfishness (Smith). Wealth is advantage (Ricardo). Wealth is luck (Malkiel). Wealth is security (Fourier). Wealth is utility (Edgeworth). Wealth is production (Mill). Wealth is consumption (Keynes). Wealth is incentive (Laffer). Wealth is trade (Bastiat). Wealth is empire (Lenin). Wealth is futility (Malthus). Wealth is pleasure (Jefferson). Wealth is obligation (Galbraith). Wealth is guilt (Marx). Wealth is power (Nietzsche). Wealth is need (Freud). Wealth is status (Veblen). Wealth is information (von Mises). Wealth is revolution (Schumpeter). Wealth is possibility (Gilder).

Each of these metaphors is helpful. Each comes from real stories that arise out of real ways of life. We can think of people whose lives symbolize them. We emulate some of these stories and abhor others. We can look upon our own families and peoples and see ourselves in them. Yet as valuable as these classifications are, to Christians they are incomplete, because their stories do not tell the whole story. These theorists leave us restless, because we sense a powerful reductionism in their storytelling. They have noticed important details, but in the end those details captivated them and blinded them to the big picture.

In the whole story of the world as creation, rebellion, salvation, and perfection, wealth is *relationship*. Wealth is one set of expressions of the eternal relatedness of all things under, then against, and finally in the Father, Son, and Holy Spirit.

> You have made [humanity] a little lower than God,
> and crowned him with glory and honor.
> You have given him dominion over the works of your hands;

you have put all things under his feet,
all sheep and oxen,
and also the beasts of the field,
the birds of the air, and the fish of the sea,
whatever passes along the paths of the seas.

(Ps. 8:5-8)

The honor has been unrequited, the glory forsaken, the relationships ruined, and the creation oppressed. Sin rebels against the originally good relationships God ordained, turning wealth into power, virtue, pleasure, luck, and the other metaphors for wealth that dominate in the cultures of the world. In these strongholds of our own making we tangle relationships into webs of structural and personal sin, and there money gains its familiar power over us.

Because the Kingdom of God is a realm of *holy* relationships, its wealth is characterized by holiness. The story of Jesus has convinced Christians that God, the alpha and omega, sustains us through the beta, gamma, and delta of our common journey out of condemnation to the righteousness of his theocracy. The name for that sustenance is *providence.* So

wealth is providence insofar as its story is the gospel story.

Bread for the World

There is a long tradition of spiritualizing the Lord's Prayer's "daily bread." We turn it into insight into the Bible, mystical relationship with God, calling to mission, the Holy Spirit, and so on. These allegories have their place (see, for instance, Luke 11:13). But they depend on the literal meaning. Daily bread signifies much more than just physical nourishment, but nourishment is still the beginning of God's faithfulness in fulfilling his intentions (Deut. 8:1-10). The good news tells of real deliverance, and anyone who is hungry knows that real deliverance is material deliverance. When angels came to Jesus in the wilderness and ministered to him (Matt. 4:11), they didn't give him Torah, or fellowship, or a mission, or even the Holy Spirit. He already had those! They gave the hungry savior what he *lacked:* the provisions he needed and refused to grant himself (cf. 1 Kings 19:4-8). Daily bread is really bread.

And what marvelous stories Israel tells with it! Bread comes up repeatedly in the Torah at pivotal moments in its stories of salvation. With the possible and significant exception of water, no other commodity does this so consistently — not gold, not livestock, not even land.

There is bread beyond Eden (Gen. 3:19). There is bread to bless the God of victories (14:17-20) and entertain God and angels (18:1-6, 19:1-3). There is bread for refugees in the desert (21:14) and exiles from the father's house (28:20-22). There is bread for gaining inheritance (25:34, 27:17) and making treaties with potential enemies (31:51-54). There is bread in Egypt for starving nations (41:53-57) and patriarchs' journeys (45:23).

There is bread in Midian for Moses the refugee (Exod. 2:20). There is bread of affliction for the exodus (Exod. 12:37-49) and bread from heaven in the wilderness (16:4-5). There is bread for the conquest (23:23-25) and bread in the land conquered (13:5-10). There is bread of divine presence in the tabernacle (25:23-30), and bread of priestly sustenance to maintain fellowship (29:31-34; Lev. 8, 24:5-9).

There is bread for commemorating Israel's holy past (Lev. 23). There is bread for fulfilling the vows of holy ones (Num. 6). There is bread aplenty when Israel obeys God (Lev. 26:5, Num. 17:21), and bread of prophetic scarcity when she disobeys (Lev. 26:26).

In the language of ethics, bread is teleological. It advances the plot. As it is in the Torah, so it is in the prophets and writings: Bread meets present needs to help bring the future.

Two Economies

The phrase "daily bread" is an awkward translation of the obscure Greek phrase *artos epiousios*. Scholars have long debated whether this petition is for our bread for today, our bread for the morrow, or our bread for the end-times. In the biblical imagination there is no dilemma, because the same bread serves all three ends. Bread's versatility in the biblical story is its sacramental ability to join the mundane to the spiritual and the present to the past and future. We may gloss the petition this way: "As you did before, so give us now what we need to see us through to the very end."

The New Testament follows the old. In 1 Corinthians 10–11 Paul describes bread, and food generally, in terms of two whole economic constellations. On the one hand, it is the "spiritual food" our ancestors ate in the wilderness (10:3), the communion loaf we break worshipfully (10:16), the sacrifice that sustains the temple priesthood (10:18), genuine hospitality to outsiders (10:25-27), the unity of believers (11:18-20), the Lord's gracious death (11:26), his promised return (11:26), the body's spiritual discernment (11:29), and Christ's saving discipline (11:32). On the other hand, it is the meal from which Israel arose in rebellion and was overthrown (10:5-7), partnership with demons (10:20-22), legalism and judgmentalism (10:28-29), division, selfishness, gluttony, and hunger (11:21-22), accountability for Christ's sufferings (11:27), illness and death (11:30), and condemnation (11:34). Quite a contrast.

Now consider the roles we give material resources in our own age. On one side, wealth is for protecting and promoting those who have it. Let us label this pole "reactionary," though in using that word I do not mean to refer to the political right. After all, entrenched interests on the left (for example, public sector unions, tenured humanities faculties, communist parties in China and the former Soviet Union) are as reactionary in this sense as landed gentry and patrician family trusts. Wealth is for buttressing a status quo. On the other side, wealth is for transferring to those who should have it but don't. Let us label this pole "progressive," though, again, I do not mean the left. After all, libertarians and entrepreneurs, commonly mistaken for conservatives, are more often actually radicals. For these visionaries economic change is its own good, wiping away the dead hand of the past that would otherwise obstruct the coming of the future. Wealth is for changing the world — by flowing to the poor, to the invisible, to the hardworking, to the entrepreneurial, to the just, to the free. Pragmatists in the middle balance the past and future to bring as much of each into the other as suits their tastes. Brooks's bourgeois bohemians, to whom most contemporary American elites belong, embody this dialectical balancing act.

All these roles construct wealth as a servant of opposition. Money distinguishes insiders from outsiders, resists change, feeds growth industries and starves sunset industries, or buries the past to deliver the future. The leaven of reactionaries, progressives, and pragmatists makes bread for the second of Paul's two economies. It is a means of rebellion, idolatry, impurity, alienation, hypocrisy, egocentrism, guilt, and perdition.

"Our daily bread" is a product of Paul's first economy because it tells a different story. The Lord's Prayer is neither reactionary, nor progressive, nor moderate. It contradicts our theories of capital because the past we remember, the present we endure, and the future we await all depend not on the acquisition or the transfer of wealth but on the providential work of Christ.

The gospel is not indifferent to wealth and poverty or the status quo and its alternatives. Far from it. Prayer arises out of a material life. In Matthew the Lord's Prayer follows a warning for disciples to give away in private rather than in public and precedes a warning to acquire in heaven rather than on earth. Jesus spends more time talking about money than about practically anything else.

In fact, the life of Christian prayer is a *constantly* material life. It is not something that follows a once-for-all divestment of possessions. In this regime, those who do not store up treasure on earth somehow still have alms to give. Those who give away their clothing on demand still have things to wear. That is because they are still receiving the daily bread and other necessities they pray for. They still give because God still provides.

Yet what God still provides is not called property, shares, collateral, income, profit, rent, interest, equity, capital gains, distributions, dividends, royalties, plunder, welfare, tax credits, benefits, winnings, loans, transfer payments, relief, or charity. Jesus has us call it our daily bread. It is what we always need now to see us through to the very end.

Of course, our daily bread may come in all these forms, as well as others. The Baptist invited Israel back into the land of milk and honey. Jesus passed around baskets full of bread and fish. Peter pulled up a staggering haul. The disciples pooled their monies. Barnabas sold a field. Destitute widows got a daily distribution or new children and husbands. Parents cared for their children and masters for their slaves. Lydia funded a mission. Paul marketed tents and raised funds for Jerusalem. The point is not the various forms, but the common substance. To be the Kingdom's providence they must be our daily bread.

Here we meet one of the eternal questions of Christian ethics. What makes these assets daily bread? How can resources from a condemned world be the Kingdom's providence? How can bad trees yield good fruit?

They cannot. Any economist who claims otherwise is a false prophet (Matt. 7:15-20). The YHWH Administration is not bankrolled by the ruler of this world. Neither feudalism, nor capitalism, nor socialism, nor any other oppositional economic order can produce Paul's "spiritual food." A tithe does not justify unrighteous income. A charitable foundation does not rectify an unscrupulous fortune. Redistributive taxes, violent revolutions, nationalized industries, privatized industries, free trade, and high technology bring neither social peace nor common prosperity. Adam Smith's and Karl Marx's efforts to turn vice into virtue are just modern schools of alchemy.

Why? Because the Kingdom *comes*. As what is personal must be born from above, so what is impersonal must be graced with a new beginning. A bad tree cannot yield good fruit, but a bad tree can be made a good one (Matt. 12:33). This is not alchemy but transubstantiation, judgment and refreshing, death and resurrection.

The point of wealth's transubstantiation from Paul's second constellation to the first, from bread as sin to bread as life, is the intersection of the two economies in Jesus' ministry. There wealth is Roman taxes, appetizers for a crowd made ready to force Jesus' coronation, embezzled apostolic funds, Caesar's denarius, a demand to divide an estate, two sons' downfalls, a rich young man's burden, a rich corpse's torment, a Pharisee's annual giving and a publican's guilt, silver for a disciple's betrayal, a plundered garment, and a potter's field. Yet wealth is also treasure from wise men, a steady if unremarkable job, angelic relief in the wilderness, supporters' hospitality, funds for a well budgeted house, a coin from a fish's mouth, a seamless robe, wine for a wedding, signs for thousands of the coming bounty, a found coin, discounted loans that win friends, a widow's mite, Zacchaeus' penance, a jar of costly perfume, an upper room, a Passover meal, and a proper tomb.

What distinguishes these two economies is also what links them. One proclaims, brings about, and celebrates the good news. The other refuses and resists it. The two economies meet in the broken flesh and spilled blood of Christ. On his cross, violence is met with peace. At his tomb, providence quells rebellion. On the road to Emmaus the covetousness that ended in murder is ended with the daily bread that yields recognition and satisfaction (Luke 24:35). In Jerusalem, the disciples devote themselves to a whole new economy of signs and wonders centered in the apostles' teaching, a fellowship of profound sharing, the breaking of bread, and prayer (Acts 2:42-47). The old has been made new.

Outwardly, wealth is ambiguous. Is my expensive home a den of thieves or a house of prayer? Is my retirement fund a big barn or an alabaster flask? Am I withholding mercy or giving in secret? It is not immediately clear — perhaps not even to me. A recent college graduate recently told me that as he drove by the gated estates of Montecito he thought to himself, "I hope I'm never so greedy that I live in one of these houses." But appearances deceive. As Quaker spiritualism rather than Anglican sacramentalism made

Pennsylvanians such successful businesspeople, so asceticism rather than materialism produced at least some of Montecito's fortunes. Some who live in those estates are astonishingly generous people, while many of the truly greedy are living in apartments and juggling massive credit card balances. Much is hidden.

Yet all will be known (Matt. 10:26). The character of our wealth can only become clear in retrospect. We identify it as good fruit from a good tree by what story we tell with it. "My family is successful," "the American Dream works," "better safe than sorry," and "life is good" are popular storylines, but the only storyline that lasts begins in Israel, centers in Jesus Christ, and spreads through the Church to the ends of the earth.

While there is no limit to our idolatrous fictions, there is also no limit to the ways we can witness to that one true story. And as all our nations will tell it in our own ways, so there must be a businesslike Russian way, an entrepreneurial Hungarian way, a thrifty Scottish way, a freely spending English way, and a familial Chinese way of testifying to the King.

Three Kinds of Accumulators

Stanley and Danko's *The Millionaire Next Door* includes a fascinating look at the way two types of Americans see money. For the "underaccumulators of wealth" whose assets lag behind their earnings, money is for earning, status-attainment, and consumption. For the "prodigious accumulators of wealth" whose assets far outpace their earnings, money is for growing, discipline, and investment. High-status careers, flashy lifestyles, and inheritance are correlated more with being a "UAW," while mundane careers, modest lifestyles, and entrepreneurship characterize "PAWs." This is a nearly complete reversal of what most people expect.

> Mr. Miller "Bubba" Richards, age fifty, is the proprietor of a mobile-home dealership. His total household income last year was $90,200. Mr. Richards's net worth . . . is expected to be $451,000. But "Bubba" is a PAW. His actual net worth is $1.1 million.
>
> His counterpart is James H. Ford II. Mr. Ford, age fifty-one, is an attorney. His income last year was $92,330, slightly more than Mr. Richards's. . . . Mr. Ford's actual net worth is $226,511, while his expected level of wealth . . . is $470,883. Mr. Ford, by our definition,

is an under accumulator of wealth. Mr. Ford spent seven years in college. How can he possibly have less wealth than a mobile-home dealer? . . .

Clearly, Mr. Ford, the attorney, must spend significantly more of his household's income to maintain and display his family's higher upper-middle-class lifestyle. What make of motor vehicle is congruent with the status of an attorney? Foreign luxury, no doubt. Who needs to wear a different high-quality suit to work each day? Who needs to join one or more country clubs? Who needs expensive Tiffany silverware and serving trays?

Mr. Ford, the UAW, has a higher propensity to spend than do the members of the PAW group. UAWs tend to live above their means; they emphasize consumption. And they tend to de-emphasize many of the key factors that underlie wealth building.[14]

These two men's treasuries arose from very different lives, in which money came to mean very different things. Because PAWs' saving habits amount to financial asceticism, they come to a place of relative detachment from the things money can buy. They live to work, not to own. They do not dream of late-model luxury cars, gourmet food, or designer clothes. Likewise, because UAWs' spending habits amount to financial indulgence, they come to a place of much greater material attachment. They work to spend. They are significantly more anxious about their future and their children's future.[15] They spend a lot of time planning new purchases and very little on financial advice or planning. Though they have smaller estates, they worry more that their children will fight over them.[16]

Stanley and Danko's profiles will remind some readers of the wise and the foolish in Proverbs (cf. Prov. 6:6-11) and the astute and inept businessmen of Jesus' parables, and there is something to the resemblance. They certainly do not match the prophets' description of the rapacious wealthy and exploited poor (cf. James 5:1-6) nor the characters of the rich man and Lazarus (Luke 16:19-31). But the point of this exercise is not to describe, let alone exalt, America's wealth accumulators. The PAW lifestyle is good for

---

14. Thomas J. Stanley and William D. Danko, *The Millionaire Next Door: The Surprising Secrets of America's Wealthy* (New York: Simon and Schuster, 1996), pp. 14-15.

15. Stanley and Danko, *The Millionaire*, pp. 88-89.

16. Stanley and Danko, *The Millionaire*, pp. 88-91.

getting out of debt and funding a family's education and security, but it is poor investment advice for rich fools building bigger barns to hold their surpluses (cf. Luke 12:13-21). Moreover, while it is tempting to think of wealthy ascetics as the quiet dissidents of American consumerism, in fact they are also its underwriters. Stanley and Danko cite an interviewee whose UAW parents smoked three packs of cigarettes a day, noting that if they had quit they would have saved $33,190 over 46 years — and suggesting if they had invested that money *in Philip Morris stock* their portfolio would have been worth over $2 million![17] A God who advocated selling rather than buying cigarettes would be a Father who answered other people's prayers with snakes and scorpions (Luke 11:11-12). America's PAW culture is at once an oppressor, a sage, and a dupe, as its UAW culture is a victim, a fool, and a perpetrator.

My point is not to identify or deconstruct heroes or villains. It is to underline that money is cultural. It is socially constructed. A dollar is not simply a dollar; it is our relationships. We make it what it is by the way we live.

The Kingdom's prayerful life reconstructs money. Providential wealth is something new and free. The true sage in Jesus' parable of the rich fool is the one who is generous toward God and so accumulates treasure in heaven (Luke 12:21, 32-34). In the parable of the prodigal son, the Father's will is to beget neither parsimonious PAWs nor decadent UAWs, but heirs who gain his own generosity and discipline.

How? As the shrewd heirs of this age hold lessons for the heirs of light (cf. Luke 16:8), so Stanley and Danko's millionaires offer us parables of the Kingdom's economy. Spendthrift UAWs pass their monetary habits on to their children in the form of unqualified financial support — undisciplined generosity — begetting new generations of coddled, undisciplined, and stressed consumers. Frugal PAWs pass their money habits on to their children in the form of discipline. But it is not a discipline without generosity. American millionaires are sparing in their material support for their progeny, with one exception: they invest heavily in their children's education. They apprentice their children through seasons of asceticism to prepare for futures of abundance. In this way PAWs tend to beget new generations of tranquil and independent owners. Those who have ears, let them hear.

The Kingdom's subjects begin as little more than slaves to their disci-

17. Stanley and Danko, *The Millionaire*, pp. 53-54.

plinarians. However, the point of their servitude is not perpetual slavery but inheritance of the Father's promise (Gal. 3:23–4:9). They receive an intensive education and a little in trust and are held responsible for both, not because God is miserly but so they can prove themselves faithful and become trustees of much (Luke 19:17). They are not to *spend* what they have, but to *give* it as freely as they received (Matt. 10:8), to share the King's teaching and treasure with all who would train with them.

UAWs grow up in cultures of consumption, into perpetual and deepening servitude. Few of them own their own businesses, so they depend on employers. Few have enough savings to tide them over in emergencies, so they depend on their own earning power. Many have grown used to regular gifts from parents they now consider part of their normal income, so they depend on patronage. The future becomes a source of worry, stress, and strife. By contrast, PAWs grow up in cultures of empowerment, into financial self-sufficiency. They are more than twice as likely to be entrepreneurs who own their own businesses and employ others. They face the future with confidence. UAWs expend wealth; PAWs create with it. UAWs live for today and so defer their future; PAWs look to the future and so reorganize their present. Similarly, like royal schoolchildren, the Kingdom's PAWs beg not as panhandlers who are one meal from starvation but as tenants and slaves who are destined to reign as heirs.

Isn't something backwards? How can begging for bread three times a day produce a culture of self-sufficiency?! Yet it does, because *the begging is not for bread alone* (cf. Deut. 8:3 in Luke 4:4). The Kingdom's gifts are for building up Christ's whole body, not consuming his creation. Jesus taught us to beg not just for our individual selves or just for today's rations but for the whole body — and for the Name to be made holy, the Kingdom to come, the Father's will to be done, sinners to be made righteous, and evil to be defeated. They keep the entire story in view.

This economic metanarrative changes everything. Money ceases to be just consumption or capital and becomes what it should always have been: our daily bread, what we have always needed today to see us all through to the very end. Jesus' mission in America's material cultures is to release their captives (Luke 4:18). We worldly poor, even we high-earning poor, are released from our indiscipline. We worldly rich, even we low-earning rich, are released from our parsimony. Both are set free from the distraction wealth has become in our lives so we can become faithful trustees of the Kingdom's far greater treasure.

Proper trusteeship demands Spiritual, Filial, Paternal discipline *and* generosity. There lies the challenge, for none of the American financial subcultures whose roots we examined in the first section and none of the subcultures that have descended from them have God's wealth of discipline and generosity. Our financial cultures and ideologies have no words for *artos epiousios,* no sense of its happy ending, no vocabulary of providence. They need judging, convicting, forgiving, and healing. As a child of these cultures and ideologies, I do too.

When we embrace God's vocabulary and beg for our daily bread, not only do we receive sustenance, but material things also receive significance. Land and currency and all the rest gain the opportunity to become our daily bread. They take part in the great story of salvation that is not just for our sake but for theirs too, and especially for the sake of the Lord's name (Ps. 23:3). The salvation is twofold: we are freed from wealth's grip, and wealth is freed from ours.

Consider the illustration that follows the Lord's Prayer in Luke (11:5-13). We are desperate neighbors who need bread for unexpected visitors. Everything is going wrong! Our guests will be insulted. We will be humiliated. We will resent our ungracious friend. The friendship will be strained, if not broken. His loaves stored away for tomorrow will be . . . what? The last answer is not supplied. But whatever the loaves turn out to be, they will have the bitter taste of unrighteousness. What sets the relationships aright and rescues everything is our incessant begging and the answer of transubstantiating grace. When the sleepy friend is finally roused and lends the bread, the guests are welcomed, we are honored, our friend credited and glorified for his sacrifice — and the bread becomes not just bodily nourishment but the delicious currency of fellowship.

Is this scenario a tale of maximized utility? Managed scarcity? Benefits exceeding costs? Spontaneous order? Sure. But these accounts hardly scratch the surface. However economists might see it, theology must see it as a story of the Kingdom's righteousness. Our work and gratitude for daily bread is the mundane middle of a prayer that strives first and last for divine holiness, the Kingdom's advent, accomplishment of the Father's will, universal forgiveness, and deliverance from evil.

> You cannot serve God and wealth. . . . So do not worry, saying, "What will we eat?" or "What will we drink?" or "What will we wear?" For it is the nations who strive for all these things; and in-

deed your heavenly Father knows that you need all these things. But strive first for the kingdom of God and his righteousness, and all these things will be given to you as well. (Matt. 6:24, 31-33)

Wealth is made providence when God reframes it in the Kingdom's righteous economy, the Spirit renarrating it as the Father's daily bread for the Son and all his charge.

A Parable of Disciplined Generosity

Accepting the Kingdom's invitation by praying the King's prayer calls Americans of every economic culture to forsake both the conservative idolatry of free-market consumerism and liberal idolatry of welfare-statism. Both sacrifice the future for a more comfortable present. Global democratic capitalism runs through resources at an unprecedented and probably unsustainable rate. Transnational progressivism bankrupts societies with transfer payments that sap productivity and initiative and place an ever increasing burden on immigrants, the young, and the unborn. Both are terminal conditions, capable only of falling.

Can these patients cure themselves? Evangelical libertarians like Doug Bandow recommend strengthened property rights and entrepreneurship as a means of empowerment.[18] Doing this has helped lift unprecedented numbers of people out of poverty, and doing it in more places would surely help even more. Yet Christian convictions soften and fade as income and wealth grow, and western consumerism and familial coddling of their own underperformers tend to break down both ethnic and familial PAW cultures within a couple of generations. Evangelical progressives like Ron Sider advocate, among other things, massive material support directed toward the poor.[19] Doing this has changed many lives for the better, and doing it in more places would surely change even more. Yet socialism's rise has coincided with the precipitous fall in European faith and hope, and statism and bureaucratic coddling of society's underperformers mainly reinforce de-

18. Doug Bandow, *Beyond Good Intentions: A Biblical View of Politics* (Wheaton, Ill.: Crossway, 1988).

19. Ronald J. Sider, *Rich Christians in an Age of Hunger: Moving from Affluence to Generosity,* 20th Anniversary ed. (Dallas: Word, 1997), pp. 216-19.

pendencies and shatter communities and families. It seems the world's material cultures and ideologies are too powerful for either worldly discipline or worldly generosity to overcome or even withstand their destructive capacity. No economic alchemy will rescue wrong relationships.

What will rescue them is justification by grace[20] and sanctification by fire.[21] Here too the discerning may find parables of the Kingdom. The bipartisan welfare reform bill that a Republican Congress worked through the Clinton Administration is the single most effective recent collective effort to lift Americans out of poverty. It confirms Stanley and Danko's finding that "economic outpatient care" — the bequest of material resources apart from discipline and accountability — is counterproductive. Indulgence doesn't justify. Yet it also confirms that faith and hope come through attention to the poor — through grace — rather than neglect. Isolation doesn't sanctify.

Why has the last decade's welfare reform worked? It avoids both the undisciplined generosity of classic Democratic politics and the disciplined parsimony of classic Republican politics. While it is more libertarian than statist, its provisions still transcend both ideologies to suggest the disciplined generosity of the Father's Kingdom. He reassures his obedient son at the prodigal's return that "all that is mine is yours," meaning that there will be no further division of the estate to benefit his underachieving brother (Luke 15:31). Yet the Father's discipline is generous: the prodigal son gains his ring and his best robe, for he is alive again (15:32). The Father does not weaken the weak as many UAWs do, nor does he merely strengthen the strong as many PAWs do. His wise providence strengthens both. The treasure that accumulates is not just higher incomes and greater assets — in fact it may not lead to these at all — but more marriages and fewer births out of wedlock, stronger families and neighborhoods, and prouder heritages — the relationships, traditions, and peoplehood that financial practices only begin to signify.

Disciplined generosity characterizes all of life in the Kingdom. The Church is not collectivist, and it is not individualist. It is personal, and therefore communal. The Son is obedient to the Father, and the Father highly exalts the Son with the name above every name. When we desperate neighbors come to knock on the Father's door, our real capital is the Son's

20. See below, "The Mercy of God."
21. See above, "The Reputation of God."

relationship with him that he had imputed to us. As in the parable, the help we receive does not jeopardize that relationship but strengthens it for the Son's sake. The greatest blessing that an heir can receive is neither life-support nor independence, but the benefactor's authority and virtue. Another word for them is relationship.

Wealth is relationship, and we are heirs entrusted with the Holy Spirit. Bread from heaven and living water is the Father's ultimate gift. The Kingdom's relationships are heavenly treasure that will never depreciate.

CHAPTER 6

The Mercy of God

She was Charlotte Simmons. Could she ever have that conversation
with herself, the way Momma told her to? Mr. Starling put "soul" in
quotes, which as much as said it was only a superstitious belief in the
first place, an earlier, yet more primitive name for the ghost in the
machine.

So why do you keep waiting deep in the back of my head,
Momma, during my every conscious moment — waiting for me to
have that conversation? Even if I were to pretend it were real, my
"soul," the way you think it is, what could I possibly say?

Tom Wolfe, *I Am Charlotte Simmons*

The Soulless World of Tom Wolfe

As I read Tom Wolfe's latest novel, *I Am Charlotte Simmons*,[1] I could have
sworn I heard a faint voice saying, "Bless me, father, for I have sinned."
How can that be? Wolfe isn't a believer, and this is a work of fiction. Am I
imagining things? You be the judge.

In one of a series of essays he published in 2000 as *Hooking Up*,[2] Wolfe
claims that this century's two deepest thoughts are headed for a collision.
Neuroscience and evolutionary psychology are uncovering the physiologi-

1. New York: Farrar, Straus and Giroux, 2004.
2. New York: Picador, 2001.

cal basis of all human behavior. Wolfe believes that they are thus closing in on solutions to the timeless riddle of human existence. "Here we have the two most fascinating riddles of the twenty-first century: the riddle of the human mind and the riddle of what happens to the human mind when it comes to know itself absolutely."[3]

Their successes are squeezing philosophy's now-unfashionable traditions of self-knowledge into a determinism far more radical than anything sixteenth-century Calvinism envisioned.[4] Determinism already has severe consequences for whether and how human beings ought to be understood as moral agents. In addition, evolutionary psychology's treatment of thought as mere evolutionary adaptations deposes traditional categories of truth for utility. Wolfe thinks Nietzsche's fulfilled predictions of the bloody consequences of twentieth-century nihilism will pale in comparison to what will happen once we realize that "transcendence" is just a misnomer for mental impressions that once had survival value.

> I suddenly had a picture of the entire astonishing edifice [of modern scientific knowledge] collapsing and modern man plunging headlong back into the primordial ooze. He's floundering, sloshing about, gulping for air, frantically treading ooze, when he feels something huge and smooth swim beneath him and boost him up, like some mighty dolphin. He can't see it, but he's much impressed. He names it God.[5]

Our interest in the self continues to thrive. Yet our intellectual culture offers less and less room for the self as a thing of enduring interest. Our age already senses that final twilight, into darkness or light we cannot yet tell, approaching but not yet arriving. What will happen to us after whatever happens to "us"? As a student of the trend, Wolfe makes a good early indicator.

For decades Wolfe's writing has been driven by a sociological "Theory of Everything" that declares that we are all constantly absorbed with social status. "We're all motivated, and I certainly include myself here, far more than we want to admit, by group expectations," he told *Time* magazine. "How other people view us has an important effect on how we view our-

3. Wolfe, *Hooking Up*, p. 107.
4. Wolfe, *Hooking Up*, pp. 97-98.
5. Wolfe, *Hooking Up*, p. 109.

selves."[6] Wolfe's social-scientific journeys led him to Edward O. Wilson, who connected the genetically determined social behaviors of ants to rhesus macaque monkeys and finally to human beings. Wilson is the father of sociobiology, "the hottest field in the academic world."[7] Wolfe realizes that his old-school Weberian Theory of Everything stands challenged by Wilson's new Theory of Everything — toe to toe, so to speak. Wolfe claims to be a skeptic of Wilson, but he allows that he is ready to exchange one for the other as the evidence comes in.[8]

Who Is Charlotte Simmons?

A little evidence just came in. Wolfe's latest novel *I Am Charlotte Simmons* is an artistic test of Wilson's vision. Does the new paradigm work as well as the one that put Wolfe on bestseller lists for decades? Does a novel need a self? Or will a sociobiologically constructed "self" suffice?

Judging from the book's sales, "selves" with quotation marks are not enough. Hardcover sales peaked at a fraction of Wolfe's first two novels. Poor reviews had little to do with it; Wolfe's first two novels were similarly panned by reviewers irritated with his style and political incorrectness, but buyers devoured them. *Simmons*' realistically obscene collegiate vocabulary and its generational distance from the middle-aged fiction-buying public were undoubtedly contributing factors. Yet what was really different this time was that the word-of-mouth was lukewarm.

Why? Wolfe's "ravenous curiosity" about all things American[9] is still infectious. His reliance on realism as the best conveyer of life's riches,[10] reminiscent of the fundamentalist thinker Francis Schaeffer's contempt for late modern ideologies, works its usual magic. His scrupulous attention to detail captures again the mystery of the mundane. He populates his collegiate landscape with his typical array of tragic characters. But this time the book's anthropology turns them more than ever into *things*. They resemble people I know, but the resemblance ends right at the line where they

6. Paul Gray, "A Man in Full," *Time*, November 2, 1998; available online at http://www.time.com/time/archive/printout/0,23657,989469,00.html.

7. Wolfe, *Hooking Up*, p. 96.

8. Wolfe, *Hooking Up*, p. 87.

9. Wolfe, *Hooking Up*, p. 170.

10. Wolfe, *Hooking Up*, p. 168.

would become personal. Even in their interior monologues, Hoyt, Jojo, and Adam are eerily two-dimensional collections of social and physiological attributes. They are the literary equivalent of computer generated image (CGI) characters from the movies. It is as if Wolfe were playing *Sim University* using Wilson's axioms of ant behavior rather than telling a story of human beings.

Astonishingly, this is even true of his protagonist. Rephrasing the title tells the story: "I, Charlotte Simmons, Am." Charlotte is the star in a story of tenuous and finally futile assertion of Nietzschean selfhood against a deterministic tide. And as she slides from insecure self-righteousness into disorientation, loneliness, surrender, humiliation, depression, and reconstitution as someone else's girlfriend, we feel for her. But we do not really feel *with* her. She remains on the other side of an unbridgeable distance. In fact, Wolfe has not really provided a 'her' to whom to bridge in the first place. Her mechanistic qualities signal Wolfe's inability to exploit the new sociobiological paradigm, even with his marvelous authorial gifts. And if he cannot do it, who can?

This tells us something important about neuroscience's new Theory of Everything: it doesn't work. It seems to explain a lot about us, but it does not render *us*. Something is still missing. Perhaps it is that old Hellenistic *deus ex machina*, a soul. Or it might be a complexity of the physical that no reductionism can capture. Maybe it is merely a knot that the relentless tweezers of scientific inquiry have yet to unravel. The apostolic faith has room for all of these possibilities and more. But whatever is missing, it seems to be the key to a story worth telling.

The fizzling of Wolfe's project is a portentous development in sociobiology. In his audacious conclusion of *On Human Nature*, Wilson himself called for a reconstruction of the humanities and social sciences atop the biological sciences, according to the "evolutionary epic" that Wilson consider the best mythology we will ever have. If this is what sociobiology offers literature and social psychology, then perhaps they are better off declining the offer.

Wolfe's failure to render a compelling protagonist has a second, even more ominous significance. After all, in Charlotte he says he has written his most autobiographical character yet. She is in many ways a fictionalization of him. A close reading of his life and interests draws a veritable map of Charlotte's psyche. Wolfe is culturally and politically conservative, like Charlotte. For his whole life he has shared her shock at modern sexual behaviors.[11] His contempt for intellectuals ("Rococo Marxists," he calls them)[12] despite his own doctorate in American studies echoes her forsaking of Adam's intellectual clique, the Millennial Mutants. He is a Virginian who lives in a sumptuous Manhattan penthouse; she is a North Carolinian from the Blue Ridge Mountains who goes off to an elite university in Pennsylvania. The two southerners are more American than either New York's insular "literary world"[13] or the "obedient colony of Europe" that is American academia.[14] He and she are both socially ascendant, obsessed with status, and preoccupied with clothing. In 1996 after bypass surgery he suffered a bout of depression like hers; similar friendships rescued both. Wolfe confesses that if he were in college today he would go into neuroscience, the subject that most fascinates Charlotte. He is not a religious man, but finds religion morally useful in others; she inherits the severe morals but not the spirituality of her mother. Both are haunted by "the ghost in the machine" of Cartesian dualism and disturbed by the Nietzschean prophecy of what will follow its demise,[15] but neither really has any alternative to forging ahead through the storm.

The book's title can thus be read in a second way, as the key to decoding a parable: "I, Tom Wolfe, Am Charlotte Simmons." The book is then a fictionalization of Wolfe's lifelong encounter with America's cultures. Charlotte's submission to society becomes Wolfe's own temptation to submit to the social and physiological principalities and powers of life, and the novel becomes a confession of his surrender to them.

Are these, then, an atheist's confessions? Not to God, of course, but to the higher power of the group — to his public and to his own vanishing self?

A Chilling Harbinger

On the first meaning of the title, *Charlotte Simmons* disappoints. This is not because Wolfe has lost his edge as a writer. His nonfiction reporting in *Hooking Up* is as sharp as ever. His characterizations of real people in that volume — William Shockley, Robert Noyce, Pierre Teilhard de Chardin,

11. Wolfe, *Hooking Up*, pp. 3-16, 72.
12. Wolfe, *Hooking Up*, pp. 113-30.
13. Wolfe, *Hooking Up*, p. 161.
14. Wolfe, *Hooking Up*, p. 12.
15. Wolfe, *Hooking Up*, pp. 107-9.

Edward O. Wilson, Frederick Hart, and Americans of all kinds at the turn of the millennium — remain splendid. His perceptions of college life strike me (as they have struck most collegiate readers) as dead-on. It is his fictional characters that come up short. They cannot compete with real human beings. After a few pages into each chapter I would find myself leafing ahead to see when it would end. This is not how I read either Wolfe's nonfiction or *Bonfire of the Vanities*.[16] Something is amiss.

On the second meaning of the title, though, everything changes. The clues suddenly line up, details from other writings and interviews find new places in the narrative, and the story comes to life. Suddenly we are peering not into a social scientist's diorama, but into the world as an eighteen-year-old Wolfe would enter it. We are seeing him live again, not as a ghost or mere construction or type or composite but as a real *self*.

I might be reading too much into the resemblance. Yet Charlotte is a lot more interesting as an allegory for Wolfe than as a mere character in her own unhappy story. That is disturbing, because it means Wolfe's social theory has robbed him of the ability to convey even his own authenticity. *I* must supply Charlotte's selfhood by making her nonfictional.

As I rehearse the novel and reread passages in this new light, a new fear haunts me: Can it be that Wolfe wants to write of his inmost self as a person, but he is no longer sure there is a person to write about? Confession requires a penitent, a confessor, and a penitential narrative. In *Charlotte Simmons* the forms are present — an author, an audience, and a life story — but not the substance. After all, if we are nothing more than what Wolfe calls "conscious little rocks," what is there to do but tumble? Does this septuagenarian want to confess his sins, but cannot find either a confessor or even his own voice, let alone the sins? Is this the cry for help of a de-centered and dissolving self?

When read as Wolfe's veiled aspirations, the novel is not a bore but a harbinger, and a chilling one. It seems hard to believe that one of the most observant and insightful observers of human life in the late twentieth century could find himself so opaque as to portray himself as a mere simulacrum. Wolfe may be personally experiencing the collision of social scientific self-knowledge and the consequences of gaining it. But rather than coming to absolute self-knowledge, he is mystified. Like Adam reap-

16. New York: Farrar, Straus, and Giroux, 1987.

ing thorns and thistles, his production is an unreal autobiographical artifice, not to mention a rare literary failure.

Lost and Found

Throughout his career, Wolfe's world has been our world. That means *we* are Charlotte Simmons too. When we no longer live in ways that make confession intelligible, our faith decomposes in the same way as hers into reputation, our hope into ambition, and our love into belonging. We cease to be persons and become units of social science. We no longer confess, but only ruminate on fleeting glories and lingering shames. We make others the measure of ourselves. We revel and we agonize. We vanquish and we capitulate. We analyze and resolve as if heroically but we finally yield to the Zeitgeist. We become characters in a Tom Wolfe novel. And ultimately we submerge into the primordial ooze.

Or maybe into the ancient myths. Wolfe's project chronicles our cultural regression from the introspective consciousness that Augustine's *Confessions* gave the west back into the un-self-conscious ambition and fatalism of pagan Rome. In *City of God* Augustine described that city's characteristic vice as the love of praise. The modern research university is one fitting embodiment of that, but there are many others. Our poor reviews and receptions of *Simmons* are ultimately appraisals of our own future.

What will happen as that future ripples out from academia into wider and wider circles? Wolfe predicts that

> in the year 2010 or 2030, some new Nietzsche will step forward to announce: "The self is dead" — except that being prone to the poetic, like Nietzsche the First, he will probably say: "The soul is dead." He will say that he is merely bringing the news, the news of the greatest event of the millennium: "The soul, that last refuge of values, is dead, because educated people no longer believe it exists." Unless the assurances of the Wilsons and the Dennetts and the Dawkinses also start rippling out, the madhouse that will ensue may make the [Nietzschean] phrase "the total eclipse of all values" seem tame.[17]

17. Wolfe, *Simmons,* p. 107.

In a less dramatic moment Wolfe forecasts a "great relearning" in the twenty-first century in which the world swears off the twentieth century's disastrous projects of ideological reinvention and lapses into social somnolence.[18]

Sleeping off a cultural hangover may be the best outcome a secularist like Wolfe can expect. But can't there be another option besides these two? Isn't there a way that doesn't lead back into the endless cyclicality of Hobbesian nature or pagan antiquity?

Of course there is. Ironically, Wolfe himself provides the sign. There is one point in *Simmons* in which true humanity erupts from beneath the social theory. It is on the novel's dedication page, in which Wolfe dedicates his book to his children, "my two collegians." He tells them:

> You have been a joy, a surprise, a source of wonderment for me at every stage of your young lives. So I suppose I shouldn't be astonished by what you have done for me and this book; but I am, and dedicating it to you is a mere whisper of my gratitude. I gave you the manuscript hoping you might vet it for undergraduate vocabulary. That you did. . . . What I never imagined you could do — I couldn't have done it at your age — was to step back in the most detached way and point out the workings of human nature in general and the esoteric workings of social status in particular. I say "esoteric," because in many cases these were areas of life one would not ordinarily think of as social at all. Given your powers of abstraction, your father had only to reassemble the material he had accumulated visiting campuses across the country. What I feel about you both I can say best with a long embrace.

There is no paragraph in *Simmons'* six hundred pages more powerful than that one. The way out of the sociological madhouse is a father's love.

Sure, theory has its proper place. Wolfe employs it in his dedication as many a dad has used a baseball and mitt to bond with his kids. But no theory will domesticate or even describe the love that shines here, in the most interpersonal lines in the entire book. What we meet here is a human echo of the Father's love for the Son, an eternal person-making embrace that we can only receive as the gift of all that we finally are and pass along as all that we finally have.

18. Wolfe, *Simmons*, p. 144.

Long ago the pagan Roman world discovered that a person is neither a moral architect nor a helpless puppet, but a *subsistent relation:* a locus of relationships with other persons whose mutual reality and otherness image the Triune God. It learned this not through a flash of philosophical insight but through the blood and breath of the one who loved us to the end. Perhaps the extraordinarily interpersonal life and legacy of Jesus might still yield the Theory of Everything that a writer could find truly fruitful.

It's an awfully good story too. Coincidence? I don't think so.

"Forgive Us . . . as We Forgive"

"We are beggars. This is true," Luther said at the end of his life. It *is* true — but we are more than beggars. Saying that we have nothing to offer God but neediness is a pious-sounding slander of our Lord. Like the Son himself, we bring resources to each petition of this prayer: the relationship that knows God as our Father, the awareness that recognizes holiness, a place in God's reign, our will, the fruit of labor, gratitude and generosity, and a willingness to go wherever God puts us. To be sure, we bring these gifts only by the Creator's grace, but we do bring them, and for that God justly receives credit.

However, we also bring something to prayer that has no analogue in the Son himself: our own barrenness.

> Ephraim is stricken, their stock is withered; they can produce no
> fruit.
> Even if they do bear children, I will slay their cherished offspring.
> My God rejects them because they have not obeyed him,
> and they go wandering among the nations. (Hos. 9:16-17)

Look for barrenness and you will find it everywhere.

One year one of my students, aspiring to become a social worker, became an intern at a local rape crisis center as part of an independent study. She loved her work, despite its somber nature. She admired her fellow workers, few of whom were Christians. She was delighted to be able to help women in need. But one thing vexed her for her whole semester: getting women back on their feet physically and psychologically and helping them through the horrors of the legal system could do no more than minimize the damage from an irreparable relationship. Forgiveness and reconciliation were not in her job description. As she read her textbooks — *Exclusion and Embrace* by Miroslav Volf,[19] *Embodying Forgiveness* by L. Gregory Jones,[20] *Ethics* by James Wm. McClendon Jr.,[21] and even the novel *Mr. Ives' Christmas* by Oscar Hijuelos[22] — she was at a loss for what to do with them. She was allowed only to assist rape victims, not to get involved in reconstructing their shattered relationships with members of the opposite sex. Devictimization was out.

That same semester, a distraught student visited my office. He was not a believer, but said he wished he could be. "Just ask for a relationship with God," his friends kept telling him, "and wait until you experience him." All his life he had heard this. But he didn't know how to ask someone who did not exist. He also knew he could wait forever without feeling anything. And he had noticed that other religions' followers had their feelings as well. What would make the resulting experience an authentic sign of the truth of Christian faith? "You'll just know," they told him. He longed for his life to come together, and he was tempted to "believe" just to overcome the emptiness of his life, but his integrity would not let him. "How am I supposed to make a relationship with God?" he asked.

Not long afterward, Westmont held a screening of *Garden State,* a film that is doing for the Millennial Generation what *The Graduate* did for their parents: providing compelling images of their world's emptiness. The film opens up the subterranean cavern of late modern doubt that saps the strength of even my most faithful students. One student told me later that the scene in which the film's main characters scream into a quarry's infinite abyss moved her to tears. Several others thanked us for initiating a genuine discussion about the effect the film had had on them, then pleaded with us for advice on filling the void it had exposed. "What do we do?" they all asked. Their expressions ranged from frustration to panic.

It is futile to try to make something out of nothing; only a Creator can do that. It is specious to try to turn something wrong into something right; only a Redeemer can do that. It is pointless even to try to transcend the nothingness. Only a Perfecter can do that. While our world identifies us as

---

19. Nashville: Abingdon, 1996.
20. Grand Rapids: Eerdmans, 1995.
21. Nashville: Abingdon, 1986.
22. New York: HarperCollins, 1995.

individuals organized in relationships of contested power and status, the Lord's Prayer insists that we are bankrupt debtors struggling to survive in a moral Great Depression, and announces that

judgment and forgiveness are God's new creation
of those formerly barren relationships.

The Death and Life of Israel

In the days of the judges and the dawn of Israel's monarchy, the former prophets saw the early signs of Israel's impending death and foretold the need for something new. The era had begun with such gifts! Such promise! Such enthusiasm! Such good intentions! Every one of God's promises to Israel had been fulfilled (Josh. 23:15). Even the land rested from war (Josh. 14:15). Yet chaos followed. "Everyone did what was right in his own eyes" in the time of the judges, who were little more than action heroes of questionable character (Judg. 21:25). The priests became corrupt and the kings rose to preside over Israel's disintegration. The story, from Joshua to Kings, is a long, slow, excruciating political death in which the sins of the children outweighed even the worst sins of the fathers (cf. Hos. 9:9 on Judg. 19). As their pulse faded, God's exiled people finally began to comprehend their need. It was not for power, status, fame, pleasure, comfort, freedom, or wealth. None of these had slowed their slide into morbidity. The latter prophets rehearsed Israel's story to announce that in perverting justice, what Israel had destroyed was its relationship with God, and what it had lost was its very life. The wages of sin were estrangement, oppression, corruption, vengeance, calamity, panic, starvation, defeat, slavery, torpor, idolatry, decline, sterility, *death.*

Israel's Canaanized sensibilities were liable to take all this negativity as another turn in the wheel of life, the interminable cycle of natural creation and destruction. That is a common pagan way of seeing things. But the prophets intercepted that misinterpretation with another timeline that led not *back* to primordial chaos but *out* to a new and mysterious future.

Sing, O barren one who did not bear;
    burst into song and shout,
    you who have not been in labor!

> For the children of the desolate woman will be more
>   than the children of her that is married, says the LORD.
>
> (Isa. 54:1 NRSV)

Of course, before these happy tidings come, the audience must endure chapter after chapter of condemnations to sensitize its numb conscience to failures it had not even thought to be ashamed of. The old contraceptives and abortifacients must be abandoned before the new mercies can bear their fruit.

Paul invokes Isaiah 54:1 to warn the Galatians not to rely on any other security but God's grace, not even the Torah itself (Gal. 4:21–5:1). He puts his audience through another long diagnostic of sin: "For the works of the flesh are plain: fornication, impurity, licentiousness, idolatry, sorcery, enmity, strife, jealousy, anger, selfishness, dissension, party spirit, envy, drunkenness, carousing, and the like. I warn you, as I warned you before, that those who do such things shall not inherit the kingdom of God" (Gal. 5:19-21). Why the list? Surely to help his audience identify the causes of their malady. Yet this list also serves as a compact historiography of Israel tumbling into paganism.

Against these sterile works of empty desires Paul opposes *new creation* (6:15) — the fertile fruit of the Creator Spirit: "love, joy, peace, patience, kindness, goodness, faithfulness, gentleness, self-control" (5:22-23). The Torah offers no condemnation of this standard, for the Spirit rules "the Israel of God" (6:16) for which all of Israel's prior history, as well as the prior histories of all other nations, have been preparation (3:6–4:11). The end of the old and beginning of the new — the omega and the alpha, I like to call it — is the gift of Jesus Christ.

Forgiveness as Atonement

That gift of newness sometimes goes by the name "atonement," referring to God's new work reconciling the world to himself in Christ (2 Cor. 5:17-19). In our characteristic love of fine distinctions, we theologians have developed a host of different metaphors for atonement: sacrifice, victory, moral influence, and the like.[23] We have also carefully distinguished be-

---

23. John McIntyre, *The Shape of Soteriology* (Edinburgh: T&T Clark, 1992); Colin Gunton, *The Actuality of Atonement: A Study of Metaphor, Rationality and the Christian Tra-*

tween atonement (which is "the work of Christ") and other theological categories such as Trinity, creation, incarnation, salvation, and ecclesiology. These distinctions are important, but we must keep in mind that the biblical writings work harder to associate such words than to differentiate them (Eph. 3:18-19). An adequate theology must emphasize how atonement, new creation, and the apostolic ministry of reconciliation relate (2 Cor. 5:16-21), not just how they differ. Christ's task of atonement *is* new creation, which *is* the apostolic ministry of reconciliation, for in the righteousness of God we all work together in a common task (5:21–6:1).

Much was said about God's Kingdom in the first half of this book, and its righteousness is the main theme of the current half. Unless these two come together and come first, things go terribly wrong. The Sermon on the Mount lists the consequences. Without God's righteousness (which is the Kingdom's righteousness, however the translator construes Matthew 6:33), God's Kingdom could bring only an end to the old order, spawning a false Christian triumphalism that leads only to the judgment, the council, and the hell of fire (Matt. 6:21-22). Without God's Kingdom, God's righteousness could be only an unbearable imposition of the new upon the unvanquished old, spawning a false Christian moralism of piety corroded into public relations, dependency soured into anxiety, and judgment withheld in hypocrisy — holy things thrown to dogs (6:1–7:6). The proper relationship between God's Kingdom and its righteousness in the lives of his disciples is embodied in the two halves of the petition to "forgive us our debts, as we have forgiven our debtors." These two halves come together so profoundly that we need not make either half radically prior to the other. Luke can put the second half in the present tense (Luke 11:4), and Matthew can put God's forgiveness first (Matt. 18:23-35). They are as one.

Things *have* gone terribly wrong. Debts imply lost wealth. Sins imply missed opportunities. Forgiveness implies lost investment, trust, and power. These are things we had but failed to keep. Much had been given, and much is now required, but we have nothing to offer. Our indebtedness twists our good relationships into forces of destruction.

Jonathan R. Wilson associates the various Christian visions of atonement with corresponding visions of sin. Where sin is rebellion and guilt, atonement is Christ's sacrifice to pardon the guilty. Where sin is enslave-

---

dition (Edinburgh: T&T Clark, 1988); Jonathan R. Wilson, *God So Loved the World: A Christology for Disciples* (Grand Rapids: Baker, 2001).

ment and victimization, it is Christ's triumph over the powers. Where sin is ignorance and alienation, it is the example that opens us up to God's gracious love.[24] Where sin is barrenness and destruction, what is atonement?

The question is a pressing one in theology. Not long ago Anselm's satisfaction theory of atonement and its Protestant varieties dominated western theological imaginations after dislodging the patristic ransom theories that had characterized atonement in the first Christian millennium. Today both satisfaction and its cousin substitution theory are in steep decline in academic circles, disgusting theologians with their vision of a Father requiring violence against his Son. Ransom theory is caricatured as a primitive, quaint, and utterly unpersuasive theory in which God either tricks the devil or pays him off through Jesus' death. Taking their place are alternative visions that appropriate the Scriptures selectively to disown all forms of divine violence (sometimes widely defined to include racism, sexism, poverty, psychological harm, and even damage to self-esteem) and recast the cross as everything from a protester's martyrdom to something utterly absurd whose senselessness can only make its meaning negative. In short, our era is probably as confused as any over whether and how Jesus has saved us.

The problem has an unavoidable cultural dimension. Irenaeus interpreted the cross in terms of antiquity, Anselm in medieval feudalism, and Calvin in Renaissance mercantilism. Our world is different from all of these. How might *we* describe atonements in our social-scientific age?

Adopting in a very basic way contemporary sociology's language — we are following up on the world of Tom Wolfe, after all — the world is an overlapping patchwork of communities with reciprocal roles, powerful orders, conventional rules, socially constructed cultures, reified institutions, personal networks, formal and informal procedures and authorities, negotiated identities, and the like.[25] We could even call Wolfe's Dupont University one imaginative world with a basis in the realities of twenty-first century collegiate America, and the Gospels another imaginative world with a different basis in the realities of first-century Palestine. The historical and literary differences are vast. But as we shall see, they are not two wholly different realities.

Both Dupont University and the Palestine of two thousand years earlier are self-perpetuating social worlds. Like all social worlds, whether idyl-

---

24. Wilson, *God So Loved*, pp. 79-136.
25. Steve Bruce, *Sociology: A Very Short Introduction* (New York: Oxford, 1999).

lic or horribly demonic (like North Korea today, for example), they are both the products and the means of human adaptation and ingenuity. They are legitimate insofar as they provide the structural necessities of human life. However, even where they are relatively just and good, their legitimacy is radically deceptive.[26] For even the best of these worlds lacks the resources to do anything else but finally decline and fall. They are barren.

This barrenness turns even the "good" roles, orders, relationships, and identities of these worlds into means of servitude and suffering. Joseph and Mary are exploited and tossed around their own country by the empire's tax assessors; Charlotte Simmons is a cashless, hapless freshman "sexiled" from her own home by her libidinous roommate and date-raped by a fraternity brother. Roman slaves' identities are tied to the prestige of their masters; Jojo's life is tied to the fortunes of the basketball team that fights like mercenaries to satisfy alumni and grow his school's endowment. The Torah turns ill innocents into desperate outcasts; the poverty Jojo's tutor Adam inherits because of his parents' divorce forces him to write Jojo's term papers at risk to his own academic and professional career. Herod and the Sadducees are puppet rulers, the Pharisees and Zealots hypocritical revolutionaries, and John the Baptist a persecuted prophet. Coach Roth's hands are tied by the sheer institutional momentum of the modern research university, Professor Jerome Quat is an aging sixties radical who can do little more than torture powerless undergraduates, and Charlotte's mother is a truthteller reduced to a thin long-distance voice and a ghost in her daughter's conscience. All these people — even each world's "winners," such as the Gospels' rich ruler and Dupont's millionaire coach — are at each other's mercy, caught in webs of accrued power and powerlessness that drive them to fear and ambition and empty them of hope for gaining anything more than more desirable parts in the same sordid drama.

The social sciences offer whole catalogs of different constructions of reality that rationalize this collective indebtedness, slavery, and suffering. We need not evaluate these proposals here — even Wilson's sociobiology — except to note that the gospel's power lies in *not* rationalizing it. Instead Jesus trains us to offer and seek forgiveness.

The King's and his subjects' grace *justifies*. Its plenitude, its weight of divine glory, its sheer *substance* renews the old that otherwise passes away.

26. Oliver O'Donovan, The Ways of Judgment (Grand Rapids: Eerdmans, 2005), pp. 165-85.

Where sin is barrenness, atonement is replenishment. The relationships that sin bankrupts, forgiveness refinances. Grace reconciles the estranged, fertilizes the sterile, refills the empty, rights the skewed, reconstructs the ruined, re-creates the destroyed, enriches the impoverished, and revives the dead. It restores the wealth of providential relationship,[27] not just among the good and the just but also the evil and the unjust.[28] Where much was forsaken, now much is forgiven, and much loved is the forgiver.

Jesus comes into these social worlds proclaiming God's jubilee year, in which the land rests, debts are cancelled, slaves are liberated, and families return to their homelands.[29] He bears the good news that Israel's corrupt roles, orders, relationships, and identities are refreshed. Moreover, this is not just another periodic Sabbath that would have left things basically as they would have been in some idealized holy past, but "as a 'refreshment,' prefiguring the 'reestablishment of all things'" — as a sign of the arrival of God's promised new creation.[30] The old order is experiencing the advent of a new one.

In this new regime, relations are radically redefined over against the structures of the old and impoverished ones. What is coming is not just the restoration of prior social obligations — John the Baptist's good advice of generosity to the poor and justice among leaders (Luke 3:10-14) — but new creation (3:15-17). It does not simply *re*form social structures to meet the highest expectations of the status quo, but *trans*forms them into the new and unexpected. The Son's arrival accomplishes the unprecedented realization of the Father's eternal prerogative, the gift of the indwelling Holy Spirit, not only in his original historical setting but in every corner of the Father's mission.

Wherever the Messiah journeys, things around him simply cannot go on as before. They break down in the face of his righteousness and peace. This is God's judgment on the whole present age: that it cannot tolerate his full presence. Christ is foolishness and a stumbling block (1 Cor. 1:18-25). Hostility inevitably results, from both the "good" who respect our world's constructed boundaries and the "wicked" who violate them.

When through his apostolic ambassadors he comes to somewhere new, the messianic pattern repeats. Let us set the story not just in the fa-

27. See above, "The Providence of God."
28. Matthew 5:45, see above, "The Character of God."
29. John Howard Yoder, *The Politics of Jesus*, rev. ed. (Grand Rapids: Eerdmans, 1994), pp. 60-75.
30. Yoder, *The Politics of Jesus*, p. 70.

miliar scene of the Gospels but also in a place like Dupont — or my own school, Westmont College.

A department secretary comes back from a brief staff retreat and suddenly proclaims summer break in March — not just to help faculty, staff, and students recover from the fatigue of college life and prepare for the next academic year, but to rearrange the school from the ground up. On her own and working from her cubicle or impromptu settings in the library or dining hall she begins appointing a new administration, hiring a new faculty and staff, devising a new curriculum, admitting a new student body, adopting a new tuition and salary structure, revolutionizing residence life, and forging a new presence in the surrounding community.

You can imagine the commotion. A few believe it — three average students, a groundskeeper, an assistant in the development office, the editor of the school newspaper — and spread a conspiracy theory that she was planted by the board of trustees and will really pull it off. When she enters a classroom and dismisses the class, and when her followers lead teach-ins and visit depressed and maladjusted students in their dorms and befriend them, greater numbers react with incredulous admiration. Yet most keep their heads down and look toward the administration building to see what will come next.

What comes next, inevitably and from all quarters, is opposition. Like the exodus that foreshadowed it, Christ's career inevitably has the quality of a showdown. The cross is definitive of both Christ's gracious presence and the world's failure along every line of engagement between our social worlds and the Kingdom. This sense hangs over every word of the Scriptures, from the Old Testament's perennially postponed resolution of conflict among human beings and against God to every Gospel's apocalyptic tone to the reverberation of the cross in every other New Testament writing from Acts through Revelation.

Order breaks down more and more wherever the secretary or her ambassadors go. Some rethink the assumptions of their roles at the college and begin to live differently. They feel refreshed until their colleagues begin to suspect they are with "her," and then they are treated with suspicion. The less mature students and the crazier faculty begin to envision the school of their dreams and compare it to the humdrum reality, and decide this is one of those rare and mysterious revolutionary moments that must be acted upon before it passes and the momentum subsides. Yet when they seek out campus believers to let them know they are on the secretary's side, her people rebuke them and lump them in with the establishment! Before long nearly everyone is missing the harmony of last semester and wishing this movement would just go away. The secretary's most insistent critics generally come from the insiders — the citizens to whom the community had always looked for guidance in times of crisis. They have different reasons for regarding her declaration as ridiculous and dismissing her vague descriptions of what it will inaugurate as absurd, but they agree that she is refusing to play by the rules of the community and overstepping her bounds. The unfolding public relations fiasco angers the department heads and faculty council, and where everything might lead worries campus security, the alumni office, and the student senate.

Why is that? Because all of Christ's opponents are invested either in the way things are or in the way we wish them to be. By our reckoning, Christ *is* unrighteous. This secretary is defaulting on her community obligations, saying and doing things she has no right to. She is a troublemaker who claims to make things better but makes them worse. The paths of disorder and destruction she leaves behind are impossible to ignore. Christ's presence unsettles because it suggests a better world yet makes us cling to the one we have more tightly than ever. Moreover, it encourages messianic imitators who will start new and inevitably more dangerous movements of their own.

Rather than go away, the secretary raises the stakes beyond the bearable. Just as parents and alumni are arriving on campus for the spring playoffs, she rides onto campus in a rented limousine, wearing doctoral regalia and acknowledging astonished spectators with the confident waves and handshakes of a newly inaugurated president. As she and her handful of true believers enter the administration building she shouts, "I declare this academic year closed." Yet rather than occupying the president's office with the other followers in the kind of sit-in everyone is expecting, she looks around and retreats from the campus. This anticlimax irritates the onlookers and vexes her dwindling supporters.

The next morning she comes again, tears the "reserved" sign off the president's parking space, and then waits quietly and patiently in the administration building's waiting room. When deans and the president finally bring her in for an audience, she treats them respectfully but says little besides asserting her superior authority, repeating the mission statement of the college, and inviting them to join her movement. Her bizarre conduct exhausts the patience and sympathy of even her own followers. She is not a trickster or a typical campus protestor. She makes no sense to any of them, other than provoking their disgust. The authorities agree to fire her, and campus security produces a restraining order and gleefully escorts her off campus.

Two systems thus collide in an ultimate contest. But what about this defining moment is atoning? How do the cross and its lingering persecutions reconcile (Col. 1:21-29)?

Grace calls our righteousness into question at the most radical level. The inability of any social order to cope with the Messiah's disruption is God's definitive interpretation of our life as sinful. In rejecting Christ's justice, identity, and life, opponents reject our own flourishing, humanity, and future. Yet God's favor still restores us and grants us new and eternal standing in God's Kingdom.

The metaphor of sin as barrenness is not all-inclusive, nor is the metaphor of replenishment adequate as a replacement for the other common images of atonement. However, these terms have several handy advantages. They are organic rather than abstract, closing the gap between formal declarations of justification and physical realities in the created and living order. They are forward-looking: as fertility connotes hope, barrenness connotes hopelessness — precisely the mood of the contemporary west and many of its sufferers. And their connotations point to ways of reinvigorating unpopular satisfaction and ransom theories and making them plausible again in our culture.

The atonement theories of Anselm, Luther, and Calvin are helpful interpreters of the story's inner logic. These have faltered as we have cooled to the idea of the Son as a sacrifice who suffers the Father's violence. Nevertheless, every life and every society is ordered, and thus sacrificial, even the Kingdom; and Christ is a sacrifice from every possible point of view.[31]

Sacrifice gives one thing for another. Some things come to an end so other things will not. So pure is the Son's trust of the Father that he surrenders even his own present to invite the Father's future. He does this by submitting to the world's wayward human structures of justice, honoring their fundamental but abused legitimacy as God's political providence and so guaranteeing their (and humanity's) future. Christ is also the sacrifice of the Father who has sent him to rescue us, and the sacrifice of the Spirit who hands him over to mortality at his conception and withdraws at his death.

From the world's perspective, Christ is a sacrifice too. Its powers sub-

---

31. Gunton, *The Actuality of Atonement.*

ordinate him to their own sinful ends. No heavenly plague or priestly act in the Temple kills Jesus, but only the God-given power that the rulers wield abusively (Heb. 13:12-13). The perceptive thief on the cross knows the authorities who punish Christ as a sinner are legitimate (Luke 23:41) and divine (23:40). Their sterile legitimacy helps explain Christ's refusal to yield to his temptations to overthrow them forcefully.[32]

Since God's legitimate guardians of human life and righteousness cannot bear the Messiah's presence, they must sacrifice something else: their own integrity, to preserve the orders they guard. Caiaphas pursues expedience over justice in resolving that one man die for the sake of the general welfare (John 11:49-50). Pilate declares Christ innocent but does nothing about it (John 18). His disciples betray and deny him. The centurion at the cross confesses the dead Jesus as just. All of these thereby default on their legitimate authority as stewards of the created order (Matt. 21:33-46). They turn their own dehumanizing barrenness upon Christ's rehumanizing fruitfulness and expose themselves and their orders as radical failures. They mediate God's judgment to Jesus *as* a curse, *as* a debtor, but it is they who really deserve the sentence. As in that archetypical act in the Garden of Eden, the good and the righteous turn themselves into enemies of goodness and righteousness, and their personal moral authority is stripped away.

The sacrificial cross reveals the insoluble impasse between the old and the new. Politics may be "the art of the possible" (so Otto von Bismarck), but there is no finessing the conflict between injustice and God's peaceful Kingdom. The cross is the radical failure of all human possibility. It all really does end there in Golgotha.

Yet salvation is the art of the impossible. Jesus' death finally exhausts our resistance. After all, what more can rebels do but rob, murder, bury, and forget? Sacrifice ends one thing that another may continue. What ceases (logically, not chronologically) at the cross is our opposition. What outlasts it is God's grace. On the cross Jesus graciously takes on God's legitimate foreclosure on behalf of the debtors he loves, and at the tomb the risen Jesus picks up where he left off. Jesus' resurrection ultimately confirms and extends God's favor, not just in spite of but *right through* our refusals. The ultimate creditor renews his offer of the Kingdom's replenishment, first to his own destitute sheep and then through them to the ends of the earth.

---

32. Yoder, *The Politics of Jesus*, pp. 21-59.

The result is a social revolution — something not seen since these dying powers began their futile reign. They continue to have roles in Christ's new arrangement. It was he who held them together; without him they could do nothing but fail; against him they could not prevail; with him again they are remade. Christ is put to death for our sins and is raised for our justification (Rom. 4:24-25). He is our eternal high priest (Heb. 4:14-16), interceding on behalf not just of his worlds of fallen institutions but also of their broken inhabitants.

The secretary has been gone for several days. Things have quieted down, but they have not gone back to normal. One morning the phone rings in the president's office. It is the chairman of the board of trustees: "Do you want the bad news first or the good?" It turns out the rumors are true. The secretary was herself a quietly named trustee — an event recorded in the minutes that no one else seemed to have noticed. Her mission was not a test, nor a trick, but a profound invitation for the school to recognize and heed its true authorities' vision. She remained faithful to the last, securing both her future as the school's chairman of the board and the school's future under her gracious leadership.

The president starts offering to resign, but the chairman continues. What's done is done. This school that pursued righteousness according to its by-laws did not succeed in fulfilling it, because it pursued it not through faith but by formalities and fudging, stumbling over the very promise on which it was founded (Rom. 9:31-33). The school massively failed to rise to the opportunity, and all have suffered for it. Because of this, nothing can ever be the same. But this bad news is also good news! The school can finally make the real improvements that had always been impossible. There will of course be — has already been, in fact — a change in administration. Yet there does not need to be a change in personnel! She wants the school's faculty, staff, and students to stay on. All she requires is that they play by the trustees' rules.

"So!" the new chairman asks the president. "What would you all like to do?"

Forgiveness as Mission

Answering that question — which is addressed to all of us — moves us from forgiveness as atonement to forgiveness and thus atonement as an apostolic office. The showdown continues as the apostolic church bears Jesus' gospel. The Gospels' world is the Epistles' world, and Tom Wolfe's, and mine, and yours. Evangelism and its consequences extend the original atonement by announcing the arrival of the new creation. This plays out the old confrontation in new settings, threatening the old order with its precarious rules, provoking it to persecution, and exposing its bankruptcy even as it invites the impoverished enemies into newly funded relationships of righteousness and peace. Because the apostles' forgiveness is the Lord's own, Christ's sheer perseverance frustrates all efforts to justify ourselves by any means other than repenting and receiving him. Left with no avenue of self-justification in the face of his grace, every knee ultimately bows and every tongue confesses to the Father's glory that Jesus is Messiah and Lord. Whatever the cultural specifics, the forgiveness that Jesus' subjects show to each other and to every neighbor, stranger, and enemy extends the fruit of the Kingdom to the ends of the earth, actualizes the atonement, and renews the creation.

Atonement as *apostolic* office? I feel Protestant pulses jumping. Works justify?! Of course (Matt. 11:19). The many practices of righteousness in the Sermon on the Mount (Matt. 6:1) are available only as the Kingdom's gracious gifts. If we beg for God to forgive our debts, we do not justify ourselves. Yet we do set relationships right when we forgive our debtors. And we can do so only when we act through the Son to whom all things have been delivered (Matt. 11:25-30) — by passing along his Father's grace. God's forgiveness and ours come together as the Son's new cloth, new wine, new treasures, and new covenant (Matt. 9:16-17, 13:52, 26:28). We who receive forgiveness are newly created and newly restored, and we who offer it are co-creators and co-redeemers, deputies of the King who act by his name alone (Matt. 28:18-20).

Prayer for persecutors and love of enemies presupposes forgiveness of debtors. Jesus has prefaced his prayer with the command to go to any brother or sister or accuser who has something against us and be reconciled (5:23-26). Replenishing our bonds with others is something we *do* out of the replenishment God has already granted us.

Apostolic forgiveness is thus mission, and apostolic mission is forgiveness.

We seek replenishment of "our" debts — the debts of all the Father's children. I do not just pray for my sins and you for yours. *We* pray for *our* Father to forgive *us*. But we grant replenishment of "theirs" — the sins of brothers and sisters as well as strangers. Here the absence of a distinction between fellow Christians and strangers is critical. Sometimes "we" and "they" are the same group, sometimes not. Sometimes the forgiven are believers, sometimes not. Sometimes the forgivers are believers, sometimes not. It is not just Christian networks that make the Kingdom visible on earth, but any of the old creation's networks of holy *and* unholy roles, orders, relationships, and identities.

The apostolic life of prayerful forgiveness makes that whole web the place of God's new creation. As persons beget new persons through relations, so relations among persons beget new relations through persons. As the atonement of persons populates the Israel of God, so the atonement of their relationships reveals the Kingdom beyond the boundaries of Christ's family and outward to the new gestation and birth of all peoples.

A stubborn flaw in much theology has reduced "the Kingdom on earth" to holy persons distinguished from others as "the Church," which then becomes not the center of redemption but its exclusive location. Inside the Church is where personal salvation is found, forgiveness happens, reconciliation takes place, atonement becomes actual, and creation becomes new. Mission goes to where the Church is not to plant forgiveness and salvation in a new place. This picture is close to the truth, but it fails when it artificially separates persons from their relationships, making salvation pertain to the former but not the latter. After all, persons are inherently relational — a classic Christian definition of a person is a "subsistent relation" to other persons — and relationships are inherently interpersonal. Persons cannot be treated in isolation from the relationships that constitute them. The Son of Man came not just to save sinners (Matt. 9:9-13) but also to forgive sins (9:1-8).

The Apostles' Creed refuses to isolate the salvation of persons from the salvation of relationships. The good news has to be about both. "I believe in the forgiveness of sins" means "I believe in the rebirth of relationships." "I believe in the resurrection of the body, and the life everlasting" means "I believe in the new creation of persons." Their communities are new creations too: "I believe in the holy catholic Church, the communion of saints." Justification involves more than either that Protestant favorite, the salvation of persons, or that Catholic favorite, the salvation of the Church. It also involves "the forgiveness of sins" — not *sinners* but *sins*. We confess the restoration of relationships that involve the brother or sister, the debtor, the accuser, the enemy, and the persecutor.

Theological and practical distinctions are necessary to the clarity and integrity of the good news. But when we turn distinctions into disconnections — isolating individual salvation from reconciliation, atonement from eschatology, Israel from Church, Church from world, justification from sanctification, creation from salvation — we leave them divided and conquered. We leave sins undiscerned, unjudged, and unforgiven. We leave the creation old and powerless against the bands of rebels and thieves, the powers and principalities, that enslave and pillage it. We make Christ's story untellable.

But when we honor God's love not just for relational persons but for personal relations, the opposite happens. The Church pursues its mission, mission reveals judgment, judgment invites forgiveness, forgiveness ushers in justification, justification brings sanctification, and sanctification creates Church, the sign of God's future prayed into the world's present. "Behold, I am making all things new" (Rev. 21:5).

Forgiveness as Rehumanization

Remember the opaque CGI figures of *Charlotte Simmons?* God's judgment-with-mercy grants us the access to profound self-understanding with which Augustine constructed the Christian self at the end of pagan antiquity. In the face of our era's emerging sociologies of depersonalization, the rebirth of relationships through forgiveness is nothing less than *rehumanization.* Let me illustrate this with a story.

Recently I found myself in urgent need of a passport. The only way to get it in time was to get in and out of the county recorder's office before the Federal Express deadline. But purchasing tickets, arranging appointments, finding documents, and taking a photo took just long enough that I arrived at the recorder's office three minutes after closing time. I got in the door only because the last customer left through it.

"We're closed," all three workers at the vacant front counter told me sternly. "Come back tomorrow."

I told them that I could not, that I absolutely had to make the FedEx drop.

"Then you should have come on time. We're closed."

I didn't raise my voice, but I didn't leave either. I was too desperate to do either. So I just stood there filling out my form while my fellow Santa Barbarans averted their eyes.

"I can't help you," one of them told me, as if doing so would have broken the laws of physics. "You'll have to come back tomorrow."

"I can't," I said. "I have to get this out today."

"Sir, we're closed," they each said again, in the matter-of-fact way of all who enjoy monopoly power.

"I know you are," I told one of them reassuringly, still not leaving.

Finally a woman from the back of the office quietly stepped up to the counter and gestured me to come forward. "Our registers are closed," she told me, "so you will have to come back tomorrow for a receipt." And she helped me.

When I walked through that door, I entered a relationship in which I was a debtor. If it had been 4:29 I would have had a right to service, but at 4:33 I had nothing but my own failure. The proper thing would have been to turn and leave. But I remained in the recording officers' presence. This went outside the rules of the formal power relationship and thus redefined it. I was no longer a customer; I was a debtor begging his creditors for mercy. And one of the officers there forgave me my debt. The grace she showed me was an act of new creation. May she find forgiveness in the age to come.

I returned the next morning for my receipt and quietly gave her a potted flower as a sign that I appreciated the extraordinary thing she had done. I waved, she smiled, and I left. The replenishment of our relationship from both sides had transformed an acted-out social role into a bond of gratitude and honor between persons.

Can any social scientist's Theory of Everything describe the new life in that office better than the storybooks of the Kingdom of God? What is missing in the soulless world of Tom Wolfe turns out not to be souls but *agapē* — the person-making love of our Triune God.

Christ's mighty act of atonement renews creation at every level: the cosmic, the tribal, the communal, the familial, the personal, and the relational. His forgiveness rehumanizes us and empowers us to rehumanize others. His death and life bring us back from the brink of death-by-dismemberment to the life of fellowship.

An extraordinarily powerful parable of forgiveness as the refreshing of relationships is — don't laugh! — the 1989 film *Field of Dreams*. Its surreal story turns a baseball diamond in an Iowa corn field into a place of re-membering, rejuvenation, revivification — and ultimately of reconciliation between a middle-aged man and his father beyond the grave. The son's teenage rebellion left the two not speaking, and the father's early death left the breach unhealed. What sets things right is a simple game of catch between the prodigal son and his father's ghost. An apology and an absolution would leave audiences satisfied, but *catch* is a conversation in a far better tongue. In a couple of nearly wordless minutes the relationship is reforged and all transgressions forgiven — and grown men are weeping in theaters and family rooms (and I am tearing up as I write). We have awakened to a vision of an eschatological future we suddenly realize we have been longing for almost all our lives.

Being an Israelite, Jesus didn't play baseball. To dethrone sin and death he used a table rather than a diamond. On the night he was betrayed, with his disciples he united the cup of blessing to the cup of wrath and made all of them newly fruitful.

Scholars debate whether the Last Supper was originally a Passover Seder or an anticipatory feast of celebration.[33] Whatever the answer, all the biblical accounts stress the connections between the Passover overshadowing Jesus' final week and his last night with the apostles. The historical shape of any such feasts in the first century is hard to recover, and the discrepancies among the Last Supper accounts in the New Testament leave most critics pessimistic about recovering Jesus' actual words.[34] Exactly what happened that night remains mysterious. Nevertheless, Jesus chose the Jewish way of remembering the escape from slavery to foretell his own story's climax, in which his blood is for the forgiveness of sins.

It is not hard to see why. In the Seder the cup is poured not by oneself, but by others, so that all have servants (cf. Matt. 20:20-28).[35] The cup is used throughout the celebration, uniting many seemingly disparate points into one story.[36] In today's standardized Seder — likely a distant descendant of the Seder Jesus would have said, and at any rate a kindred rite — the first cup of wine is drunk for blessing God as Israel's sustainer. The second is lifted up as symbol of God's steadfast protection against Israel's enemies, spilled in remembrance of the signs of wonders of Joel 2 (cf. Acts 2:16-22) and the plagues of Exodus 7–12 (cf. Acts 3:18-26), then lifted again and drunk in praise to God for his redemption from slavery and in antici-

33. See, e.g., Jerome Kodell, *The Eucharist in the New Testament* (Collegeville, Minn.: Liturgical Press, 1988).

34. See, e.g., John Reumann, *The Supper of the Lord: The New Testament Ecumenical Dialogues, and Faith and Order on Eucharist* (Minneapolis: Augsburg, 1985), pp. 2-11.

35. *Mishnah Pesahim* 10:1.

36. *Pesahim* 10:7.

pation of new liberation in the future. Finally (with only the *afikoman matzah* or bland bread remaining), the third is poured in grateful expectation of "when Hashem brings back the exiles to Zion" and with a plea for God to end Israel's indebtedness to all but him, then drunk in hope that God will "make us worthy to attain the days of the Messiah and the life of the world to come." The fourth is poured as the cup of God's wrath upon Israel's enemies (though significantly the fourth cup may have originated after the first century) and drunk at the conclusion of the Hallel, an immense matrix of biblical texts of assurance, gratitude, deliverance from death, loyalty, ultimate sacrifice, worship, remembrance, exultation, supplication, heralding, universal salvation, and Messianic expectation. Three times the wine is described as "the fruit of the vine" of the promised land.[37]

Whatever actually happened in that upper room, all of these echoes explode with significance for those trained to hear Jesus' fundamental message: that he is the fulfillment of Israel's blessings and dreams for replenishment. "Drink of it, all of you; for this is my blood of the new covenant, which is poured out for many for the forgiveness of sins," he says in Matthew's version, the only one in which "the forgiveness of sins" appears. "I tell you I shall not drink again of this fruit of the vine until that day when I drink it new with you in my Father's Kingdom" (Matt. 26:17-29).

A fundamentally refreshed humanity is the abundant fruit of his vine. Its members are not just the band of disciples who drank on that night but *many* — saints and sinners, servants and rebels, believers and unbelievers, trustees, and students and everyone in between. It springs as one from Christ's open side, quickens at his resurrection, takes its first breaths from his Spirit, is nourished by his apostles' teaching, and grows and grows into the fullness of the one who fills all in all.

> Before she labored, she was delivered; before her pangs came,
> she bore a son.
> Who ever heard the like? Who ever witnessed such events?
> Can a land pass through travail in a single day? Or is a nation
> born all at once?
> Yet Zion travailed and at once bore her children!
> Shall I who bring on labor not bring about birth? — says YHWH.

37. Cf. *Mishnah Berakoth* 6:1.

The Mercy of God

Shall I who cause birth shut the womb? — said your God.
Rejoice with Jerusalem and be glad for her, all you who love her!
Join in her jubilation, all you who mourned over her —
That you may suck from her breast consolation to the full,
That you may draw from her bosom glory to your delight.
For thus said YHWH: I will extend to her prosperity like a stream,
The wealth of nations like a wadi in flood; and you shall drink
    of it. . . .
The time has come to gather all the nations and tongues;
They shall come and behold My glory.
I will set a sign among them, and send from them survivors
    to the nations . . .
That have never heard My fame nor beheld My glory.
They shall declare My glory among these nations. . . .
For as the new heaven and the new earth which I shall make
Shall endure by My will — declares YHWH —
So shall your seed and your name endure.
And new moon after new moon and sabbath after sabbath,
All flesh shall come to worship Me — said YHWH.

(Isa. 66:7-12, 18-23, JPS)

Drink of it, all of us.

CHAPTER 7

The Victory of God

For where God built a church, there the Devil would also build a chapel. . . . Thus is the Devil ever God's ape.

Martin Luther, *Table Talk* 53

Woe, Woe, Woe

And yet.

There are times when it all seems like foolishness. I am not deaf to the other stories my world tells. There are times when they catch my ear, and the good news of Jesus Christ becomes remote — not just unfashionable or countercultural but bizarre, dated, worn out, driven out of me, the mythical tale of a marginal and slightly crazy remnant of an ancient culture.

One doesn't feel like praying at such times. In fact, the tendency to pray feels like a shadow of a dying past, the force of a habit that still has a residual pull but no longer a viable place in my life.

Many Christians know the feeling, even if we are reluctant to admit it. Craig M. Gay contends that our society so emphasizes human agency, human potential, and the demands of the here and now that it tempts us to "practical atheism," the living of our lives as if God either did not exist or did not matter. Our whole world "is an interpretation of human life that is largely void of the *living* God" whose institutions are structured in ways that make God irrelevant.[1] This feeds a vicious circle: even in our churches our social practices and languages make the claims of the Lord's Prayer unintelligible, pulling us back out of its reach and strengthening our habits of unbelief.

Those other claims are invalid — they stand against the gospel of the risen Christ — so they fail. But they are still powerful. The story of practical atheism in the contemporary west has been a tragic fall from Renaissance and Enlightenment *triumphalism,* which assumed humanity would solve the problems of the human condition, to cascading *failures* of the modern project in the nineteenth and twentieth centuries and a growing *defeatism* among the children of modernity who, having given up on their utopian futures, cannot see any other. Because every stage embodies the same practical atheism, our failing world still denies the very possibility of the good news and bars our way out like an abusive and jealous husband.

So, as modernity's battered and imprisoned wife, we believers lament the eclipse of our faith . . .

> The breath of our life, YHWH's anointed,
> was captured in their traps —
> he in whose shade we had thought
> to live among the nations.
>
> (Lam. 4:20)

I have three woes to pronounce over my flagging modern world.

The Woe of the Lie

Theodore Dalrymple (the pen name of one Anthony Daniels) is a prison doctor in the U.K. and an essayist for the conservative quarterly *City Journal.* His essays in *Life at the Bottom: The Worldview that Makes the Underclass*[2] focus on domestic decay in the west. This is a common topic, but Dalrymple does not supply common answers.

Dalrymple's grim book is a journal of England in a time of plague.

---

1. Craig M. Gay, *The Way of the (Modern) World; or, Why It's Tempting to Live as if God Doesn't Exist* (Grand Rapids: Eerdmans, 1998), pp. 2-5.
2. Chicago: Ivan R. Dee, 2001.

Through his patients he reckons he has learned about the lives of at least fifty thousand people —

> lives dominated, almost without exception, by violence, crime, and degradation. . . . Day after day I hear of the same violence, the same neglect and abuse of children, the same broken relationships, the same victimization by crime, the same nihilism, the same dumb despair.[3]

In light of his prior experience as a doctor in impoverished locales in Africa, the Pacific, and Latin America, Dalrymple's encounters at his hospital in a British slum and at its nearby prison have convinced him that "the mental, cultural, emotional and spiritual impoverishment of the Western underclass is the greatest of any large group" he has ever encountered anywhere.[4]

This is not because of the pressure of unemployment or capitalist contradictions. It is neither genetically nor racially determined, for the British underclass is both new and majority white. It does not derive from the welfare state, though the welfare state is its patron, offering thousands of pounds in financial disincentives for a couple to marry or stay married. No, Dalrymple diagnoses the disease that afflicts the British underclass as ideological. "It is the ideas my patients have that fascinate — and, to be honest, appall — me: for they are the source of their misery." Their common genus is moral, cultural, and intellectual relativism. They were spread among the poor by earlier generations of intellectuals and are now creeping back up the social scale to the elites.[5]

Ideological plague is not confined to England or even to the English-speaking world. It shows up as both the hype and the despair of global democratic capitalism.[6] It manifests itself in the incorrigible utopianism of progressivism, the narcissism of millions of little Nietzschean *Übermenschen*, and the defeatism of abused women and primal aggression of their men. It builds the dream palaces and dictatorships of the Muslim world,[7] con-

---

3. Dalrymple, *Life at the Bottom*, pp. vii-viii.
4. Dalrymple, *Life at the Bottom*, p. viii.
5. Dalrymple, *Life at the Bottom*, pp. viii-ix, xii-xiv.
6. Brian J. Walsh and Sylvia C. Keesmaat, *Colossians Remixed* (Downers Grove, Ill.: InterVarsity, 2004), pp. 15-37.
7. Fouad Ajami, *Dream Palace of the Arabs: A Generation's Odyssey* (New York: Vintage, 1999).

structs conspiracy theories implicating the all-powerful west, multinational corporations, and "the Jews," and opens up the memory hole of Arabizing Islam as it wipes away what it calls the rabid ignorance *(jahiliyyah)* of its cultural predecessors.[8] It drives nationalist and tribalist mafias that rule the communist and ex-communist world, eschatologies both fundamentalist and secular that see every new turn of events as the prelude to the final revolution, the romanticism of every past from royalism to fascism to Stalinism, hysterical partisan politics in the world's settled democracies, and the worldwide cult of celebrity. It kindles warriors' imaginations and inspires peace activists' countermeasures.

Its many strains fall into two varieties: messianism (here meaning loyalty to any figure, system, or cause that is taken as a savior in some sense), and the nihilism that follows when messianism is abandoned. While they are endemic all over the world, Dalrymple finds the plague particularly devastating in his home country. He reports that his fellow physicians who emigrate from India and the Philippines are at first delighted with the capabilities and generosity of British medical care. However, as they experience the ingratitude of their patients, discover the breadth and depth of their pathologies, and compare underclass "families" to the intact family structures of poorer immigrants from former British colonies, they change their minds. "'On the whole,'" one Filipino doctor told Dalrymple, "'life is preferable in the slums of Manila.' He said it without any illusions as to the quality of life in Manila." Dalrymple's professional conclusion, and the conclusion of his immigrant colleagues, is "that the worst poverty is in England — and it is not material poverty but poverty of soul."[9]

In *After Virtue* Alasdair MacIntyre describes three indispensable characters of modern society: the aesthete, the manager, and the therapist.[10] We all know them well (especially those of us who have or are leaders in the American Church): lampooned in the black humor of *The Simpsons,* *South Park,* and Dilbert, these types are ubiquitous and socially indispensable. As *characters,* they fuse a psychological profile and a social role into one powerful unity that embodies their culture. MacIntyre locates these three modern characters within an underlying philosophical culture of

---

8. Marshall G. S. Hodgson, *The Venture of Islam,* vol. 1 (Chicago: University of Chicago Press, 1974), p. 174.

9. Dalrymple, *Life at the Bottom,* pp. 142-43.

10. 2d ed., Notre Dame, Ind.: University of Notre Dame Press, 1984, p. 30.

emotivism, which reduces moral judgments to the expressions of personal preferences.[11] (In the words of Mormon moral philosopher Napoleon Dynamite, "Just follow your heart. That's what I do.") Emotivism flourishes among the social classes, institutions, and professions whose purposes it serves most naturally and organically.[12] These groups benefit from emotivism's reduction of ethics to self-expression. Emotivism is a twentieth-century British invention,[13] and MacIntyre's characters are also of course the principal authorities in Dalrymple's world. They spread its moral ideology among all who entrust themselves to them, catechizing both their cultures' natives and its new arrivals in the dogma that moral truth boils down to authentic self-expression.

Emotivism is immensely advantageous for powerful classes, institutions, and professions. It goes beyond even the divine right of kings in absolutizing their authority. Cultivated taste, proven effectiveness, and earned credentials are their own justification. However, emotivism pressures the powerless into the role of a very different character: *the victim.* The moral choices of a victim are radically constrained by the choices of the powerful. It is tempting to consider the victim a fourth character in emotivist culture. After all, what would aesthetes be without vulgar masses, managers without worker-drones, and therapists without patients?

The greatest comfort to emotivism's elites, the absolute sovereignty of the emotivist self, is the sorest spot for emotivism's victims. You see, if victims are moral agents too, then at least some of their failures should reflect the choices they have made. This is the conviction Dalrymple's patients and inmates cannot bring themselves to face. They plead with Dalrymple that they fail because they are too easily led, or fell in with the wrong crowd, or took drugs because they were widely available. They refuse to take the blame for their mistakes.

> They go to some length to provide an answer other than that they liked it and found pleasure in doing what they knew they ought not to do. "My grandfather died," or "My girlfriend left me," or "I was in prison": never do they avow a choice or a conscious decision. And yet they know that what they are saying is untrue: for they grasp the

11. MacIntyre, *After Virtue*, pp. 11-12.
12. MacIntyre, *After Virtue*, p. 29.
13. MacIntyre, *After Virtue*, p. 14.

point immediately when I tell them that my grandfather, too, died, yet I do not take heroin, as indeed the great majority of people whose grandfathers have died do not.[14]

They grasp Dalrymple's point because they too are players in an emotivist drama.

Like yin and yang, a common moral axiom creates emotivism's winners and losers in one stroke and pits them against each other. Each group's existence drives the other to hypocrisy. Elites must pay lip service to the determinism that comforts victims, but they dare not direct it at themselves. Victims can acknowledge the moral agency they share with their successful neighbors and superiors, but they prefer to shift blame to structures both personal and impersonal.

> This is the lie that is at the heart of our society, the lie that encourages every form of destructive self-indulgence to flourish: for while we ascribe our conduct to pressures from without, we obey the whims that well up from within, thereby awarding ourselves carte blanche to behave as we choose. Thus we feel good about behaving badly.[15]

Put simply, both sides live a lie.

In the final chapter of *Life at the Bottom,* Dalrymple describes the lengths to which both the elite architects of the disaster of modern Britain and their victims go in order not to see what they have wrought. They use *denial,* abusing statistics and flatly contradicting inconvenient evidence. They use *tendentious historical comparison or precedent* to fabricate a past that compares favorably to the present, often by magnifying the awfulness of carefully chosen past abuses. They *refuse to draw conclusions* when they are finally forced to admit the applicability of contrary evidence. The lying that keeps the peace between modern society's powerful and powerless depends on imaginative nothingness to relieve the discomfort of intransigent reality.

But what's wrong with denial, fabrication, and non-inference, a good emotivist will ask. After all, moral judgments are just expressions of personal preferences! And true to form, there is an interesting psychological

14. Dalrymple, *Life at the Bottom,* p. 121.
15. Dalrymple, *Life at the Bottom,* p. 122.

literature on the Darwinian utility and physiological basis of these coping mechanisms. Roy Baumeister's moral calculus tallies the costs and benefits of overconfidence and denial.[16] David Nyberg, philosopher at a graduate school of education, offers a utilitarian apologia for deception insofar as it seems basic to "a healthy, livable human lifetime of relationships with others," along with the touching reassurance that "the mind does not evolve in ways harmful to itself."[17] Others embrace mythologies such as Freudianism that allegorize lies into other kinds of claims. For instance, Daniel Goleman considers denial and other modes of social and personal deception to be analgesics that have helped human beings deal with pain in situations where it would be counterproductive.[18]

These rationalizations only magnify the pathologies and entrench the powerful. Like the state in Orwell's *1984* that sponsors its own resistance to keep it under control, intellectuals have seized on and co-opted the diagnostic tools of social science in order to rule from the culture's high ground. The middle-class intellectuals who now hold power in Britain wield ideological critiques to stigmatize and destroy their Victorian, aristocratic, ecclesiastical, and capitalist rivals. But they do so selectively, ignoring the rise and spread of the underclass across class, ethnic, and gender boundaries and refusing to acknowledge their own part in the mess they have helped make.[19] This sophisticated hypocrisy both comforts them and conveniently extends their own political hegemony:

> Every liberal prescription worsened the problem that it was ostensibly designed to solve. But every liberal intellectual had to deny that obvious consequence or lose his Weltanschauung: for what shall it profit an intellectual if he acknowledge a simple truth and lose his Weltanschauung? Let millions suffer so long as he can retain his sense of his own righteousness and moral superiority. Indeed, if millions suffer they are additional compassion fodder for him, and the more of their pain will he so generously feel.

16. Roy Baumeister, "Lying to Oneself," in *Lying and Deception in Everyday Life,* ed. Michael Lewis and Carolyn Saarni (New York: Guilford, 1993).

17. *The Varnished Truth: Truth Telling and Deceiving in Ordinary Life* (University of Chicago Press, 1993), p. 2.

18. Daniel Goleman, *Vital Lies, Simple Truths: The Psychology of Self-Deception* (New York: Simon and Schuster, 1985), p. 43.

19. Dalrymple, "Seeing Is Not Believing," in *Life at the Bottom,* pp. 244-56.

The Liberal Democrat Party, Britain's third party, which is dominated by the middle-class intelligentsia and is gaining an unthinking popularity born of disillusionment with the [Labour] government and the patent incompetence of the official [Conservative] opposition, recently held its annual conference. And what were the most important proposals put forward there? The legal recognition of homosexual marriage and shorter prison sentences for criminals.

Nero was a committed firefighter by comparison.[20]

Every culture rationalizes or tolerates certain practices of deception as the necessary lubricant of a healthy society. Yet no culture *is* perfectly healthy. Lying ruins our person-making relationships[21] by transmitting the intellectual plagues that darken our minds and turn us into willing fools (Rom. 1:18-25). Whatever their basis, whatever their mechanics, whatever their apparent social utility, lies hold us in thrall. They seduce us. And we long to be seduced. We are not lies' passive victims; we are their creators and sponsors. We fabricate them and in turn they bind us together. In the language of Goleman's psychological guild, we liars and our lies are codependent.

Dalrymple refuses to indulge these strategies of rationalization. Instead he stays fixed on the moral agency of the perpetrators and victims of Britain's underclass culture. A lie by any other name is still a lie. In this way he renders the victims and perpetrators a far superior service than emotivist compassion: he leaves room for truth.

Yet in reducing moral agency to individual choosing — what James Wm. McClendon, Jr. calls "decisionism"[22] — he is still obeying emotivist rules. He is right that suffering cannot be reduced to a function of race, class, gender, or the other usual stock items in the formulary of modern intellectualism. Yet there *is* a structural evil behind his tragic stories, a cultural and ideological one that has taken these people captive. It is the social construction of emotivism itself, which roots truth in human hearts.

20. Dalrymple, *Life at the Bottom*, pp. 255-56.
21. See above, "The Mercy of God."
22. James Wm. McClendon Jr., *Systematic Theology*, vol. 1: *Ethics* (Nashville: Abingdon, 1986), pp. 56-59.

The Woe of Evil

Bruce S. Thornton, a classics and humanities professor on Dalrymple's side of the political spectrum, adduces that "we are just as prey to misinformation, half-truths, gratifying superstitions, pleasing myths, and outright lies as any seventeenth-century Salemite reaching for a torch as he eyes suspiciously the neighborhood crone."[23] We carry "plagues of the mind," intellectual diseases that comprise a "new epidemic of false knowledge."

Thornton draws out a whole list of diagnoses, of which we must concentrate on only one: "the abandonment of the idea of evil."

> The idea that evil doesn't exist, or that it is a metaphor for some as yet unknown material phenomenon, is the most dangerous piece of false knowledge circulating in the modern world — for the simple reason that inexplicable evil *does* exist, not just in the atrocities of monsters but in every one of our own hearts.

Evil, Thornton says, mysteriously lurks in each and all of us. This is "the reality from which both the Enlightenment and Romantic visions turn their eyes — the former because it believes knowledge is virtue, the latter because it believes that humans are naturally good."[24]

Goleman's psychology of lying roots human deception in the *lacuna* — what a person or a culture cannot say or even notice in order to avoid pain. Thornton identifies a big one in intellectuals' refusal to name evil as such — a bigger one, in fact, than the lacuna Dalrymple identifies in intellectuals' and victims' denial, concealment, and avoidance of the problems of modern Britain. Consider the irony of a social-scientific literature on lies and deception that rarely mentions, let alone addresses, the phenomenon of evil! Evil is our intellectual culture's ultimate lacuna.

M. Scott Peck is one of those laboring to fill that void. In *People of the Lie,* he regards the absence of a body of scientific knowledge about human evil in the therapeutic profession as one of the chief obstacles to treating a class of patients who failed to respond to the typical approaches of psychi-

23. Bruce S. Thornton, *Plagues of the Mind: The New Epidemic of False Knowledge* (Wilmington, Del.: ISI, 1999), pp. xvi-xvii.
24. Thornton, *Plagues,* pp. 82-84.

atry.[25] Peck draws on his own clinical experience and on the work of neo-Freudian Erich Fromm (but keeps Freudian psychobabble tolerably muted in his own work) to define evil as a variety of mental illness that warrants rigorous scientific investigation (67). He even identifies evil as a psychological disorder (129). Evil is a quintessential form of scapegoating, using power to destroy the spiritual growth of others for the purpose of defending and preserving the integrity of a sick self (119).

Peck extends his account of evil beyond the personal level to the group, which he regards as an analogous organism whose status as a group depends on unity and cohesiveness (224-25). Because groups tend to distribute their collective conscience among their members, evil manifests itself as moral fragmentation (217), the narcissism and false consciousness of group pride (225), regression to childlike dependence on authority (223), construction of others as enemies (225), and intolerance for group self-criticism, especially in times of weakness (226). Social evil manifests the very symptoms Peck associates with evil as a mental illness.

Even to a theologian like me, Peck's suggestion sounds like a category error. A particular variety of mental illness or social pathology is *evil?* That sounds odd, because our culture has trained us either to spiritualize evil into some nonscientific realm of demons and devils or to dissolve it into pathologies with their own scientific terminology. Remember, we tend to be dualists or monists with respect to spiritual things.[26] Why not just coin a new syndrome — say, "Radical Narcissism Disorder" — keep things in the realm of the psychological, and leave evil out of it? Or, on the other hand, why confine evil to such a narrowly psychological manifestation? Is it not more than a social-scientific phenomenon?

Sure, evil has a wider provenance than Peck's proposal allows. And his argument reflects the inexperience and awkwardness of a new Christian struggling to bring together the estranged languages of his professional culture and the Christian tradition. Yet if we respect these shortcomings, we can appreciate Peck's case as not only scientifically persuasive, but also thoroughly Christian. It reunites the practices of goodness, healing, and deliverance. These have been aspects of the good news of Jesus Christ since

---

25. *People of the Lie: The Hope for Healing Human Evil* (New York: Simon and Schuster, 1983), pp. 39, 178. Subsequent references to this work are indicated by parenthetical page citations in the text.

26. See above, "The Reputation of God."

the Lord himself commanded his disciples to preach the Kingdom with healings, cleansings, and exorcisms (Matt. 10:7-8). We sense with Peck that falsehood, malady, and evil refuse to respect the disciplinary distinctions we try to impose on them.

Since lying and evil always come together (135), they are best treated together. Stanley Hauerwas draws on Thomas Aquinas and James Alison in his essay "Sinsick" to undo the modern divorce between sin and sickness that has driven our language about health apart from our language of salvation and evil. The result, he says, will be a practice of deliverance that cannot fall simply into either clinical or liturgical categories.

> Nothing could be more important today than for Christians to recover a Christian practice of medicine shaped by the practices of the church, and in particular baptism. For . . . it is through baptism that we are introduced to undistorting desire through the pacific imitation of Christ. That this is not a voluntaristic exercise is clear from the fact that exorcisms, which free us from Satan's kingdom, are celebrated as intrinsic to baptism. Thus through baptism simultaneously we are incorporated into the church and our sins are forgiven.[27]

In baptism God declares an end to the reign of the lie in us and we embrace the truth of all things in light of his revelation in Jesus Christ, vowing to abide in him that we may know his truth and gain our freedom.

Peck almost always relies on psychotherapy, "a light-shedding process par excellence" (77), to bring truthfulness to the consciences of his patients. But he too advises that some of his most stubborn clinical cases might be appropriate candidates for the additional strong medicine of the now largely abandoned techniques of exorcism and deliverance (181). He describes these as therapeutic processes with different conceptual frames and, more significantly, the overt use of power. Deliverance and exorcism are practices Peck likens to surgery — power-psychiatry, so to speak — which offer remedies volitional psychotherapy does not (and which require analogous safeguards against their abuse) (185-89).

For many this goes too far. Exorcisms? Devils? Even if the word "evil" were worth revitalizing, what possible place could these relics have in scien-

---

27. Stanley Hauerwas, *A Better Hope: Resources for a Church Confronting Capitalism, Democracy, and Postmodernity* (Grand Rapids: Brazos, 2000), p. 199.

tifically responsible medicine? Yet the very same question could be asked about prayer, whose role in medicine is enjoying a comeback. Perhaps a little suspension of scientific disbelief is in order, at least among those who pray.

Peck describes the devil as "a real spirit of unreality" (207). It is powerful, malevolent, deceitful, and vain, and its voice of nihilism is at the heart of psychological evil and the head of a hierarchy of lies, confusions, and heresies.[28] Psychiatric experience of the webs of lies, negations, confusions, and self-deceptions of the mentally ill matches both the Christian epithet for the devil as "the Father of Lies" and the repeated results of exorcisms in which "demonic voices will propound nihilism of one variety or another" (39). Some people are at one with the demonic in a state of "perfect possession": these are Peck's "people of the lie." Others are not evil but in conflict with evil, submerged into the demonic but "imperfectly possessed" and still want deliverance: these are candidates for deliverance and exorcism.[29] Peck's admittedly sparse anecdotal evidence still confirms the traditional Christian sense that "Satan has no power except in a human body," and that "the only power that Satan has is through human belief in its lies" (206) — in our complicity with unreality. I have no grounds to doubt it; I have even witnessed these traits personally.

The devil is making a comeback in the West, along with the void he personifies. Robert Jenson's foreword to *Sin, Death, and the Devil*[30] diagnoses nihilism as the inevitable consequence of a culture that, having been trained by the gospel no longer to worship the creature, then ceases to believe in a Creator. In that case "there is precisely nothing to believe in. And that, it seems, is what our culture is coming to" (4). Toying with paganism and trendy spiritualities as some do is just unserious "emptiness trying to cover itself with pretense known, deep down, to be pretense" (5). Jenson claims the threat of nihilism is the defining evil of our age. Nihilism underwrites the killing of the unborn and the elderly, complacency at leaders' immorality, the collapse of school systems, and the trivialization of the Church itself. Moreover it is "one enemy we cannot co-opt" (6) — though some Christian postmodernists try.

This fits the first woe we have identified. Nihilism is the root of emotiv-

28. M. Scott Peck, *Glimpses of the Devil: A Psychiatrist's Personal Accounts of Possession, Exorcism, and Redemption* (New York: Free Press, 2005), pp. 113-14, 127-29, 238.

29. Peck, *Glimpses*, pp. 98-99, 196, 239.

30. Carl E. Braaten and Robert W. Jenson, eds. (Grand Rapids: Eerdmans, 2000). Subsequent references to this work are indicated by parenthetical page citations in the text.

ism and its pathological corollaries. If the self's own arbitrary choosing makes it the ultimate moral agent, then there can be nothing prior to it.[31] This is to say that emotivism's moral ultimate *is* nothing. That which the choosing self attends to is an empty set. It must be if it is to be free in the way emotivists claim. Emotivism's winners and losers, its enablers and vandals, its messianic revolutionaries and anti-messianic counterrevolutionaries are all worshippers of a void.

This is precisely what nothingness seems to want — attribution; the status of somethingness. Deceivers work ceaselessly to earn others' trust. Lies invite belief that might harden into conviction. Demons seek habitation, and demoniacs invite them in. In the Gospels the demons plead not to be cast out of human bodies because human consent is all the access to power they have, and exorcists report the same behavior today.[32] One finds the same relationship of codependence between nothingness and its champions as between lies and their liars.

The constitutive practice of deceivers is called *lying*. What should we call the constitutive practice of the champions of nothingness?

The Woe of Sloth

Kevin Vanhoozer quotes Dorothy L. Sayers' words that sloth "believes in nothing, enjoys nothing, hates nothing, finds purpose in nothing, lives for nothing, and remains alive because there is nothing for which it will die."[33] He diagnoses the spiritual condition of fading modernity as pride and that of postmodernity as the deadly sin of sloth.[34] R. R. Reno offers a similar Augustinian diagnosis of postmodernity as a cynical "Petronian" reaction against "Promethean" modernity that distances oneself from anything that threatens to change one's life.[35] Both these terminologies neatly fit the

31. MacIntyre, *After Virtue*, p. 33.

32. Peck, *Glimpses*, p. 181.

33. Dorothy L. Sayers, *Christian Letters to a Post-Christian World: A Selection of Essays* (Grand Rapids: Eerdmans, 1969), p. 152, quoted in Kevin Vanhoozer, *The Cambridge Companion to Postmodern Theology* (New York: Cambridge University Press, 2003), p. 23.

34. Kevin Vanhoozer, "Theology and the Condition of Postmodernity: A Report on Knowledge (of God)," in *The Cambridge Companion*, pp. 23-24.

35. R. R. Reno, *In the Ruins of the Church: Sustaining Faith in an Age of Diminished Christianity* (Grand Rapids: Brazos, 2002), pp. 41-43.

global plagues of messianism and post-messianiac nihilism. Sloth is the utopian's hangover.

Sloth is certainly a sin I have struggled with lately. As I write, I am unproductive, burnt out, worried, numb. Despite outward health, I have not shaken a nagging feeling of massive failure. I spend way too much time in ways I regret even while I do them. I put off necessary duties with aimless diversions that quietly accrue into weeks of life simply surrendered to the void.

"That sounds like depression," the clinically savvy will say; "you should seek professional counseling." Even if the diagnosis fits (and it probably does, though only in a very mild form), this response just means that psychology would prefer to use a different word with merely medical rather than fully moral connotations, as if I need only to be *treated* rather than *saved*.

"That sounds like a mid-life crisis," others will say, and my forties have indeed arrived. Yet the sources of happiness in my life — teaching, family, theology, friends — are still sources of great happiness. Far from being dissatisfied with this season of life, as I raise my children and work at school I already miss it. I would not change a thing in my circumstances — except for one: I want *fully* to embrace these exceptional blessings. I don't want to hear psychological or social-scientific descriptions of my condition; even if they are apt in their own ways, they are also way too convenient. Sloth is a far more demanding and satisfying diagnosis. It tells me that I am distancing myself from my sources of life. I am salt that is losing its saltiness and light that is hiding out of sight.

I see the same dynamics in many of my students. College campuses across the country are reporting a dramatic increase in the numbers of students with depression, sleep disorders, anxiety disorders, eating disorders, substance and sexual abuse, and suicidal behaviors.[36] Showered with social, intellectual, spiritual, and material blessings, they suffer from a spiritual poverty like the one that haunts the slums of Britain. They feel disconnected from their families, disillusioned with the youth culture they are just leaving, alienated from the artificial community of the college campus, too mature for the youth-culture Christianity that lured them in only a few

---

36. See Richard Kadison and Theresa Foy DiGeronimo, *College of the Overwhelmed: The Campus Mental Health Crisis and What to Do About It* (San Francisco: Jossey-Bass, 2004).

years ago, but not yet ready for the life that will begin after they graduate. As if all this stress were not enough, they are raised in a culture that delivers a daily barrage of publicity about stubborn problems across the world and in their own immediate neighborhoods. Like me, they have been trained to think in terms of either *fixing* or *ignoring* such problems — of responding to bad news with Promethean messianism or Petronian anti-messianism. College only intensifies both the relentless consciousness-raising and urgent appeals of the one and the escapisms, from tokenism to the party scene, spiritualism, and careerism of the other.

My own fatigue is just a more advanced case of the same cycle of conscientization, frenzy, and distance that seems to afflict them. Our idealistic twenties give way to pragmatic thirties and familial forties and fifties. As awareness and pressure grow, the scope of our ambition contracts to the width of a nuclear family, an office desk, a pub, a checking account, a voting booth, or a newspaper. Modern depression and mid-life crises are, at least in some cases, the cognitive dissonance between our crumbling sense of obligation to fix everything and our building sense of ineptitude and impotence. Apathy, burnout, inactivity, and hopelessness shrivel childhoods of pride into adulthoods of sloth. Once our resignation finally breaks through our messianism, there is finally nothing to do but retire as comfortably as possible and wait for the end to come.

As there is ever deepening cooperation between the deceived and their lies and between the void and its children, so sloth requires a pact between death and the living where each accommodates the other. Like these other woes, sloth does not afflict victims so much as recruit willing partners. I have no primordial innocence to fall back on for self-justification when I squander another precious moment of my life. Like Augustine, what I have done is love my fall — "not the object for which I had fallen," for sloth has no such object, "but the fall itself."[37]

Is There a Cure?

Examining these three woes has left us with a tangle. Peck's psychological demonology, MacIntyre's emotivism, Dalrymple's psychic poverty, Gole-

37. Augustine, *Confessions*, trans. Henry Chadwick (New York: Oxford, 1992), 2.4.9, p. 29.

man's evolutionary lacunae, Thornton's modernist plagues of falsity, and Jenson's nihilism are all facets of one vast affliction that extends beyond the unfolding tribulations of the modern world to encompass a universal, fundamental state Paul aptly called "wretched" (Rom. 7:24). In the words of Paul's interpreter Augustine:

> In adversities I desire prosperity, in prosperous times I fear adversities. Between these two is there a middle ground where human life is not a trial? Cursed are the prosperities of the world, not once but twice over, because of the fear of adversity and the corruption of success. Cursed are the adversities of the world, not once or twice but thrice, because of the longing for prosperity, because adversity itself is hard, and because of the possibility that one's endurance may crack. Is not human life on earth a trial in which there is no respite?[38]

It is indeed. Any one of these woes is debilitating. It makes the Lord's Prayer unprayable by making the prayer itself senseless. *What* temptation? There is only my will. *What* evil? There is only the physical world as it has come to be. *What* deliverance? Ever since the fathers fell asleep, all things have continued as they were from the beginning (2 Pet. 3:4).

These woes are not redemptive sufferings. They lead not out of ruin but only further into it, and they block the path back to health. We are wretches. We need more than better therapy, managerial technique, better ideas, deeper reflection, and stronger medication.

The tried-and-failed formulas of the Christian past don't seem to offer the healing we need either, at least not if they are viewed as guarantees. The coercive power of Christian civil government has brought more corruption than Kingdom. Catholic and Orthodox worship's regularly infused grace and Protestant worship's constant reminders of imputed grace have licensed cultures of apathy and low expectations. Pietism's warm feeling and revivalism's fleeting ecstasy have imprisoned God in our collective and individual mood-swings. None of these strategies has been a real solution. In fact, each is now a temptation of its own, a religious recipe to which we turn out of convention and convenience as much as conviction, which has fostered at least as much abuse as deliverance, and which has the same ring of remoteness from our plight.

38. Augustine, *Confessions* 10.28.39, p. 202.

Gone is the joy of our hearts;
our dancing has turned into mourning.
The crown has fallen from our head;
woe to us that we have sinned!
Because of these things our hearts are sick,
because of these things our eyes are dimmed.
Because of Mount Zion, which lies desolate;
jackals prowl over it.

(Lam. 5:15-18)

At first our prayer's striking final petition (treated as two by Roman Catholics and Lutherans, but one by Orthodox, Reformed, and the text of both Matthew and Luke) appears only to make things worse. But that is only because, providentially, it fits neatly into none of these confessional schemes. The very quality that makes the Lord's Prayer so odd and senseless in the post-Christian west — its place in the gospel story — makes it potent in the Kingdom.

"Do Not Lead Us into Temptation, Rather Deliver Us from the Evil One"

A Disturbing Finale

On the eve of the Battle of Agincourt, Henry V inspired his troops with talk of looming glory. By contrast, Jesus deflates his people with a final plea that God *not* test our mettle. It is a disturbing anticlimax. The awkward syntax of "do not lead us into temptation" seems to blame God for putting us in unbearable situations, as if, as Gerhard Ebeling claims, "God has to be appealed to against God."[39]

"Father, please don't let us down"?! Is this any way to end a prayer?

No wonder interpreters have bent over backwards to smooth out the language. Many assure us that Jesus *really* means "keep us away from temptation," or "lead us out of temptation," or "remind us that you never tempt us." Of course none of these things is what Jesus actually said. He told us to beg God not to put us to a test, presumably because we would

---

39. Gerhard Ebeling, *The Lord's Prayer* (Brewster, Mass.: Paraclete, 2000), p. 87.

fail it. What a vote of confidence in us! What a vote of confidence in God! What a way to conclude a conversation!

And no wonder a properly reassuring doxology was almost immediately appended. The first- or second-century *Didache* already closes the prayer with "for yours is the power and the glory." Later tradition further added "the kingdom" and gave the prayer its familiar form. Without those postbiblical flourishes, the prayer leaves us with a pallor of doom: "do not lead us into temptation; instead deliver us from the evil one. . . . Amen."

You cannot blame people for wanting to end the Lord's Prayer with a proper bang. However, my exercise in prayerful theology will not imitate them. There will be no chapter on the doxology. It is not that it is wrong to say more — Hebrew prayers traditionally concluded with a spontaneous doxology (cf. 2 Tim. 4:18).[40] Tertullian picked up on this by using the Lord's Prayer as "the foundation of further desires," meaning the basis on which the congregation would now go on and pray for its specific concerns. The problem is that the Christian tradition's usual ending reverses the rhetorical course of this prayer that has purposefully shifted focus from the Father to us. Matthew's and Luke's prayers end with not the crescendo and soaring notes of Albert Hay Malotte's musical setting but the duck-and-cover of a disaster preparedness drill.

This seems to be the point. As a collect, the Lord's Prayer both sums up where we have been and leads us to where we should be next. And where it leads us is not to dwell on God's majesty like Peter camping out at the Transfiguration (9:28-36) — or like a pagan ingratiating himself with his many words to get the outcome he wants — but to prepare for the treacherous road to Jerusalem (Luke 9:51). In the Gospels Jesus' prayer ends on an ominous note of evil's tenacity and power. That we have not wanted to conclude here is a further sign that perhaps we should. The biblical Lord's Prayer is not a conquest, celebration, reassurance, love letter, or revival. It is a lifeline. Its ending should not disturb any who grasp its grace.

Worlds collide in these words. A plagued earth is encountering the Kingdom of Heaven and finding there an end to its bondage. Tracing the collision will take us in a circuit that examines the apocalyptic character of the good news, Jesus' ministry as an apocalyptic prophet, his unique life

---

40. Ulrich Luz, *Matthew 1–7: A Continental Commentary* (Minneapolis: Augsburg, 1992), p. 385.

within the prophetic pattern of disaster and deliverance, our complementary roles as beneficiaries and partners of his grace, and finally the passing of our woes through God's leadership and deliverance.

An Apocalyptic Prayer

The "temptation" or "time of trial" of the prayer's final petition seems to refer to the tribulation at the end of the age (Matthew 24–25, Luke 21). No wonder we need a lifeline. The eschatology that pervades the Lord's Prayer is an apocalyptic eschatology of disaster and deliverance. And in an age swinging from triumphalism to defeatism, that is just what we need.

Apocalyptic prophecy rips the veil off of an age of stubborn incompatibility between the Kingdom's rule and the world's rebellion. Here there are no holy cities, only holy fellowships *in* cities (Rev. 2:1, 2:8, 2:12, 2:18, 3:1, 3:7, 3:14). Here the temptations of holy fellowships are also temptations *within* holy fellowships (Rev. 2:4, 2:10, 2:14-15, 2:20, 3:1, 3:11, 3:15). Just to survive with integrity is to conquer.

God might seem far away, but the faithful do not experience God as simply absent. The stories of oppressed believers from the days of Daniel throughout history and across the world share a startling juxtaposition of divine estrangement, divine absence, and divine presence.[41] The saints await the Lord's coming. Yet the Lord is already present in Spirit, in prophetic speech and Scripture (as, for instance, the prophet John is told to write what he sees and send it to Jesus' churches), in the saints themselves, and in their deeds. Suffering churches and their peoples do not yet enjoy Christ's full presence, but they do know Christ's real presence.

The Bible's apocalyptic passages are sometimes treated as oddities and either obsessed over or neglected (John Calvin, like many before him and many since, gave the book of Revelation a pass when writing his expansive commentary on the Bible). But apocalyptic prophecy is only as weird as the gospel itself. It merely rearranges the old prophetic visions that assured Israel that God had not abandoned it to evil, specifying that the Lord of the world's final reckoning is the Lord Jesus Christ.[42] Apocalyptic sensibil-

41. Richard Bauckham, *The Climax of Prophecy: Studies on the Book of Revelation* (Edinburgh: T&T Clark, 1993), pp. 150-73.

42. Bauckham, *The Climax of Prophecy,* pp. x, 174-98.

ity is *typical* of the convictions of the apostolic Church. It permeates all four Gospels, the Acts and Paul's letters, and the so-called general letters because all of these traditions share the convictions and possibly the common apocalyptic traditions of the first Christians.[43] If the Lord's Prayer makes any original sense at all, it must make sense in this setting. And of course it does, as any persecuted Christian will joyfully attest.

Jesus, Prophet of Apocalypse

If the Father's Kingdom comes with Jesus as king of kings and his forgiveness comes with Jesus as eternal priest, then his deliverance comes with Jesus as prophet *par excellence*. In both the Gospels and Revelation Jesus is the paradigmatic heir of the prophetic tradition. As Moses had only a staff with which to free a whole people, so Jesus' only weapon is the sword of his own mouth whose truth confutes our world's lies and dispels our illusions (Rev. 1:16, 2:12, 2:16, 19:11, 19:15, 19:21). As Moses' long-awaited successor (Deut. 18:15-22 in Acts 3:17-26), Jesus' liberating signs and wonders and reconciling fellowship with God are unrivaled (Deut. 34:10-12, Acts 2:22-36). The Anointed One does not just foretell deliverance; he delivers and then leads his people. So he is both the worthy subject of the original song of Moses (see how Rev. 1:18 transposes Deut. 32:40) and the subject of a new song like it (Rev. 15:3-4).

If Jesus is the new Moses, we at his rear are the new stiff-necked people. We balk at his signs, whine at the trouble his grace causes us in Egypt, forget our freedom, forge false gods, grumble in the wilderness, put him and his Father to the test, and presume to offer our own unholy or unauthorized fire. As in the days of Nadab and Abihu and of Korah, our obstinacy invites plagues and open graves (Lev. 10:1-7, Num. 16:32-33, cf. Rev. 12:16 and 19:20). The Torah is not just a chronicle of deliverance; it is also a chronicle of failure in the face of temptation. It recounts the woes that come when Israel goes its own way.

Like a frustrated (and fallible) parent, Moses at first coaxed, commanded, nagged, goaded, and threatened his people to the banks of the Jordan. These techniques were enough to get Israel *to* the land of promise. But he knew they would not be enough to keep Israel *in* the land of prom-

---

43. Bauckham, *The Climax of Prophecy*, pp. 92-117.

ise. Not even the Torah's blessings and curses would cure Israel's weak faith. So, with one hundred and twenty years of wisdom and forty years of seasoning behind him, Moses employed a new strategy for making Israel's settlement a permanent one: he wrote a proclamation of disaster and deliverance for Israel's future generations (Deut. 31:16–32:47).

The Song of Moses in Deuteronomy 32 forecasts an apostasy so severe that conscious memory alone will not remind the Chosen People of their identity and destiny. It will take a new cycle of exile and return to break the sinful habits that will have immersed God's people in ignorance. Only disaster will destroy the ways of life that enable those habits and overturn the deception of their false gods when they fail to rescue. Only deliverance will provide new ways of life for nurturing new habits and another true story to counter the lies that still want to be believed. The prophetic future is theological chemotherapy — bitter medicine for an otherwise terminal disease.

Moses' song of providence, comfort, idolatry, curse, exile, and eschatological return became the pattern of the latter prophets (e.g., Isaiah 45). These truth-tellers served as Moses' accompanists to help dispel the fog of Israel's self-deception and willful ignorance. Apocalyptic prophecy is merely the most dramatic variation on the prophetic theme of disaster and deliverance. It intensifies the melody line with notes of radical universality, finality, inevitability, imminence, urgency, hope, and unity.[44] Not just Israel but the whole world is judged. Justice is only a matter of time. Its coming presses in with urgency that demands repentance for the unjust of every age and readiness for the just. Its power is assured, dispelling anxiety and raising hope. It is one encompassing judgment, even if meted out across centuries and nations, that comes to a sure and eternal climax.

The penultimate apocalyptic prophet, John the Baptist, foresees the awaited day with new and sudden proximity: "Repent, for the kingdom of heaven has approached. . . . Even now the ax is laid to the root of the trees" (Matt. 3:2, 10). The Kingdom's coming is Jesus' coming: "He will baptize you with the Holy Spirit and with fire. His winnowing fork is in his hand, and he will clear his threshing floor and gather his wheat into the granary, but the chaff he will burn with unquenchable fire" (3:11-12). So it is to the office of apocalyptic prophethood that the Father anoints Jesus with the

44. Telford Work, *Living and Active: Scripture in the Economy of Salvation* (Grand Rapids: Eerdmans, 2002), pp. 159-61.

Holy Spirit. The Son wields Moses' words (Deut. 6 and 8 in Matt. 3:16–4:11) and later his own (Matt. 5–7) in triumph against the evil one. When Jesus appropriates the prophetic tradition he rearranges its earlier promises of disaster and deliverance around his own ministry of judgment and mercy: "repent, for the kingdom of heaven has approached" (Matt. 4:17).

It is as an apocalyptic prophet that Jesus plans for disaster. He has his disciples baptized to put an end to their old and futile ways and bring them into his own new beginning. He warns them to recognize the world's liars. He forbids them to submit to either their lies, especially the messianic ones (Matt. 24:3-8, Luke 21:7-10; Matt. 24:21-28, Luke 17:23-24), or their threats, especially the anti-messianic ones (Matt. 24:9-14, Luke 21:12-19). Especially as his own end nears, he prepares his followers to face their coming failure:

> Simon, behold, Satan demanded to have you all, that he might sift you all like wheat. But I have prayed for you [the word is singular] that your faith may not fail; and when you have turned again, strengthen your brothers and sisters. (Luke 22:31-32)

> You will all fall away because of me this night; for it is written, "I will strike the shepherd, and the sheep of the flock will be scattered." But after I am raised up, I will go before you to Galilee. (Zech. 13:7 in Matt. 26:31-32)

So the Father answers the Son's prayer by delivering from evil, but only after leading him alone through his temptation and time of trial (Matt. 26:47-68, cf. Matt. 26:41). None of us wants an answer like this — not even the Son himself (Matt. 26:36-46). Yet it fits the prophetic pattern. The Scriptures must be fulfilled (Matt. 26:53-56). Exodus' pattern of deliverance through disaster cannot be broken.

Accordingly, as YHWH gives his stiff-necked people at the Jordan's east bank a last song to see them through their scattering, so the Lord gives his stiff-necked disciples in Roman-occupied Jerusalem a final supper for which to reunite after their dispersion and remember their deliverer (Matt. 26:26-29, Luke 22:15-20). And as the first songwriter stays behind to die in the wilderness while his fellow Hebrews go on without him, so the Lord who includes us in his prayer to the Father now writes a liturgy in which his role and theirs are radically distinct. In Lesslie Newbigin's incomparable words:

The final conflict with the prince of the world was at hand. The faith of the disciples was crumbling. In a few short hours all understanding and all obedience would be carried away in the flood of disaster. They would all forsake Him, and He would have to go forward utterly alone to make the final offering of obedience on behalf of all men, and win on behalf of all men the final battle. At that moment, when all faith was crumbling, he staked all upon a deed. He took bread and wine, told them, "This is my body given for you, this is my blood shed for you. Do this in remembrance of me," and then went out to suffer and die alone. And on the first Lord's Day, when the victory was won, but the disciples were defeated and broken, it was in the breaking of the bread that He was made known to them in His risen power. When all landmarks were submerged in the flood of disaster, and stories of His resurrection seemed but an idle tale, it was this utterly simple word, "Do this," which rallied them, and gave them the place at which the meaning of what had happened could be made plain.[45]

Triumphalists and defeatists alike, take note: As the whole Israelite past was a failed history except for the steadfastness of God, so the whole cosmic future is a failed future except for the victory of one Son of Israel and Son of Man. As the Song of Moses and the Tabernacle and Temple built into Jewish faith a firm respect for the chronic disaster that is Israel, so the Lord's Prayer and the Eucharist build into Christian life an enduring respect for the chronic disaster that is the Church. Their most significant difference is that the old signs point forward and the new ones backward to the One who beat the temptation into which the Father led him. The final petition is a constant prayer for mercy to spare us from the trouble we cannot handle; the other is a constant covenant renewal to get us out of the trouble we keep getting into, through the blood with which he prevailed over it. This is the Lord's disaster plan.

The Lamb and the Multitude

An axiom of Christian faith pervades every tradition in the New Testament, including the Gospels of Matthew and Luke:

---

45. Lesslie Newbigin, *The Household of God* (New York: Friendship Press, 1954), p. 70.

Jesus Christ alone is our Savior.

Obviously! Yet it is less obvious how this is so. The distinction between Jesus' role and ours in the Father's answer to our final petition is the key to understanding it.

Translations of the Lord's Prayer usually render the word for "lead," *eispherō,* as *causing someone to enter into* something. But the word literally means *to bring in* or *to carry in* something, as a shopper arriving home carries in the groceries. If the sense of accompaniment is meaningful — and I think it is — then this petition does not ask God to cancel our trial. It asks God not to carry us along into what Christ has made *God's* trial.

Here again, Trinity solves the mystery. The Spirit leads the Son on behalf of both the Father and wayward Israel to heal the breach between them. His act of intercession brings truth into the realm of lies, presence into the void, and life into the grave. So he will be, must be, borne into the trial of human life on earth so that sinners may have a respite. In the language of Hebrews, the one whose deity is proclaimed in the Scriptures (Ps. 45:6 in Heb. 1:8) tastes death apart from God for others' sake.[46] The Son learns obedience to the Father by sharing our sufferings (Heb. 5:8), yet the forsaken one does it only through the eternal Spirit (9:14). The Father's Spirit does not carry *us* along into that trial but only *him.* God_1 answers God_2 by sending God_3 to carry God_2-without-God_1 through disaster and from the evil one. This is an act only God can initiate, only God can bear, and only God can conclude.

This unsurpassed sacrifice is the resolution of apocalyptic prophecy. By sharing with us his prayer and his victory, our apocalyptic conqueror initiates us into his one universal, final, inevitable, imminent, urgent, assuring victory over temptation and evil. Our trials are no longer ours alone but in Christ, after him, and through him. There are no longer isolated, personalized temptations for us to avoid on our own. There is only one long trial that Jesus has already taken on for us and won. The Spirit led Jesus through it in order to spare us from failing. Nothing can separate us now (Rom. 8:39).

However, apocalyptic's resolution is not its denouement. Temptation

---

46. Heb. 2:9, in a textual variant treated in Bart Ehrman, *The Orthodox Corruption of Scripture: The Effect of Early Christological Controversies on the Text of the New Testament* (New York: Oxford, 1993), pp. 146-50.

and evil must still visit Jesus' brothers and sisters. They even set up strong-holds in the Church. The prophetic pattern persists even now. Peck is hardly alone in noticing a correlation of excessive piety and criminality, especially among clergy and Christian volunteers: "Since the primary motive of the evil is disguise, one of the places evil people are most likely to be found is within the church."[47] The name for their behavior is blasphemy — a common apocalyptic sign.

Yet temptation and evil visit us in a different eschatological setting than they visited Peter or the other disciples on the night they betrayed and denied Jesus. Once Christ has risen, the threat that pervades the Sermon on the Mount and the apostolic travelogues of Luke and Acts and still haunts the fellowship of saints has lost its power. Whatever trials we face now are just hints of the joy to come (James 1), reminding us that Christ our only Savior remains with us to see things through to their foregone conclusion (Matt. 28:20).

But then wouldn't this petition be obsolete? Why are we praying this way, if the Father has already answered? Because the Lord's Prayer is *Christian* prayer.

The Lord's Prayer repeatedly makes requests that are obvious to the point of absurdity. Jesus points this out himself: Why *wouldn't* the Father give his children their daily bread (Matt. 6:25-33)? For that matter, why *wouldn't* the Father sanctify his name? Why *wouldn't* the Father realize his will? The final petition is just as obvious. Why *would* God lead us into fatal temptation or *not* deliver us from the evil one? These things are simply what God does, right?

Right. Interpreters get into trouble when they treat this prayer as less obvious than it is. For "Amen," think, "Duh!" The clarity and authenticity of the prayer are a function of its bone-headed straightforwardness.

Then is this prayer just a teaching device, a clever way for Jesus to get us to recognize the obvious truth that God is our holy Father who realizes his will and who feeds, forgives, and delivers us? Many take it to be that. Yet if that were the whole story, it would not need to be a prayer; a statement of faith would be enough. This prayer does teach us, but it teaches us *to pray.*

Why pray what is obvious to God and even to us? To make it so. This is a prophet's prayer. Prophecy is not just reality-depicting, but reality-making. Its words of new creation call into being the things that *are* to be.

---

47. Peck, *Glimpses,* pp. 147-48, 207-8.

Thanks to Jesus, justice *is* found in God's Kingdom. Thanks to Jesus, God's name *has* been sanctified. Thanks to Jesus, God's will *was* realized on earth after all. Thanks to Jesus, our sustenance *is* now daily bread for eternity. Thanks to Jesus, our sins *are* atoned for. Thanks to Jesus, God *is* our deliverer from the evil that threatens us not at God's bidding but ours.

Jesus' prayers are an irreducible part of his work bringing about these realities in the created order. They are not our appropriation of some independent salvation; they are the saving words of the Triune God appropriating us. What would the Gospels be without them? Jesus prayed these things into being because he was the Father's missionary. We get to pray them into being too because his grace has made us *his* missionaries, witnesses, and deputies (John 20:21). We now matter in a whole new way. The Creator has given his failed fellow creatures roles in his ultimate work of eternal creation. Who would not accept such an offer?

To accept that offer is to accept it in its totality. When the final petition is read or lived in isolation from the rest of the prayer, it suggests a life of social divestment or withdrawal and compulsive personal purity — defeatism.[48] When the rest of the prayer is read or lived in isolation from the final petition, it suggests a life of social investment and assimilation that defeats on its own the compromise and corruption of the present order — triumphalism. These strategies attempt to outlast or terminate the present evil age as if history's turning point had not already arrived. But Jesus does not lead his disciples into either kind of life — in fact, he condemns them as two foolish responses to persecution (Matt. 5:11), like hiding light or diluting salt (5:13-15) — because in him the turning point has already come. Truly apostolic life is neither defeatist nor triumphalist, but simply and powerfully evangelical. It hears the Son's words and does them: "let your light so shine before people that they may see your good works and give glory to your Father who is in heaven" (5:16). With the Spirit, the Son made the Father's plan a reality. With the same Spirit, we now make the Son's reality manifest.

The Theater of Truth

Accepting the task of manifesting the Son's reality puts the Son's messengers ever on the margins. Mission draws us to the edges of the obvious

---

48. See above, "The Reign of God."

where the true and the false are just now being exposed as such, and pushes back the boundaries of the darkness where the truth is still unknown and the false dominates. As knowledge serves faith and praise serves love, so *prophesying kindles hope* (cf. 1 Cor. 13) that defuses both the nihilistic resignation and the messianic arrogance that plague our world. The witness of the Church is the front line in the apocalyptic theater of truth.

Here the prophetic pattern of disaster and deliverance becomes persecution and victory. Matthew and the other more Jewish writings of the New Testament dwell more on persecution and "the evil one" darkening our hearts and punishing our righteousness. By contrast, Luke and the other more Hellenistic writings focus more on victory and temptation's incapacity to halt the front's advance at the Jordan, the wilderness, Palestine, Jerusalem, or the pathways to the ends of the earth. These are just variations on a common theme. They both score the same war. Matthew's defensiveness may be more amenable to pessimists, but it is not defeatism, because Christ Almighty is risen and present to the end of the age (Matt. 28:18-20). Luke's aggressiveness may be more amenable to optimists, but it is not triumphalism, because worthy apostles still suffer (Acts 5:41). The temptations and evils do not yet end, but they never prevail. God's people often fail under pressure, but the news is still good.

Praying the Lord's Prayer shapes our lives according to this pattern. It prepares us not for a decisive defeat nor for a cascading victory but for a long tribulation, for a continuation of the prophetic pattern of both the Old and New Testaments. We need the training. Every prophetic drama features ungodly characters who rely on their own devices and whose love grows cold (Matt. 24:12). Faithful ones rely on God their savior and endure to the end (24:13).

Luther preached that "our whole life is nothing but temptation by these three, the flesh, the world, the devil. Therefore pray: Father, let not our flesh seduce us, let not the world deceive us, let not the devil cast us down."[49] Luther's three temptations are not so different from this chapter's three woes. Lies are love fleeing to the void and made unreal. Evil is love curved back on itself and fallen into hate. Sloth is love seduced by pain and grown cold.

49. John Dillenberger, ed., *Martin Luther: Selections from His Writings* (New York: Doubleday, 1962), p. 226.

These are sad things. We would rather not think about them. But avoidance is itself a self-serving and slothful lie. So the Lord's Prayer reminds us again and again about temptation and evil — not to intimidate us but to frame them in the context in which we can finally think about them in the right way.

> Take us back, O YHWH, to yourself,
> and let us come back;
> renew our days as of old!
> For truly, you have rejected us,
> bitterly raged against us.
>
> (Lam. 5:21-22)

God's grace purifies. It trains us away from our passions and toward godly lives that wait for our Christ's glorious return (Titus 2:11-14).

Much recent history in and out of the west has told a tragic story of messianic triumphalism, failure, and disillusionment that corrodes into anti-messianic defeatism. That is not the Church's story. When the Son of Man comes (cf. Matt. 24:30) our woes are ended. The final petition reveals an alternative storyline that is ours for the taking in which truth overcomes lies, good overcomes evil, and joy overcomes sloth.

The first woe passes. The power of the lie is real power. This is not because the lie itself is anything, but because we creatures seize on the void as a place to become "creators" of our own. We arm its empty unreality with our God-given reality and power and so make ourselves its slaves. But *Truth* loves all that was, is, and will be. Neither the Torah of Moses, the Word of the prophets, the Wisdom of the writings, nor the gospel of Christ submits to our common sense, our self-evident truths, or our constructions of reality. Instead each enacts a life of freedom that respects the power of the lie but never the lie itself. The lie falls before the all-surpassing power of the Truth who rules at the Father's right hand.

Jude warns that as God had once saved a people out of Egypt but soon destroyed those like Korah who did not believe, so God has determined to uproot the ungodly who travel in Christ's circles but deny Christ as Lord and pervert his grace (Jude 4-5, 11). The worldly ones in Jude's churches will not prevail against those who pray in the Spirit, remain in God's love, wait for Christ's mercy, and speak truth to win back doubters (Jude 16-25).

Truth is told through Christ's witnesses, but it is less often heard. I have disputed a variety of issues with dear friends who are fellow Christians. Our conversations are hospitable and free of acrimony. Yet they still usually end in stalemates or polarized truces. These exchanges leave me amazed at the distance that separates us and convinced that more time together will not resolve our differences. She is a radical; I am a conservative. He is a premillennial; I am postmodern. She distrusts businesspeople; I distrust politicians. He is mainline; I am evangelical. She is a USC fan; my family roots for UCLA. He is European; I am American. None of these qualities is a matter of indifference or relativism. Radicalism and conservatism are not morally equivalent, let alone USC and UCLA. Yet logic and persistence will not reconcile us. The problem is not our diversity; that is a precious gift. The problem is that self-serving lies hide behind and within our perspectives, using our diversity as an impenetrable refuge from each other's truth-telling. What do we do then?

In these situations Christ the prophet still speaks truth. The one who asked Saul, "Why do you persecute me?" and told Simon Peter, "You are not on the side of God but of human beings" rebukes us all. It is hard for me to hear the correction of a friend with different politics or institutional loyalties, and for good reasons. Yet even when we judge each other and fail, Jesus can still judge each of us and succeed. Together or alone my friends and I go before his pulpit, baptismal font, communion table, and heavenly throne. There we lay down our perspectives, convictions, and hypotheses for him to come and judge. It is in many such situations that the Spirit has worked prophetic disaster and deliverance in my hardened heart, or guided me back to the words of a brother or sister I could not hear at the time, or overturned the whole framework of our dispute.

Diversity ceases to be a stronghold in these settings because Jesus is the Lord of *all.* Jesus is everyone who is in his body the church (Eph. 1:22-23). He is a radical, premillennial, mainline politician. He is a conservative, postmodern, evangelical businesswoman. He comes to Catholics as a fellow Catholic. He comes to Americans as a fellow American. He comes to Hispanics as a fellow Hispanic. He comes to mothers as a mother (as Julian of Norwich unforgettably showed). He comes to you and me in sympathy as well as disapproval, as someone who was carried along into suffering and temptation as well as delivered from evil. Jesus understands (2 Cor. 2:9-16)! He honors all that is honorable in us even while judging all that is reprehensible. Thus the word of truth breaks down the lies that keep us walled off from each other's worlds.

The second woe passes. Sin is undone by replenishing its barren relationships and rescuing its debtors, but the evil one is undone only by being overthrown. The Church does not forgive demons any more than it casts out sins! The taproot of evil is self-centeredness. But if evil is love turned inward on itself to the exclusion of others, *good* is love extended even at its own cost. Defeating evil supplants its taproot with new roots in the love of God and neighbor. Baptism is the revolution that overthrows evil by turning away from the devil and his works, submitting to exorcism, confessing trust in the Triune God of love, and entering into Jesus' death and resurrection for his befriended adversaries.

Yet how many baptisms sweep a house clean only to yield to more unclean spirits? How many tribes and cities submit to the good news but sooner or later return to the old ways? How many times has the faith faded and died where it had flourished? How many institutions say "Lord, Lord" but refuse the Father's will? Revolutions come and go.

Jesus is the vine (or in some translations the vineyard) and his disciples are the branches (or the vines) who abide in him and thus bear fruit. Yet some branches do not. They must be cut off, wither, and burn (John 15:5-6). Apocalyptic prophecy reveals a world so stubbornly evil, so thoroughly schooled in self-centeredness, that our only part in its conquest is the difficult work of perseverance. One must *keep* evil starved of its sources of power, or it is sure to grow back.

Jesus does not hesitate to warn his disciples about the dire consequences of unreadiness and inattention. He lists five in a series of apocalyptic parables near the end of Matthew: His servants will be invaded and find themselves powerless (Matt. 24:43). They will harm one another and intoxicate themselves (24:49). When time runs out they will be caught unprepared (25:10). They will be paralyzed by fear (25:25). They will neglect their duties to each other (25:42-44). Is this not the state of much of Christianity, especially in the west? Are not many of our Christian communities undefended, abusive, ill-equipped, fearful, and negligent in precisely these ways? Are we not the shorn Samson, abusive Abimelech, the Levite and his concubine, the routed Benjaminites, and the wrathful Jephthah in the time of the Judges? Some consider these failures evidence against the Kingdom's reality, but not Jesus. He calls them comparative signs of the Kingdom (Matt. 25:1). Again the prophetic pattern is fulfilled.

That is good news! It means that deliverance from our most disastrous problems is ever at hand. We think we need revival, but revival implies death. Jesus still sees signs of life, and so he commands us merely to awaken (Matt. 24:42, Rev. 3:2). Being not overcome by evil simply means overcoming evil with good (Rom. 12:21). That might sound impossible, but all that is actually required of us is readiness — vigilance, attentiveness, diligence, confidence, righteousness — because God's grace has supplied everything else we need (cf. Rom. 12:3-13).

The third woe passes. Our faith may not be literally dead, but sloth's dreadful momentum is a kind of living death. Who wants to be the weeds or the wicked servants in Jesus' parables? And yet we let our love run cold. But *joy* celebrates deliverance that has already come, with love that moves forward in the face of even mortal opposition. The woe of sloth is undone not because we pray or work ourselves out of depression — we cannot — but because Christ lives and reigns in spite of all opposition.

The best reason not to treat the prayer's doxology, "For yours is the kingdom and the power and the glory," in a separate chapter is that it belongs in *this* chapter. In fact, it belongs in every chapter — not as the Lord's words, for they are not the Lord's words, but as *our* words of worshipful response to all the Father has done for us in the Lord Jesus Christ. Because Jesus alone is our Savior, our life is joyful celebration that worships God alone.

Precisely because the final petition prays the obvious, inviting the Father to do the kinds of things that are consistent with his deity, the Father's answer arouses our worship. The prophetic pattern of disaster and deliverance fits into a more fundamental pattern of salvation and devotion: "I am YHWH who brought you out of Egypt, the house of bondage; you will have no gods besides me" (Exod. 20:2-3).

Prayer, deliverance, and worship are inextricable from each other. The Hebrews' desire to worship the God of Israel was the pretext for Exodus' disasters (Exod. 5:1), and their freedom to worship was the consequence of its deliverance (Exod. 15). Impure worship led to Israel's exile, and Israel's return will lead to purified worship (Deut. 32, Isa. 45:20-25, Zech. 14:16-21). Deliverance through disaster led the disciples to worship Jesus both before and after his resurrection (Matt. 14:33, 28:9, 28:17). Worship of the risen Jesus immediately distinguished "Nazarenes" from their fellow Jews who discerned nothing new in the world.[50] The New Testament's apocalyptic

---

50. Richard Bauckham, *God Crucified: Monotheism and Christology in the New Testament* (Grand Rapids: Eerdmans, 1998); Larry W. Hurtado, *At the Origins of Christian Worship: The Context and Character of Earliest Christian Devotion* (Grand Rapids: Eerdmans, 1999).

passages are drenched with the worship of Jesus.[51] And in every age the most joyful worshippers of the Triune God are those who realize they have been delivered from disaster. Sloth has no defense against their joy.

This chapter began with Theodore Dalrymple's reporting on the disorder that has produced Britain's malevolent underclass. A bright ray of light pierces those hundreds of bleak pages: Dalrymple's description of the Pentecostal churches of African and Jamaican immigrants that lend their people dignity and hope and fortify them against the enemies assembled roundabout them.[52] The heart of these communities is always a worship of the Lord Jesus that bursts with joy. Consider this excerpt:

> The congregants were dressed in all their finery, immaculately turned out in elegant hats and dazzling dresses; the older among them wore veils and gloves. . . . The preacher, a young woman, called the congregation for testimony to the Lord, and an old lady with a limp, whom I had passed several times in the street, came forward. She thanked the Lord in trembling voice for all the blessings that He had showered upon her, His servant, among which was the great gift of life itself. "We thank Thee, Lord! We thank Thee, Lord! We thank Thee, Lord! . . . We thank Thee, Lord, for the gift of healing. . . .
>
> "But we are all sinners, Lord. Therefore we pray for forgiveness. We do not always follow Your ways, Lord; we are proud, we are stubborn, we want to go our own way. We think only of ourselves. That is why there is so much sin, so much robbery, so much violence, on our streets." . . .
>
> Murmurs of assent were heard everywhere. It wasn't the police's fault, or racism's, or the system's, or capitalism's; it was the failure of sinners to acknowledge any moral authority higher than their personal whim. And in asserting this, the congregation was asserting its own freedom and dignity: poor and despised as its members might be, they were still human enough to decide for themselves between right and wrong.[53]

---

51. "The Worship of Jesus" in Bauckham, *The Climax of Prophecy,* pp. 118-49.
52. Dalrymple, *Life at the Bottom,* pp. 92-98.
53. Dalrymple, *Life at the Bottom,* pp. 93-95.

Dalrymple thinks he is witnessing a religiously styled assertion of self-determination over against encroaching fatalism. There is something to that. As we have already seen, Christian faith is not determinism. However, Dalrymple fails to understand the truest revelation in this display. These poor immigrants gather not to assert their free will against a tide of determinism but to confess and worship the God of grace.

Social scientists take note: "Religion" is not the same as joy. Religion is not the answer to the pathologies of western underclasses, Peck's troubled patients, or Thornton's and MacIntyre's technocrats. Not even Christian religion. After all, alongside Dalrymple's accounts of healthy immigrant churches are sad stories of impotent clerics of a Church of England that is well advanced along the road from irrelevance to extinction (a somewhat unfair characterization), totalitarian cults like the Jesus Army,[54] and spiritualists like Marie Therese Kouao who drove her daughter to destruction through exorcism and torture.[55] Christians know very well that our religiosity can turn toxic. No, the answer to sloth, evil, and the reign of lies is *grace:* the deliverance that comes through Christ alone. The *response* is Christian religion: the further grace of a new and healthy life that heeds the prophet Jesus rather than the tempter and worships the deliverer rather than the evil one. Grace has made us limited partners and unlimited beneficiaries. God has granted our request to deliver us from evil without carrying us along into Christ's temptation. A whole kingdom is ransomed to worship the Lamb who alone is worthy.

So it is that God offers a happy ending to our modern and postmodern tragedy. Truth overcomes lies, good overcomes evil, and joy overcomes sloth. These three call us to know, serve, and worship the living God and to renounce every other competitor for glory. And what else *are* my three woes but spurious, vacuous, and lifeless idols? Who am I for serving them but a fool? My reluctance to leave them behind in the water of my baptism is necessarily a refusal to proclaim, worship, and reign with God.

When prayer summons me back to his presence, I suddenly find my little idols far less appealing and far less threatening than I had supposed. The real world had not exposed the Lord's Prayer as unintelligible after all! No, the Lord's Prayer has been leading us out of yet another labyrinth of our own making. Over and over again I learn what Augustine realized long ago:

---

54. Dalrymple, *Life at the Bottom*, pp. 98-101.
55. Dalrymple, *Life at the Bottom*, p. 169.

Many and great are those diseases, many and great indeed. But your medicine is still more potent. We might have thought your Word was far removed from being united to mankind and have despaired of our lot unless he had become flesh and dwelt among us.[56]

We have much to pray and much to do. But we have much more to celebrate.

---

56. Augustine, *Confessions* 10.43, 69, p. 220.

Amen

BIBLE STORIES YOU DIDN'T OUTGROW: JONAH

A sermon delivered at Hope Community Church,
Santa Barbara, California, February 17, 2002

THIRD IN A THREE-PART SERIES

We live in a post-Christian society. Many Bible stories are no longer well known. However, a few live on. Even many people who aren't all that familiar with the Bible or interested in Christianity know them. Jay Leno may still be able to embarrass people who don't know the name of Adam's wife, but he probably has to work a little harder than usual with these.

I am glad these stories are still well known. But when the *broader context* of these stories is no longer well known, the stories themselves lose their place in the larger story. They float free, becoming little self-contained fairy tales, and start meaning something new (and *less*). They also get left behind with the other stories of our childhood.

The writers of the New Testament saw these stories differently: as little details of a big picture. We have spent three weeks looking at some of them, but we could have spent fifty-two, because the big picture is still the same. After a year of sermons, it would be exquisitely detailed and vibrantly colored. But you would still see the same thing.

That big picture is the good news of Jesus Christ. It is often summarized at ball games in the words of John 3:16: "For God so loved the world that he gave his only Son, that whoever believes in him should not perish

206

but have eternal life. For God sent the Son into the world, not to condemn the world, but that the world might be saved through him" (John 3:16-17).

Some people don't buy John 3:16. It all sounds too easy. What about the one who abused me as a child? What about me after what *I* have done? What about Timothy McVeigh? What about Osama bin Laden? "God so loved al-Qaeda that he gave his only Son"?

If you are one of those critics, I think you have a good point.

Jonah

A Bible story "for kids" will help us see that John 3:16 really *isn't* too easy to be true. It is the story of Jonah.

Maybe you know the story. Jonah gets a word from God: "Go at once to Nineveh, that great city, and proclaim judgment upon it; for their wickedness has come before me" (Jonah 1:2). Nineveh is an ancient and powerful enemy of Israel. Jonah makes a beeline in the opposite direction and sails away from the city. God raises a storm that endangers the whole crew. Jonah has them throw him overboard. This would normally kill Jonah. But God sends a fish to swallow him, and Jonah remains in its belly for three days and nights. Jonah prays for deliverance, and God commands the fish to spit Jonah onto dry land.

Most people tune out here. But this is Jonah, not Pinocchio. We are only halfway through the story. God reiterates the command. This time Jonah obeys. He goes and proclaims, "Forty days more, and Nineveh shall be overthrown." The king, too theologically naïve to know that an immutable God cannot take things back, advises everyone, "Who knows? Maybe God will take it back," and the people repent. And guess what? God takes it back!

Happy ending? Not for Jonah! He's ticked. He prays — actually, he rants: "This is why I fled! For I know you are a compassionate and gracious God, slow to anger, abounding in kindness, renouncing punishment. Kill me now — I'd rather die than live." Jonah stalks out of the city and waits, hoping something bad will happen to Nineveh. Nothing does. Instead, God starts sending more things to Jonah — little irritating things: a plant for shade, then a worm to kill the plant. A pleasant wind, then a punishingly hot sun. The story has become a farce.

The book ends with God lecturing Jonah like a spoiled child: "You care about some stupid plant that you didn't even grow. Am I not supposed to care about Nineveh, and its innocent animals, and its 120,000 clueless people?" The moral of this story is that God loves the enemies of his people Israel, whether Israel likes it or not.

Greater Than Whom?!

It is amazing that Israel would be telling this humiliating story about itself. It is downright phenomenal that it would end up in its own Bible. And it is just *incredible* where Jonah shows up in the New Testament:

> Some of the scribes and Pharisees said to [Jesus], "Teacher, we wish to see a sign from you." But he answered them, "An evil and adulterous generation seeks for a sign; but no sign shall be given to it except the sign of the prophet Jonah. For as Jonah was three days and three nights in the belly of the whale, so will the Son of Man be three days and three nights in the heart of the earth." (Matt. 12:38-40)

Wait a minute! Is Jesus really comparing himself to *Jonah*, the whiny runaway? Why reach down to just about the sorriest excuse for a prophet? Why not pick Moses, Elijah, Jeremiah, Isaiah, Ezekiel? In prophet school they don't teach you to be like Jonah.

Sure, Jesus is predicting his death and resurrection. But why cast it in terms of Jonah? Why take an impressive sign like resurrection and sully it with Jonah the loser? That is like Jesus doing signs and wonders and then comparing himself to Penn and Teller.

Here is what I think is going on. It will help us overturn two common misconceptions of God.

God So Loved

First, you often hear that *people* are loving and *God* is strict, especially in the Old Testament. That is why belief in God is an obstacle to world peace. But think about it: Aren't *we* pretty harsh on those who oppress us? Like Jonah wanted to be? Jonah runs away because he knows that if Nineveh repents, God is *too* compassionate to follow through on his threat.

The story tells it differently than we often choose to hear it. Jonah *did not* so love *Nineveh* that he gave them *God. God* so loved *Nineveh* that he gave *Jonah* — not to condemn it, but that it might be saved through him. (And Jonah didn't like it one bit.)

Second, you *also* often hear that the one Jesus calls "Father" is the one who holds a grudge against all humanity, and that *Jesus* is the nice one. The Father is fearsome and angry. We have Jesus on our side to soften him up.

The story tells it differently. After all, what makes us think that love of God's enemies is something that comes effortlessly to Jesus? This is a guy who is living under Roman occupation. His own puppet king has overseen a mass murder of two-year-olds to get *him.* Every day he sees Roman abuses of power against his people. By the time he is thirty, how many horror stories do you think Jesus has accumulated that would make our blood boil?

Forgive the Romans? Proclaim peace to Israel's oppressors? Are you kidding?

And in fact, Jesus *is* a rather reluctant prophet when it comes to extending God's mercy outside Israel. He can be curt with Gentiles, and when he does help them, he usually reminds them that they are beyond the scope of his original mission.

We do not have to work too hard to imagine the world Jesus lived in, because it is still here. Jews are being blamed for 9/11. Anti-Semitism is coming back into fashion in Europe. Suicide bombings in Israel are regular events. Why should Jesus, who is as Jewish today as he was two thousand years ago, be any nicer today? Who is going to soften *him* up?

Maybe the Father isn't the bad guy after all, but the steady source of Jesus' sacrificial love and compassion. "*God* so loved."

The World

But would that mean that like Jonah, Jesus has — *issues?*

Well, wouldn't you? Wouldn't you have a problem with the world? *Don't* you honestly have a problem with the world?

Let me read from an article by Tony Parsons in yesterday's *Mirror:*[1]

---

1. Feb. 16, 2002. Available online at http://www.mirror.co.uk/news/allnews/page.cfm?objectid=11314790&method=full.

"Did you see the yuppies flying out the windows of the trade center?" laughed a young man outside a mosque in North London. "That was so funny."

And I can't tell that young man how angry he makes me feel. And I can't tell him how wrong he is. And I can't explain that there are many of us who have been sickened by the slaughter of Palestinian children, who will probably now care a little less about the injustices of the Middle East now that we have an injustice of our own, now that we know that young man would be amused if our own loved ones were burned alive, buried in rubble, torn to bits.

We are being forced to choose sides. The evil idiots who crashed those planes, their grotesque cheerleaders like that young man, are forcing us to harden our hearts. That's the real tragedy of that unforgettable Tuesday.

Think for one honest minute about what we do to each other in this world. And then ask yourself why Jesus should find it easy to forgive the Romans who are crucifying him like they have crucified so many who came before him, and who will soon destroy his homeland.

On the night that everyone betrays and denies and sentences and abandons him, Jesus tells his few remaining companions, "My soul is very sorrowful, even to death" (Matt. 26:38). Those are Jonah's very words after Nineveh had repented and God had withered Jonah's favorite plant. Again Jesus puts himself in Jonah's place. He has issues.

Tony Parsons is dead right. Suffering from sin forces us to harden our hearts. That really *is* a real tragedy of 9/11. Al-Qaeda and all its sympathizers have hardened my heart. I studied Islam for years under a beloved professor who had converted to Islam from Christianity. My fellow students were mostly Muslims, and they were all, without exception, wonderful people. Now, when I think of Islam, I think of people rejoicing at the deaths of thousands of innocent people. I want to condemn Nineveh, not see it saved. I have issues. *Legitimate* issues.

This puts me in the position of the scribes and Pharisees who demand a sign from Jesus. They have legitimate issues too. So they are demanding that Jesus show himself to be *their* kind of deliverer. They want a movie hero. Their hardened hearts want vengeance. That is what makes them "an evil and adulterous generation." Sorry, Jesus says. My sign will disappoint you. It will trouble your souls even to death, as it troubles my own.

Jesus is promising the sign of Jonah. He will be the gift to "*the world* God loved." Even to Nineveh. Even to Israel's enemies. Even to us.

That He Gave His Only Son

September 11 *has* left me feeling a lot less warm and fuzzy about the world. It has created a new need in me: a cure for a hardened heart. But it is here that Jonah offers more resources for healing than Tony Parsons' compelling journalism and optimistic resolve. It is here precisely that the sign of Jonah offers concrete help.

For one thing, the sign of Jonah reminds us of the prayer Jonah prayed while waiting to die under the sea:

> Jonah prayed to YHWH his God from the belly of the fish. He said:
> In my trouble I called to YHWH, and he answered me;
> from the belly of Sheol I cried out, and you heard my voice.
> You cast me into the depths, into the heart of the sea, the floods engulfed me;
> All your breakers and billows swept over me.
> I thought I was driven way out of your sight:
> Would I ever gaze again upon your holy Temple?
> The waters closed in over me, the deep engulfed me.
> Weeds twined around my head.
> I sank to the base of the mountains;
> the bars of the earth closed upon me forever.
> Yet you brought my life up from the pit; O YHWH my God!
> When my life was ebbing away, I called YHWH to mind;
> and my prayer came before you, into your holy Temple.
> They who cling to empty folly forsake their own welfare,
> But I, with loud thanksgiving, will sacrifice to you;
> What I have vowed I will perform.
> Deliverance is YHWH's!
> YHWH commanded the fish, and it spewed Jonah out upon dry land.
> (Jonah 2:1-10 JPS)

You know, that sounds like it could come from the same Jesus who moves from "My God, my God, why have you forsaken me?" (Matt. 27:46) on Friday to "Do not be afraid" (Matt. 28:10) on Sunday.

It helps to know that suffering innocently and bearing the burden of forgiving one's oppressors grieves even Jesus. In a world where heroes die senselessly, it helps to know that *my* hero died senselessly. In a world where it is so hard to learn obedience to a compassionate God, it helps that, as Hebrews puts it, even the Son "learned obedience through what he suffered" (Heb. 5:8). When news of some new outrage begins to choke off my compassion, it helps that "we have not a high priest who is unable to sympathize with our weaknesses, but one who in every respect has been tempted as we are, yet without sin" (Heb. 4:15).

When I see all over again that we don't have it in us to love enough, that *I* don't have it in *me* to love enough, it helps to know that the Father and the Son and the Holy Spirit are unspeakable love for their world, unconditional love, unpleasant love.

If God's love for the world is anything less than this, then we ought to give up hope. The world's evil *will* triumph over it. It will force us all to surrender to the rage *we* feel at the rage of others.

Jonah learned obedience through what he suffered. Jesus did too. But for all the similarities, there is a critical difference. God's love triumphed *over* Jonah. Jesus is "greater than Jonah" (Matt. 12:41) in that God's love triumphed *in* Jesus. God "gave *his only Son.*" Jonah arose from the deep, but he pouted until the story was over. Jesus arose from the tomb, and promised to go with us (Matt. 28:20) as we bring his peace even to our enemies.

Today that peace has come to us. Listen for the bittersweet power of John 3:16-17 as I read it one last time: "For God so loved the world that he gave his only Son, that whoever believes in him should not perish but have eternal life. For God sent the Son into the world, not to condemn the world, but that the world might be saved through him."

You can either celebrate this, or you can pout about it. You can surrender your hate to the one who refused to hate, or you can fight your own personal World War III, which you will lose even if you win. Why don't you bring your issues to him instead?

Generosity under Pressure;
or, How to Win in November No Matter What

A sermon delivered at Montecito Covenant Church,
Santa Barbara, August 15, 2004

The American Feedback Loop

I am glad the Olympics have started. I needed the breather from presidential politics. I'm ready for a race that is a *literal* race. One that lasts ten seconds rather than two years, without months of predictions, where a finish line does the judging. Most of all, I need a breather from all the fighting. I need a while away from statements like this, which came from two adjacent letters to the editor of the *South Coast Beacon* several weeks ago:

> "Could it be that those stolen documents [on Sandy Berger's person] strengthen Bush's case while revealing Clinton, Kerry and the Democrats to be nothing more than al-Qaeda enablers?"
>
> — R. E. Lynn, Santa Barbara

> "President Bush, with unparalleled arrogance, masquerades as a door-to-door salesman for democracy and human rights. Yet, post-invasion Iraq labors under the jackboot of a foreign military occupation and its hand-picked puppet government. . . ."
>
> — Robert Baruch, Goleta

These passages illustrate the bitter polarization right now in American politics. Robert Samuelson described it recently in *The Washington Post:*

> Politics is increasingly a world unto itself, inhabited by people convinced of their own moral superiority: conspicuously, the religious right among Republicans; and upscale liberal elites among Democrats. Their agendas are hard to enact because they're minority agendas. So politicians instinctively focus on delivering psychic benefits. Each side strives to make its political "base" feel good about itself. People should be confirmed in their moral superiority. . . .

Entertainment and politics merge, because both strive to satisfy psychic needs. Rush Limbaugh and Michael Moore are more powerful political figures than most senators, because they provide more moral reinforcement. . . .

Politics should reflect and, at its best, conciliate the nation's differences. Increasingly, it does the opposite. It distorts, amplifies and inflames conflicts. It's a turnoff to vast numbers of centrist voters who do not see the world in such uncompromising absolutes. This may be the real polarization: between the true believers on both sides and everyone else.[2]

Perhaps you are one of those True Believers. Perhaps you are one of the turned off ones. (I am a little of both.) This talk is meant for all of us.

Remember the united-we-stand days after September 11? Back then the American political dynamic was expressed as national unity. By the 2002 election it had split into two opposing varieties of the same basic message. This is the last chance to stop *our beloved America* from sliding into fascism. This is the last chance to stop *our beloved America* from losing the next Great War. *We* can protect America better than *they* can.

Many of the True Believers really hate and fear each other. Those are strong words, but I think they're accurate. These people regularly pepper their speech with put-downs, dismissals, and cheap shots. With each volley the True Believers' argument gets louder and louder like a feedback loop until the screech drowns out everything else. Our whole future is at stake! *We* need to prevail! We can't let *them* take it away! *They* aren't just wrong, they're out of touch! They're menacing! They're stupid! They're immoral! They're evil! *Screeeeeeeeech!!*

Within each tribe the tone is just as intensely loyal. True Believers love and protect their own. They pull punches, tolerate exaggerations, and correct patiently, if at all. The environment is as safe for the insiders as it is hostile to the outsiders.

This is even true among Samuelson's "everyone else." In the Turned-Off tribe the etiquette of political conversation works like this: You remain calm and a little stoical. You listen respectfully and speak softly. You don't interrupt. You refute others indirectly rather than taking them head-on.

2. "How Polarization Sells," June 30, 2004. Available online at http://www .washingtonpost.com/wp-dyn/articles/A16180-2004Jun29.html.

You get points for hedging (e.g., "Well, I dunno," rather than, "You're wrong!"), not being sure, and dropping hints of skepticism about the whole business. *Above all, you conclude the exchange within sixty seconds.* Break any of these rules and you are a True Believer. You're a zealot. You're out of the tribe and off the island.

Surrendering to any one of these tribes' logics — whether by making human flags in 2001, taking sides in 2002-2004, or opting out along the way — is addicting. Throwing yourself into the psychology of a campaign is exhilarating. "We get to be on the side of *good* versus *evil!*" Turning off and dropping out is not so much exhilarating as satisfying and liberating. "Can't we all just get along? Your bickering is ruining the country! We independents are above the fray! *We* are better than *you!*"

So far I haven't said a word about the Church. I haven't needed to. The same dynamics are tearing it apart. For decades strident politics from pulpits has motivated True Believers, fatigued loyal dissenters, driven away visitors, turned off independents, and divided congregations. Have you felt the pressure? So-called Christian radio sounds like the rest of talk radio. Every year sees new scenarios of the end-times where contemporary politics turns into chapters in the book of Revelation. Many American Christians are even more frantic than the wider electorate. Others have decided they're too spiritual for all this mess and joined the Turned-Off tribe.

Many of us would rather be with nonbelievers who agree with us politically than believers who don't. What does that say about our real identities? Partisan politics' ability to drive a sword right through the Church shows the power it has over us. The campaigns are telling us that politics is what matters in America and America is what matters in politics, *and many of us are agreeing.* They are telling us that Republican or Democratic goals are our ultimate goals, *and many of us are agreeing.* Others are resigning themselves to being ruled by True Believers and doing their best to tune them out, not so much disagreeing as giving in to the others.

A Different Spirit: Generosity through Hope

This church has been in a several-month-long series on the Lord's Prayer. A pastor friend of mine once summed up a series of his own in one profound line: "Because God is our Father, our lives are different." I want to develop that truth — that because God is our Father, our lives are different

— by contrasting the spirit of our times with the spirit of several letters of the New Testament.

Revelation is strong stuff. Its prophecies of plagues, persecutions, judgments, famines, disasters, and the end of the world dwarf even the worst threats from al-Qaeda or whatever world villain you fear most. I think it's safe to say that things are worse here than even under a Kerry or a second-term Bush administration! Yet even after all that death and destruction the book closes with these remarkable words:

> The Spirit and the bride say, "Come." And let everyone who hears say, "Come." And let everyone who is thirsty come. Let anyone who wishes take the water of life as a gift.
>
> I warn everyone who hears the words of the prophecy of this book: if anyone adds to them, God will add to him [or her] the plagues described in this book, and if anyone takes away from the words of the book of this prophecy, God will take away his [or her] share in the tree of life and in the holy city, which are described in this book.
>
> The one who testifies to these things says, "Surely I am coming soon." Amen. Come Lord Jesus! (Rev. 22:17-20)

That is about as far as it gets from a 2004 campaign ad. Revelation closes not with sunny optimism, fear, bitterness, or resignation, but with invitations, a warning, and a prayer.

I find this attitude astounding. It is not denial or cheap optimism or naïveté; the writer knows the danger. It is not the hypocritical conciliation our president-elect will offer to try to get along with the party he has beaten. After all, here in Revelation it is still October, so to speak; the battles are still raging. This attitude is something else entirely: *generosity* born of hope in the midst of evil. "Let *anyone* who wishes take the water of life as a gift," the prophet says. Even the Romans who are killing Christians. Even the people who are handing believers over.

What is this "water of life"? It is not the oppressive stuff of the Nile, the Euphrates, or the Potomac (cf. Jer. 2:13-18), but the water of God. It is the Holy Spirit (cf. John 7:37-39). It is total fellowship with the God of Israel. Generosity doesn't get more generous.

Extending such generosity is costly. This bride is the throng of martyrs in Revelation 6. It would be so easy to rise above the fray and join the sixty-seconds-or-less tribe! Keeping quiet would allow the bride to go underground and stay alive. Yet the Spirit in her is still causing her to call out, "come," and reveal her position. Hospitality matters more than security.

And consider the longing that goes along with it. The Spirit and the bride aren't just inviting the thirsty in for living water. They are also inviting *the Lord Jesus* to come and rescue *them*. Their generosity depends on the conviction that Jesus will be faithful.

(If you were listening closely, you heard something that probably sounds wrong. *The Spirit* needs the Son to rescue him? Well, why not? The Son needed the Spirit to raise him! Now that the Spirit is the Church's "down payment" on the Son's promise to come and fulfill every promise, doesn't the Spirit need the Son to return to relieve him of grieving the world's sins and interceding with groans and sighs beyond words? The Spirit is the *author* of our prayers for the Lord Jesus to come.)

This is not the logic of a campaign. A campaign inspires confidence by describing America as strong, true, unique, proud among nations, and so on. However, voters can't believe this *too* strongly, or we might feel safe to vote the other way! We have to believe our lives, finances, civil liberties, and national pride are insecure and ultimately depend on this candidate. For the election to matter, America has to be a goal as much as an asset.

Revelation's churches are not nearly as comfortable as America's. Then why is there such security in this passage? Because the goal was already reached. The good news is a celebration, not a campaign. Jesus already assured John at the beginning of the vision that "I died and behold I live, and I have the keys to death and the grave" (1:17-18). Jesus has freed us from American insecurities. The wedding is on. Crucifying the groom didn't stop it. Murdering the bride won't stop it either.

Turning from the bride's serenity back to the world's screeching political anxiety rejects God's grace. It denies the resurrection. It acts as if it matters more that President Bush or Kerry has the keys to the Oval Office than that Jesus has the keys to death and the grave.

Here is another contrast. A campaign is a balancing act between being all about *us* (meaning the nation) and all about *me* (meaning the individual). Not this passage! The bride looks to the Spirit she wants to share, and vice versa. The two of them wait for the bridegroom. They call across the world to invite strangers to be engaged too. They care not about how the bride looks to herself, but about how she looks to him (Rev. 2–3, 19:7-8, 21:2–22:5).

Voting out of our own fears or our own dreams does what Jesus refused to do. It puts our own agenda ahead of the Father's. We don't pray "Father, *our* will be done in heaven as it is on earth." That is what the devil tells Jesus to do in the wilderness! We don't turn stones into dollars, armies, diplomats, prestige, or any other thing we think we need most. We cannot *manipulate* the Spirit. We can only *receive* the Spirit. So we pray, "Father, *your* will be done on earth as it is in heaven."

You see, our works and our emotions are signs of our *real* beliefs. If our lives *aren't* different, then we don't really trust that God is our Father.

Some signs in my own life point in embarrassing directions. Since 9/11 I have been doing a lot of "checking." I check the news often — not just because it is interesting, but also out of a nagging worry that a disaster or big event might have happened since a few hours ago. I check the markets. I check the polls. That's not hope, and it doesn't yield generosity.

I think I do this because I want to feel safe. Yet what I learn usually tempts me to check even more. It feeds addictions that I don't like and don't want, but find hard to resist.

Am I the only addict in the room? Perhaps you don't even follow politics; but do a little adjusting and you will see this talk is about you too. We are a world of news junkies, sports junkies, envy junkies, sex-and-violence junkies, video game junkies, conspiracy junkies, talk-show gossip junkies, substance junkies, popularity junkies, shame junkies, and all the rest. What do *you* really believe in? Where does pressure drive you? To costly generosity, or elsewhere?

Inaction Items

Now at this point a proper sermon is supposed to shift from convicting you about what's wrong to offering a "how-to" list for making things right. Everyone ready for three action items? You're not going to get them. I'll show you why with more contrasts between American politics and Christian faith.

In an election, it is momentarily up to us, then out of our hands. What a thrill that is! But in our passage, it is never just up to the bride, because *the Spirit is with her.*

American politics cannot even dream of the assurance that conviction brings. Look at Paul's letter to the Romans:

> Therefore, since we are justified by faith, we have peace with God through our Lord Jesus Christ. . . . And not only that, but *we also boast in our sufferings, knowing that suffering produces endurance, and endurance produces character, and character produces hope,* and hope does not disappoint us, because God's love has been poured into our hearts *through the Holy Spirit that has been given to us.* (Rom. 5:1-5)

The Spirit is with us, so suffering leads to hope. Politicians try to use the word "hope," but they can't bring hope in the Christian sense at all. Hope is what you still have when your brothers and sisters are perishing for the crime of believing, the stars are falling from the sky, the seas are turning to blood, the water supply is radioactive, the sun no longer shines, and people are begging for death to come (Rev. 8–9).

Times are bad in the first century for Christians and just about everyone else. But hear the joy surging through this passage in 1 Peter, written to churches that feel like "aliens and exiles" (2:11) in a hostile world:

> Rejoice in so far as you share Christ's sufferings, that you may also rejoice and be glad when his glory is revealed. If you are reproached for the name of Christ, you are blessed, *because the spirit of glory and of God rests on you. . . .* Therefore let those *who suffer according to God's will* do right and entrust their souls to a faithful creator. (1 Pet. 4:13-19)

The Spirit is with us, so suffering leads to joy. Christians squabble about what it means to be baptized with the Holy Spirit. Do we speak unknown tongues? Do we get other gifts like supernatural knowledge and healing? Well, let's *not* squabble about this: Whatever else it does, the Holy Spirit resting on us gives us the power to do the Father's will, just as the Spirit resting on the Son empowered him to obey the Father from the wilderness all the way to the cross.

I think one reason why the Spirit and the bride are calling for the Son to come is that they need his courage. Jesus has already walked this path. He has already loved his enemies and prayed for his persecutors. They need the Son not just to return in glory at the very end to rescue them once and for all, but also to stay with them in glory until the end of the age.

They need him to lend them his patience and generosity while they suffer and grieve. They need his glory.

Falling back into fear, bitterness, or resignation acts as if we were alone when the Spirit and the Son are actually seeing us through. It forgets that Christ is faithful. It denies his gift of the Spirit. It shuns his glory. It fails to acknowledge him before others. That in turn invites Jesus to deny us before the Father (Matt. 10:32-33).

I said that *the Spirit is with the bride;* but it might be better to say that *the bride is with the Spirit.* The Spirit speaks first: "Come." In fact, the Spirit has taken the lead right from the beginning of Revelation. The Spirit has showed John the opening vision of Jesus and inspired Jesus' stack of letters to his churches. In fact, the Spirit has taken the lead in realizing the Father's will ever since brooding over the waters in Genesis 1:2!

Yet it is not just up to the Spirit. An amazing thing happened when Jesus poured his Spirit into the heart of his bride and anointed her head: he delegated the Spirit's authority. In effect, he gave us the Spirit's initiative. The bride now takes the lead! Not *from* the Spirit, of course — "the Spirit blows where he wills" — but *with* and *in* the Spirit. Having the Spirit puts us on the leading edge. We aren't just aliens and exiles; we're pioneers and settlers. The Son leads us to the Father, but we lead the Son to the nations. What *we* do on earth — testifying, forgiving, binding, loosing, opening eternity's gates, inviting the world to enter them, and calling on the Son to come too — will have been done in heaven.

The Bible uses more than one metaphor to get all this across. In the Son we follow Christ, as the body follows the head. Yet in the Spirit we lead Christ, as the bride calls for the bridegroom. That sounds wrong too — how can *we* lead God? — but remember, the Spirit led Jesus into the wilderness. In Christ we do not trade off leading and following, being in charge for two minutes and then being out of power for two years, the way Americans do on Election Day. We *always* follow and we *always* lead. "We know that we abide in [God] and [God] in us," 1 John says, "because he has given us of his own Spirit" (4:13).

What a difference this makes! Since we abide in each other, "love is perfected with us, that we may have confidence for the day of judgment, because as he is so are we in this world. There is no fear in love, but *perfect love casts out fear*" (1 John 4:17-18). Hatred and resignation too (1 John 4:20-21). Anxiety, aggression, and despair give way to the calm confidence of knowing we are never alone.

Does all this apply to the world of politics? You bet. Titus is told to

> exhort and reprove with all authority. Remind [the church] to be
> submissive to rulers and authorities, to be obedient, to be ready for
> any honest work, to speak evil of no one, to avoid quarreling, to be
> gentle, and to show perfect courtesy toward all. For we ourselves
> were once foolish, disobedient, led astray, slaves to various passions
> and pleasures, passing our days in malice and envy, hated by people
> and hating one another; but when the goodness and loving kind-
> ness of God our Savior appeared, he saved us, not because of deeds
> done by us in righteousness, but in virtue of his own mercy, by the
> washing of regeneration and renewal *in the Holy Spirit, which he
> poured out upon us richly* through Jesus Christ our Savior, so that we
> might be justified by his grace *and become heirs in hope* of eternal
> life. (Titus 2:15–3:7)

Doesn't that sound like an antidote to power politics? The Spirit is with us,
so submitting displays authority. Oh, *we* remember our old vices. That's
why we sympathize with our rulers! Yet God has freed us from having to
beat them, join them, surrender to them, imitate them, or leave them
alone. Now we can freely *respect* them as we go about our own business as
God's Church. We have gone from being fellow rebels to God's heirs. The
Spirit has given us a new style of politics: a gentle obedience that is really
authority, leadership, and evangelism.

Are you ready to abide in God and submit with courtesy, whoever
wins in November?

"But Bush is a fascist!" "But Kerry is an appeaser!" Well, first, let me
suggest very gently that those of you who feel this way *might* need to get a
grip. Your trustworthy friends who support your nemesis might not be as
deluded as you think. (You do have some, right? I do.) And remember,
there are True Believers on your side who *want* you scared. Fear puts you
under their control. What they *need* is Christians who won't be played,
who don't panic, and who hold onto our authority. *That* would change the
rules of politics.

But maybe you're right. Maybe Bush *is* a dictator. Maybe Kerry *is* a defeatist. I have trusted friends who think these things too. Then keep in mind
that Paul is referring to *Roman emperors and governors.* They are killing
Christians who refuse to worship them! Even if your worst nightmares come

true, Titus still applies. Withholding generosity towards your enemies would still be self-defeating. It would turn you back into the very people you fear.

Remember, *because God is our Father, our lives are different.* The Spirit is with the bride! This is why the mindset that a sermon's conclusion should move us from a bad place to a good one is dead wrong. God has *already* moved us into a life in his Church that frees us to be faithful under these pressures. These biblical passages are not treating our fears as either imaginary or irrational. The threats have to be as real as the cross that saves us from them. The Son was crucified so people like Simon the Zealot and Matthew the tax collector — people who worked for each other's mortal enemies — could be liberated from their sources of animosity and share the table in Christ's new community of peace. Think of that next time you see a bumper sticker you want to rip off of someone else's car. Your serenity was won by the blood of Jesus.

By the way, there is also a place at that table for the Turned-Off tribe. Nathanael speaks for jaded, above-it-all independents in John 1:45-46: "Can anything good come out of Nazareth?"

After Jesus has done this beautiful new thing to reconcile these totally incompatible people, can you imagine Simon or Matthew going back to their old rivalry? Can you imagine Nathanael going back to his old cynicism? I can imagine them being tempted to, when politics comes up around the campfire. But after all they have been through, can you imagine them giving into their temptations?

That is what we do when we surrender to conventional politics: we spurn the atonement. We shrug off the Father's will and try to secure our own salvations. We become the Galatians who yield to tribal politics and resegregate their Jews and Gentiles. No, our task is a kind of *inaction*: not to backslide into our old lives of frenzy, anxiety, alienation, and resignation.

> Formerly, when you did not know God, you were in bondage to beings that by nature are no gods; but now that you have come to know God, or rather to be known by God, how can you turn back again to the weak and miserable worldly things, whose slaves you want to be once more? (Gal. 4:8-9)

You can hear Paul's incredulity. After becoming an heir of the Spirit, you want to go back to being a hack?! "For *freedom* Christ has set us free! Stand fast, then, and do not submit again to a yoke of slavery" (Gal. 5:1).

The Spirit is with us, so we are free. If we Christian tax collectors, Zealots, and skeptics return to the old ways, we will find ourselves consumed by each other — conceited, competitive, and envious. Our nostalgia will strangle our hope. "Do not gratify the desires of the flesh," Paul says. It leads to what we see in worldly politics at its worst: idolatry, enmity, strife, jealousy, anger, selfishness, dissension, partisanship, envy, and the other bad habits of the violent world that tried and failed to defeat Christ (Gal. 5:19-21, cf. 4:29). Instead, walk by the Spirit. Then we produce fruit of the Spirit: love, joy, peace, patience, kindness, goodness, faithfulness, gentleness, and self-control (Gal. 5:22-26). And we show the world another politics — another way.

I am *not* saying not to vote! You have the authority. I am not saying whom to vote for! Reasonable people can disagree, and reasonable people can be undecided. I am not saying anything goes! There are political stands the Church has to take *as the Church* — one famous example was the Barmen Declaration in Nazi Germany. I am not saying to be unconcerned when things go wrong! *Lots* of things will go *very* wrong in the next four years, no matter who wins. Grieve them, speak up against evildoers, and work for change, all as the Spirit prompts. And I am not saying that all political views are equally valid. Mine are right!

All I mean by "inaction" is not losing our focus. Resist the reflex in American politics to become our own saviors. Christ defeated it as God defeated Pharaoh. Don't go back! Don't even think of going back! The genuine danger of giving in to that temptation is why our passage in Revelation includes that warning not to tamper with its words. Gratifying our old desires is like editing the prophecies of Revelation. It only adds to the hazards and takes away the comforts (22:18-19).

Greater Freedom from a Greater Problem

I have developed all this using national politics, and some of you apolitical types have been patient with me. But the problem is much broader and deeper, isn't it? There is power politics in the polling place, the workplace, the marketplace, the classroom, the bedroom, and at the dinner table. Fortunately, our freedom is there too. You have probably heard many times how Christ has freed us from sin and death. Well, Christ has freed us from much more than those. Christ has freed English speakers and Spanish speakers in California from having to take sides against each other. Christ has freed women and men from the battle of the sexes. Christ has freed the old and the young from the generation gap and the fight for Social Security. Christ has freed the world's peoples from the clash of civilizations. Christ has freed athletes from obsession with winning and artists from preoccupation with fame. Christ has freed the powerful and the poor from having to tie each other's hands. Christ has freed offices, schools, and churches from petty power politics. Hallelujah! All these things have been transcended — not just wished away, but put away — through the blood of the cross and the breath of the resurrection.

I find no better summary of this new reality than Paul's words in 1 Corinthians 13. "These three things remain," he tells the church in Corinth: *faith* (which means living through trust in God's goodness), *hope* (which means acting with confidence in God's power to fulfill his intentions), and *love* (which means putting God and neighbor before oneself). A trusting, hoping, loving church is a fearless, hateless, self-denying church. It truly loves its enemies and prays without ceasing for its persecutors. It does not worry about tomorrow, but acts generously out of trust in its providential Father. It does not follow its flesh back to Egypt but follows the Spirit forward to the frontier. It is a refuge for those who fear, hate, and are self-centered. It looks like the Sermon on the Mount, like Paul on his missions, like the young Church in Acts, and above all like Jesus on his way to the cross and to the Father's right hand.

When I think about how these virtues might look today, the picture I get in my mind is the black Church during the civil rights movement. Talk about fear, hate, persecution, bad faith, and all the rest — but in these people were trust, confidence, and unselfishness. Those three things remained, and so they and their movement overcame their own hatred, fears, and needs for self-assertion over others, and helped white America do the same. The Church in America hasn't seen victories like that since, I think because it has never been as faithful, hopeful, or loving as it was then. Can you imagine either "the Christian left" or "the Christian right" acting this way nowadays? I can, but only if a lot of things change.

Conclusion

Let me close with a few final questions for us all.

Are we burdened with fears, divisions, and battles like these? I certainly am. Then let's stand fast with the Spirit and the bride. Let's identify our weaknesses and repent of them. Let's live like the free people of these New Testament letters and the saints who came after them. Here's a suggestion: when you and I face temptations to turn back, let's resist them by praying the Lord's Prayer. Just those few words reframe everything.

Do we know others with these burdens? If our neighbors are breaking under the pressure of self-determination, then let's extend God's own generosity. Let's include them in the bride's and the Spirit's life of peace, security, and freedom and then invite them to stay.

Someday things will get harder, and not just because the Olympics will end. We can expect further terrorist attacks. Eventually one will probably succeed. Do we want to be generous *then?* Then let's cultivate a spirit of Christlike generosity *now.* We can do that with prayer for our enemies, forgiveness, mercy, courage, nonviolence, compassion, sacrifice, and fellowship.

And if God hasn't moved you into this new place, then come and take the water of life as a gift. Come and be our sister or brother. Our opinions will sometimes drive each other crazy . . . but it sure beats politics as usual.

God's ultimate response to these needs is as full as the Father's will and as filling as the Holy Spirit. It is the whole life of the bride. And it has already been given. Shall we receive it?

You Can Say That Again

A sermon preached at Montecito Covenant Church, August 14, 2005

A Culture of Sorrow

My son Jeremy has become a fan of the *Series of Unfortunate Events* books by the pseudonymous Lemony Snicket. Here is the back cover copy from the first volume in the series:[3]

---

3. *The Bad Beginning*, 1st ed. (New York: HarperCollins, 1999).

Dear Reader,

I'm sorry to say that the book you are holding in your hands is extremely unpleasant. It tells an unhappy tale about three very unlucky children. Even though they are charming and clever, the Baudelaire siblings lead lives filled with misery and woe. From the very first page of this book, when the children are at the beach and receive terrible news, continuing on through the end of the story, disaster lurks at their heels. One might say they are magnets for misfortune. . . . It is my sad duty to write down these unpleasant tales, but there is nothing stopping you from putting this book down at once and reading something happy, if you prefer that sort of thing.

With all due respect, Lemony Snicket

This cleverly plays to what I will call *our culture of sorrow.* It is a common sensibility that life's true character is misfortune and that sadness rules over us. It may seem far away to this room of cheerful southern Californians on a Santa Barbara morning, but it is a lot closer than we think.

In our culture of sorrow, *sadder is cooler.* Joy may be desirable, but it's not fashionable. What is? Ask the fashion industry! Does that look of aloof, disheveled, emaciated sophistication strike you as happy? Me neither. But it's cool! Or name a big pop band that has looked happy in its photos since the Beatles in 1964. Cool means hard stares, angry sneers, lust, and brooding.

The businessman in me marvels at this. Money can't buy happiness, but now it can buy unhappiness! Just spend three figures on this blouse and pout like *her.* Just buy this band's CD and wallow in the futility of the ghetto. (Or suburbia . . . whatever.) Hand over a few bucks and enter Snicket's cute, dark narrative world. More serious types can go to a prestigious school and get a whole education in angst, ennui, existential despair, cynicism, political decline, environmental catastrophe, and social alienation. Master these and you'll be the life of the dinner party. Pull enough all-nighters and you can get the strung-out fashion-model look at no extra cost.

I am not singling out our fashion leaders. After all, we're buying what they're selling. I am just pointing out which attitudes we *all* associate with coolness, as a society.

In our culture of sorrow, *sadder is wiser.* Misery has become our myth, our metanarrative. Joy is liable to be taken as immaturity or ignorance:

"Don't they know about all the suffering in the world?" If you want an Oscar, don't go with a so-called Hollywood ending. Go with a gut-wrenching tragedy like *Million Dollar Baby*. If you don't believe me, find a list of Best Picture award winners and tally them yourself.

Sadder is deeper. What moves a personal relationship from small-talk pleasantries to greater sincerity? Telling the truth, of course. And for us the deepest truth-telling generally involves the disclosure of pain, hardship, and anxiety. Relationships tend to deepen from shallow happiness to more authentic sorrow: "It's hard at home." "I'm worried about the war." "I suffer from depression." "Our finances are precarious." "I am an addict." It is usually with comments like these rather than confessions of deep, abiding joy that we "open up" to one another. They seem more authentic.

Sadder is greater. Joy doesn't make headlines. "If it bleeds, it leads." Pity and guilt raise money to help the destitute, not joy. Anger, fright, and fantasy bring out voters and volunteers, not joy. Fear and greed drive the economy, not joy. Sorrow acts and we react. It calls the shots.

I dream of writing a screenplay for an episode of *The Twilight Zone* where someone is suddenly teleported into a culture of joy rather than a culture of sorrow and doesn't know what to do. But I don't have to! It has already been done.

A Life of Joy

There *is* such a culture, with a whole different approach:

> You became imitators of us and of the Lord, for you received the word in much affliction, with joy inspired by the Holy Spirit; so that you became an example to all the believers in Macedonia and in Achaia. . . . Though we had already suffered and been shamefully treated in Philippi, as you know, we had courage in our God to declare to you the gospel of God in the face of great opposition. . . . You, brethren, became imitators of the churches of God in Christ Jesus which are in Judea; for you suffered the same things from your own countrymen. (1 Thess. 1:6-7, 2:2, 2:14 RSV)

Those are Paul's words to the Thessalonian believers. They relate a lot of pain. Yet pain is not in control. *Joy* is in charge here. Lemony Snicket could never have written this.

Plenty of bad things have already happened to Paul even this early in his career. He could be angry at God, bitter at his enemies, worried about the future, and burned out from the constant problems in his churches. Instead he writes like this:

> We wanted to come to you — I, Paul, again and again — but Satan hindered us. For what is our hope or joy or crown of boasting before our Lord Jesus at his coming? Is it not you? For you are our glory and joy. (1 Thess. 2-18-20)

This is classic Paul: suffering but joyful. Steaming mad at the Galatians for abandoning God's grace, Paul still steers his letter to them toward the *joy* of walking by the Spirit (Gal. 5:22-26). Anguished at the wretched, rebellious Corinthians, he closes 2 Corinthians 10–13 by rejoicing when he is weak and they are strong (2 Cor. 13:9). Walking the Romans at length through the problems of Jewish-Gentile relations in the church, he crystallizes the Kingdom of God into "righteousness, peace, and *joy* in the Holy Spirit" (Rom. 14:17) and encourages them to live together in joyful hope and patient harmony (Rom. 12:12-16). The only letters of Paul that don't mention joy are the ones scholars aren't sure Paul wrote.

His churches are a mess. He is usually in prison, on the run from his own people, or under arrest. His own body is literally a pain. Yet Paul is a *joy machine.* Scholars debate where he was when he wrote his various letters. Was he in Rome? Was he in Ephesus? I know the answer. He was in the Twilight Zone. Jesus called it the Kingdom of God.

A Zone of Twilight

Twilight is that moment of transition either as morning dawns or as evening becomes night. I don't have to write that episode of *The Twilight Zone* because Luke did it for me — in his account of the Transfiguration (Luke 9:28-36).

Here is the setting: The disciples know Jesus is up to something new, but he still baffles them. Not long ago Peter gave Jesus his best shot when he called him "Messiah," but then Jesus started saying that he had to suffer and be rejected and then be raised. When Peter protested, Jesus rebuked him and promised that his true disciples would face the same. Now he's

228

thinking: I left my family, I left my business, and my reward is a cross? What have we gotten ourselves into? Should I get out? The sun is setting; the future looks dark and miserable.

Then Jesus takes Peter, James, and John up a mountain to pray. As he prays everything changes. Moses and Elijah appear in their state of glory. A cloud overshadows the whole group. The whole scene is like a reverse solar eclipse: a flood of light suddenly shining in the middle of the night. They really *are* in a twilight zone! But it's not the twilight of dusk. *Dawn* is breaking.

The Transfiguration is a dose of the Father's joy, delivered just in time to a world of gloom. And what happens to the people who encounter it? Most of them don't know what to do.

Some rejoice in the wrong things. Soon the twelve will be rejoicing at their power over demons. No, Jesus tells them, you're still giving too much room to sorrow. Demons are just filthy pests. You should be rejoicing in your salvation (Luke 10:17-20). Many churches are caught up in illusions, loyalties, and battles that keep us from rejoicing at the truth. There is a word for that kind of joy: *Schadenfreude*, joy for which we ought to be ashamed.

Some rejoice in the right things but in the wrong way. Peter weakly calls Jesus "rabbi." That's like calling Mozart a piano player. This prompts a correction from above: "This is *my Son, my Chosen One*. Listen to him!" Then Peter tries to keep the prophets from leaving with an invitation to hang out and celebrate good times. That bright idea brings on a cloud that shuts down the scene like Mardi Gras at midnight.

Peter *is* right to enjoy the presence of the Father, the glory of Jesus, and the communion of saints. But his joy is complacent. He is looking back toward the old days at Sinai and the wilderness when he ought also to be looking forward to Jerusalem. Like Peter, a lot of joyful churches are rightly glad about the great things God has done for us, but we forget to press on. That's not exactly sorrow, but it is something close: nostalgia. Celebrating good times is good, but anticipating better times is better.

Some refuse to rejoice. James and John are with Peter in the Twilight Zone, but what do *they* do when they wake up? Apparently nothing worth mentioning. They represent what you might call the Church's silent majority: mute when Peter calls Jesus Messiah, in the boat when Peter walks on water, hiding when Peter is in the courtyard, and quiet when Peter preaches. Many of us feel intimidated by the power of sorrow. Powerless

Christians aren't joyful Christians. Or perhaps it is better to say that joyful Christians aren't powerless Christians.

I make all these mistakes. I don't *want* sadder to be cooler or wiser or deeper or truer. I know the culture of sorrow is a lie. Yet I am always falling for it. Are you?

Then rejoice, because there are also persons in this episode who get joy right, and more chances for people like me to get it right too.

Heading for Jerusalem

Moses and Elijah get joy right. They aren't talking about their glorious days of old. In fact, they are the ones pointing Jesus forward to the *next* exodus. Jesus, of course, gets joy right. In the gathering darkness he begs for the Father's joy. He is the one whose face and clothes are changed in his praying, as the Father shows him the glory that outlasts his suffering. And don't forget the Father! It is *his* Kingdom and power and glory, and he is joyfully showering all of them on his beloved Son.

Center on this circle. They get it. The Father enjoys the Son as the Son enjoys the Father in the extravagant fellowship of the Spirit. An ever-widening circle of joy flows from the Father to the Son and back, from the prophets to the Messiah and then to his apostles — from the mountaintop down the slope, over to Jerusalem, onto the cross, out of the grave, out to the ends of the earth, and forward to the eternal future.

The scene ends, because it must, and it never repeats. It is just a glimpse of what is to come. In the meantime everyone must endure another nightfall. You see, we who got joy wrong have another chance to get it right — but only if we do a very difficult thing. Jesus does it down below (Luke 9:31, 51). His disciples do it with him, and do it again after he rises (Luke 24:49, 52). Joyful Paul does it four times or more (Acts 9:26, 11:30, 12:25, 15:4, 21:17). They head for sad, occupied Jerusalem. Jerusalem is the place where God's purposes meet their greatest opposition — where darkness confronts the twilight and does all it can to overcome it. Yet it is also the place where the light shines in spite of the darkness and overthrows it forever. Jerusalem has to be our destination too. Transfiguration doesn't last — yet. But that one moment changes everything. In the Transfiguration the Father hurls a bright ray of hope right into the dark middle of the gospel of Jesus Christ . . . and also into the dark middles of our own lives.

Could you use a mountaintop view of eternity now and then? I sure could. Well, the Transfiguration is over, and you and I missed it. But its *power* and *light* are still available. Second Peter says we should pay attention to the Transfiguration as if it were a lamp shining before daybreak (2 Pet. 1:16-19). For Jesus and his companions it was a preview. For us on the other side of his resurrection it is a reminder. The Kingdom's twilight is just that: a glimmer rather than full sun. You can ignore it if you like, but you can see it if you search.

Would you like that transforming power? Then *pray*. That's what Jesus is doing when transfiguration happens. *Worship*. Gather with other believers and exchange reminders. *Serve*. Share Christ's light with those who are struggling to see. All of these activities invite the Father to bleach our troubles, our hopes, our needs, our questions, and our sufferings dazzling white in his glory.

Then do what 2 Peter says — and pay attention to what happens. You can tell who is following along with a storyteller because they smile and gasp and laugh at the right time. They know what to do. Jesus on the mountain is paying attention. He is awake, aware, and unafraid. Many Christians today are like him. But many others lack joy. I can think of only one reason why: We haven't been paying attention. We are like the disciples on the mountain: asleep when the glory appears, clueless about what is happening, afraid of where it will all lead, and reluctant to leave as it ends.

The disciples had another chance to behold his glory at the resurrection. Now that the Spirit has come, we have one every day. When we pay attention, the Father's transfiguration of our lives in resurrection's power and light neutralizes our misery and every other challenger. Then we know what to do. We are treated as sorrowful, Paul tells the Corinthians, yet we always rejoice (2 Cor. 6:10).

Cultures of the Kingdom

Joy is a fundamental sign of faith.[4] Healthy families, healthy churches, and healthy lives have *got to have* cultures in which joy rather than sorrow

4. Daniel W. Hardy, "Joy," *The Oxford Companion to Christian Thought* (New York: Oxford University Press, 2000), p. 354.

reigns. I began with our culture of sorrow; let's end with cultures of the Kingdom.

A true culture of joy is *reasonable*. Christian joy is never irrational exuberance, because it is always grounded in the good news. Paul commands his churches to remember Jesus' resurrection and await his return. He tells the Philippians to contemplate all that is true, honorable, just, pure, lovely, and gracious (Phil. 4:8). That is not hype or wishful thinking. It's intellectual integrity.

Lesslie Newbigin was asked once whether he was an optimist or a pessimist. "Neither," he said. "Christ is risen." That is exactly right. Optimism is blind faith that can't handle bad news. Pessimism is blind doubt that warps it into *sad* news. Paul doesn't hide his hardships or wallow in them. He rejoices even when his enemies preach Christ just to worsen his imprisonment (Phil. 1:18). That's not spin, it's confidence.

Second, joy is *varied but not artificial*. Paul commends joy in all circumstances, and he pulls it off. When Christians try to imitate him by putting on an act, it is not a pretty sight. True joy is by definition not fake joy. Paul didn't turn his letters into motivational speeches. He just received the Spirit's joy and passed it along naturally.

Paul's writing is anything but monotonous, because a life of joy is naturally rich in its variety. We enjoy ordinary things in an astonishing range of ways. Think of a ticker-tape parade, a wedding reception, a wedding night, a good day at work, a birthday party, a peaceful evening at home, and a dignified inaugural. Why not enjoy the extraordinary things of the Twilight Zone in an even more astonishing range of ways? That is what the Bible in its incredible variety trains us to do, if we heed it.

Third, joy is *obvious but not forced*. This is a joyful church. However, with our northern European heritage, we tend to keep our joy rather . . . *understated*. Yet we find all kinds of other places to be over-the-top with exuberance: games, concerts, school plays, graduations and awards ceremonies, and even just around the table. None of that is forced. Perhaps we should let our light shine even more obviously. After all, David does. Heaven does on Christmas night. Paul does. The prodigal son's father is *embarrassingly* joyful. Jesus' robe turns not just bright white, but *dazzling* white. Over-the-top white. That is the joy of the Twilight Zone. When the Father lavishes joy so expressively on his Son, why shouldn't we?

Two weeks ago Leslie, a local Young Life student, told her story of coming to faith. The key word in her testimony was joy. The joy of the Lord is magnetic. It attracts and it repels. Some people come away from joyful Christians thinking, "Those people are just too happy. Something is wrong with them." Some come away thinking, "I don't know what it is they have, but I want it."

Fourth, joy is *encouraged and disciplined.* The ultimate letter of joy in the New Testament is Paul's letter to the Philippians. He sounds like a broken record. In 2:18, "rejoice." In 3:1, "rejoice." In 4:4, "rejoice; again I say, rejoice." This got me wondering. Why does he say it again? The Philippians are doing as well as any of his churches. Do you run around telling happy people to cheer up or healthy people to get well soon?

He keeps telling them to rejoice because he needs to say it, and they need to hear it. It's that simple. Joy is a gift, and gifts are for giving. Sorrow is tempting. If joy just happened automatically, Paul would not have written this way. We need reminders, and we need *to be* reminders.

This takes effort. Kim and I vacationed this summer in Pasadena and returned to Christian Assembly, our Pentecostal church in Los Angeles. That church is *extraordinarily* joyful. God seems to have given it a special mission to spread his joy. Its worshippers cheer. They laugh. They shout and wave. They cry. They rock and roll. They whisper Jesus' name in prayer. Last Easter the worship leader led everyone in group high-fives. Several Easters earlier a few choristers improvised the electric slide during the final song. Crazy. Exuberant. Joyful. They aren't like this by nature. They are joyful because they train hard.

Montecito Covenant trains hard too. As I have thought through this message I have noticed how many ways we rejoice. Diana convenes us with words of joy, often from the Psalms. Joy has characterized just about every one of Doug's sermons in one way or another. The refreshment tables, Noah's, summer dinners, and Operation Christmas Child are just a few of many well-disciplined displays of joy. Thank you!

It startled me to realize I had overlooked so many of these reminders when I am professionally trained to notice them. Yet I *had* been missing them. I am embarrassed to confess that I need you all to be more obvious with your reminders. You may even need to be as obvious as Pentecostals. Call me to attention! I am the distracted one in the back Paul had in mind when he wrote "*again* I say, rejoice" (Phil. 4:4). I need you to say it again loudly and slowly.

I don't think I am the only one. If *I* can miss it after twenty years of faith, what about kids like Leslie who know nothing but a world of sorrow and are unfamiliar with Church customs? Young Life doesn't get results by being subtle.

Let me sum it all up: Joy is and has to be *central to our identity* as people who trust Jesus Christ. It cannot be an option, an add-on, or a half-measure. Leslie's Young Life leader Scott Lisea used the story of the paralytic lowered by his friends through a ceiling (Mark 2:1-12) to get us "on the roof" as a church. Well, on the roof is over the top. Jesus took his friends up the holy mountain to pray. On a mountain is over the top. Paul reminds the Philippians that the Father has highly exalted the Son (Phil. 2:5-11). A throne in heaven is *totally* over the top. I think these folks are telling us something.

The people I can think of who really know what to do in the Twilight Zone are over-the-top with joy: St. Augustine, who made joy cool for over a thousand years. St. Francis. Karl Barth, who said that "The theologian who labors without joy is not a theologian at all."[5] C. S. Lewis. Hans Urs von Balthasar, who said simply that "the Christian message is joy."[6] The black Church. Persecuted Christians in China, whose sufferings remind me of *Unfortunate Events* but whose lives remind me of the Philippians. John Paul II and Benedict XVI. I could go on and on. That cloud on the mountain is a cloud of witnesses.

Do you have a special reason to be sad? I bet you have *formidable* reasons to be sad. Don't ignore those troubles. But don't look at your situation as a potential installment in *A Series of Unfortunate Events*. Take it up to the mountaintop. Pay attention to that light at the horizon. The kingdom and the power and the glory all belong to the everlasting Father. They are in the best possible hands, and always will be. Join the cloud of witnesses. Rejoice! *Rejoice!* Rejoice-rejoice-rejoice!

5. *Church Dogmatics* II/1 (Edinburgh: T&T Clark, 1957), p. 656.
6. *The Glory of the Lord: A Theological Aesthetics*, vol. VII: *Theology: The New Covenant* (San Francisco: Ignatius, 1990), p. 532.

Bibliography

Abbott, Edwin A. *Flatland: A Romance of Many Dimensions*. New York: Dover, 1992.

Abrahams, Israel. *Studies in Pharisaism and the Gospels*. Jersey City, N.J.: Ktav, 1967.

Ajami, Fouad. *Dream Palace of the Arabs: A Generation's Odyssey*. New York: Vintage, 1999.

Augustine. *Confessions*. Translated by Henry Chadwick. New York: Oxford, 1992.

Balthasar, Hans Urs von. *The Glory of the Lord: A Theological Aesthetics*. Vol. VII, *Theology: The New Covenant*. San Francisco: Ignatius, 1990.

Bandow, Doug. *Beyond Good Intentions: A Biblical View of Politics*. Wheaton, Ill.: Crossway, 1988.

Barth, Karl. "The Strange New World within the Bible." In *The Word of God and the Word of Man*. New York: Harper, 1957.

————. *Church Dogmatics* II/1. Edinburgh: T&T Clark, 1957.

Bauckham, Richard. *God Crucified: Monotheism and Christology in the New Testament*. Grand Rapids: Eerdmans, 1998.

————. *The Climax of Prophecy: Studies on the Book of Revelation*. Edinburgh: T&T Clark, 1993.

Baumeister, Roy. "Lying to Oneself." In *Lying and Deception in Everyday Life*, edited by Michael Lewis and Carolyn Saarni. New York: Guilford, 1993.

Bloom, Harold. *The American Religion: The Emergence of the Post-Christian Nation*. New York: Simon & Schuster, 1992.

Book of Common Prayer. New York: Church Hymnal Corporation, 1979.

Boy Scouts of America: The Official Handbook for Boys (Reprint of Original 1911 Edition). Bedford, Mass.: Applewood, 1997.

Boyd, Gregory A., and Paul R. Eddy. *Across the Spectrum: Understanding Issues in Evangelical Theology.* Grand Rapids: Baker, 2002.

Braaten, Carl E., and Robert W. Jenson, eds. *Sin, Death, and the Devil.* Grand Rapids: Eerdmans, 2000.

Brooks, David. *Bobos in Paradise: The New Upper Class and How They Got There.* New York: Simon and Schuster, 2000.

Bruce, Steve. *Sociology: A Very Short Introduction.* New York: Oxford, 1999.

Burtchaell, James Tunstead. *The Dying of the Light: The Disengagement of Christian Colleges and Universities from Their Christian Churches.* Grand Rapids: Eerdmans, 1998.

Catechism of the Catholic Church. New York: Doubleday, 1995.

Clapp, Rodney. *A Peculiar People: The Church as Culture in a Post-Christian Society.* Downers Grove, Ill.: InterVarsity, 1996.

Cocksworth, Christopher. *Holy, Holy, Holy: Worshipping the Trinitarian God.* London: Darton, Longman and Todd, 1997.

Cone, James H. *God of the Oppressed.* Revised edition. Maryknoll, N.Y.: Orbis, 1997.

――――. *For My People: Black Theology and the Black Church.* Maryknoll, N.Y.: Orbis, 1984.

Dalrymple, Theodore. *Life at the Bottom: The Worldview that Makes the Underclass.* Chicago: Ivan R. Dee, 2001.

Danby, Herbert, ed. *The Mishnah.* New York: Oxford, 1933.

Dillenberger, John, ed. *Martin Luther: Selections from His Writings.* New York: Doubleday, 1962.

Downey, Michael. *Altogether Gift: A Trinitarian Spirituality.* Maryknoll, N.Y.: Orbis, 2000.

Ebeling, Gerhard. *The Lord's Prayer.* Brewster, Mass.: Paraclete, 2000.

Ehrman, Bart. *The Orthodox Corruption of Scripture: The Effect of Early Christological Controversies on the Text of the New Testament.* New York: Oxford, 1993.

Fischer, David Hackett. *Albion's Seed: Four British Folkways in America.* New York: Oxford, 1989.

Gay, Craig M. *The Way of the (Modern) World; or, Why It's Tempting to Live as if God Doesn't Exist.* Grand Rapids: Eerdmans, 1998.

Gilder, George. *Wealth and Poverty.* New York: Bantam, 1982.

Goleman, Daniel. *Vital Lies, Simple Truths: The Psychology of Self-Deception.* New York: Simon and Schuster, 1985.

Gregory of Nyssa. *On 'Not Three Gods.'* In *Nicene and Post-Nicene Fathers,* Second Series, volume 5, edited by Philip Schaff. Peabody, Mass.: Hendrickson, 1994.

Gunton, Colin. *The Actuality of Atonement: A Study of Metaphor, Rationality and the Christian Tradition.* Edinburgh: T&T Clark, 1988.

Hamilton, Von Gail. *Work Family History: Twelve Generations of Works in America, 1690-1969.* Park City, Utah: Publishers Press, 1969.

Hardy, Daniel W. "Joy." In *The Oxford Companion to Christian Thought.* New York: Oxford, 2000.

Hauerwas, Stanley. *A Better Hope: Resources for a Church Confronting Capitalism, Democracy, and Postmodernity.* Grand Rapids: Brazos, 2000.

————, and William H. Willimon. *Resident Aliens: Life in the Christian Colony.* Nashville: Abingdon, 1989.

Hays, Richard. "Christ Prays the Psalms." In *The Conversion of the Imagination.* Grand Rapids: Eerdmans, 2005.

Heilbroner, Robert L. *The Worldly Philosophers.* 5th ed. New York: Simon and Schuster, 1980.

Hijuelos, Oscar. *Mr. Ives' Christmas.* New York: HarperCollins, 1995.

Hodgson, Marshall G. S. *The Venture of Islam.* Chicago: University of Chicago Press, 1974.

Holladay, William L. *The Psalms through Three Thousand Years: Prayerbook of a Cloud of Witnesses.* Minneapolis: Fortress, 1993.

Huntington, Samuel P. *Who We Are: The Challenges to America's National Identity.* New York: Simon and Schuster, 2004.

Hurtado, Larry W. *At the Origins of Christian Worship: The Context and Character of Earliest Christian Devotion.* Grand Rapids: Eerdmans, 1999.

Jenkins, Philip. *The Next Christendom: The Coming of Global Christianity.* New York: Oxford, 2002.

Jenson, Robert W. *Systematic Theology: The Triune God.* New York: Oxford, 1997.

Jones, L. Gregory. *Embodying Forgiveness: A Theological Analysis.* Grand Rapids: Eerdmans, 1995.

Kadison, Richard, and Theresa Foy DiGeronimo. *College of the Overwhelmed: The Campus Mental Health Crisis and What to Do About It.* San Francisco: Jossey-Bass, 2004.

Kallenberg, Brad J. *Ethics as Grammar: Changing the Postmodern Subject.* Notre Dame, Ind.: University of Notre Dame Press, 2001.

Kingsolver, Barbara. *The Poisonwood Bible.* New York: HarperCollins, 1999.

Kodell, Jerome. *The Eucharist in the New Testament.* Collegeville, Minn.: Liturgical Press, 1988.

Kraft, Charles H. *Defeating Dark Angels: Breaking Demonic Oppression in the Believer's Life.* Ventura: Regal, 1992.

Lewis, C. S. *The Great Divorce.* New York: Macmillan, 1946.

Lindbeck, George. *The Nature of Doctrine: Religion and Theology in a Postliberal Age.* Philadelphia: Westminster, 1984.

Lindberg, Carter. *The European Reformations.* Malden, Mass.: Blackwell, 1996.

Luz, Ulrich. *Matthew 1–7: A Continental Commentary.* Minneapolis: Augsburg, 1992.

MacIntyre, Alasdair. *Three Rival Versions of Moral Enquiry: Encyclopedia, Genealogy, and Tradition.* Notre Dame, Ind.: University of Notre Dame Press, 1990.

—————. *After Virtue.* 2d ed. Notre Dame, Ind.: University of Notre Dame Press, 1984.

Marion, Jean-Luc. *God without Being.* Translated by Thomas A. Carlson. Chicago: University of Chicago Press, 1991.

McBrearty, Sally, and Alison Brooks. "The Revolution that Wasn't: A New Interpretation of the Origin of Modern Human Behavior." *Journal of Human Evolution* 39, no. 5 (November 2000), 453-563.

McClendon, James Wm. Jr. *Systematic Theology.* Volume 3, *Witness.* Nashville: Abingdon, 2001.

—————. *Systematic Theology.* Volume 1, *Ethics.* Nashville: Abingdon, 1986.

McGrath, Alister E. *The Genesis of Doctrine: A Study in the Foundation of Doctrinal Criticism.* Grand Rapids: Eerdmans, 1997.

McIntyre, John. *The Shape of Soteriology.* Edinburgh: T&T Clark, 1992.

McKnight, Scot. *The Jesus Creed: Loving God, Loving Others.* Brewster, Mass.: Paraclete, 2004.

Mead, Walter Russell. *Special Providence: American Foreign Policy and How It Changed the World.* New York: Routledge, 2001.

Meaning of the Holy Quran. Translated by 'Abdullah Yusuf 'Ali. Brentwood, Md.: Amana, 1993.

Migliore, Daniel L. *Faith Seeking Understanding.* Grand Rapids: Eerdmans, 1991.

Miles, Jack. *God: A Biography.* New York: Vintage, 1995.

Miller, Patrick D. *They Cried to the Lord: The Form and Theology of Biblical Prayer.* Minneapolis: Fortress, 1994.

Moynahan, Brian. *The Faith: A History of Christianity.* New York: Doubleday, 2002.

Newbigin, Lesslie. *Signs amid the Rubble: The Purposes of God in Human History.* Edited by Geoffrey Wainwright. Grand Rapids: Eerdmans, 2003.

―――. *Proper Confidence: Faith, Doubt, and Certainty in Christian Discipleship.* Grand Rapids: Eerdmans, 1995.

―――. *The Gospel in a Pluralist Society.* Grand Rapids: Eerdmans, 1989.

―――. *The Household of God.* New York: Friendship Press, 1954.

Nyberg, David. *The Varnished Truth: Truth Telling and Deceiving in Ordinary Life.* Chicago: University of Chicago Press, 1993.

O'Donovan, Oliver. *The Ways of Judgment.* Grand Rapids: Eerdmans, 2005.

O'Keefe, John, and R. R. Reno. *Sanctified Vision.* Baltimore: Johns Hopkins University Press, 2005.

Peck, M. Scott. *Glimpses of the Devil: A Psychiatrist's Personal Accounts of Possession, Exorcism, and Redemption.* New York: Free Press, 2005.

―――. *People of the Lie: The Hope for Healing Human Evil.* New York: Simon and Schuster, 1983.

Reno, R. R. *In the Ruins of the Church: Sustaining Faith in an Age of Diminished Christianity.* Grand Rapids: Brazos, 2002.

Reumann, John. *The Supper of the Lord: The New Testament Ecumenical Dialogues, and Faith and Order on Eucharist.* Minneapolis: Augsburg, 1985.

Samuelson, Robert J. "How Polarization Sells." *The Washington Post,* June 30, 2004.

Sayers, Dorothy L. *Christian Letters to a Post-Christian World: A Selection of Essays.* Grand Rapids: Eerdmans, 1969.

Schmemann, Alexander. *Our Father.* Crestwood, N.Y.: St. Vladimir's, 2002.

Sider, Ronald J. *Rich Christians in an Age of Hunger: Moving from Affluence to Generosity.* Dallas: Word, 1997.

Smail, Thomas A. *The Forgotten Father.* Grand Rapids: Eerdmans, 1980.

Snicket, Lemony. *A Series of Unfortunate Events: The Bad Beginning.* New York: HarperCollins, 2000.

Stanley, Thomas J., and William D. Danko. *The Millionaire Next Door: The*

Surprising Secrets of America's Wealthy. New York: Simon and Schuster, 1996.

Stevenson, Kenneth W. *The Lord's Prayer: A Text in Tradition*. Minneapolis: Fortress, 2004.

Thompson, Marianne Meye. *The Promise of the Father: Jesus and God in the New Testament*. Louisville: Westminster John Knox, 2000.

Thornton, Bruce S. *Plagues of the Mind: The New Epidemic of False Knowledge*. Wilmington, Del.: ISI, 1999.

Vanhoozer, Kevin J., ed. *The Cambridge Companion to Postmodern Theology*. New York: Cambridge University Press, 2003.

Volf, Miroslav. *Exclusion and Embrace: A Theological Exploration of Identity, Otherness, and Reconciliation*. Nashville: Abingdon, 1996.

Walsh, Brian J., and Sylvia C. Keesmaat. *Colossians Remixed*. Downers Grove, Ill.: InterVarsity, 2004.

Wells, Spencer. *The Journey of Man*. New York: Random House, 2002.

Wilkinson, Bruce. *The Prayer of Jabez: Breaking Through to the Blessed Life*. Sisters, Ore.: Multnomah, 2000.

Wilson, Jonathan R. *God So Loved the World: A Christology for Disciples*. Grand Rapids: Baker, 2001.

Wink, Walter. *The Powers that Be: Theology for a New Millennium*. New York: Doubleday, 1998.

Wittgenstein, Ludwig. *Remarks on Color*. Translated by Linda L. McAlister and Margarete Schättle. Berkeley: University of California Press, 1977.

———. *Philosophical Investigations*. Second Edition. Malden, Mass.: Blackwell, 1958.

Wolfe, Tom. *I Am Charlotte Simmons*. New York: Farrar, Straus and Giroux, 2004.

———. *Hooking Up*. New York: Picador, 2000.

———. *The Bonfire of the Vanities*. New York: Farrar, Straus and Giroux, 1987.

Work, Telford. *Living and Active: Scripture in the Economy of Salvation*. Grand Rapids: Eerdmans, 2002.

Wright, N. T. *The Resurrection of the Son of God*. Minneapolis: Fortress, 2003.

———. *The Lord and His Prayer*. Grand Rapids: Eerdmans, 1996.

Yoder, John Howard. *The Politics of Jesus*. Revised edition. Grand Rapids: Eerdmans, 1994.

Subject Index

agency, human, 103, 106-10, 152, 172, 177-79, 187, 218

al-Qaeda, 7-8, 207, 210, 213, 216

America, United States of, 5, 7-8, 28-30, 53-63, 79-103, 106-7, 109-10, 120-25, 127-29, 136-42, 148, 213-15, 217-18, 224

analogy, 35

angels, 21, 23, 33, 43-44, 68, 108, 131-32

Anointed One. *See* Messiah

Anselm, 157, 162

apocalyptic, xii, 5, 129, 160, 189-203

apostles; apostolic, 70, 78, 113, 135, 156, 164-66, 191, 197-98, 230

Aquinas, Thomas, 35, 182

atheism; atheist, 8, 55, 60-61, 148, 172-73

atonement, 24, 108, 155-59, 162-68, 222

Augustine, St.; Augustinianism, 31-32, 67, 150, 167, 184, 186-87, 204-5, 234

baptism, 182, 193, 201, 204

Baptist tradition, 32, 94, 123

Baptist, John the, xix, 42, 108, 112, 134, 158, 159, 192

barrenness: sin as, 152-55, 157-59, 162-63, 201

Bible, xvi-xviii, 5, 9-14, 21, 62, 112-13, 160, 190, 206-8. *See also* Torah

blasphemy, xxii, 29-31, 41, 196

Boy Scouts, 54-63

bread, xvii, xxii, 131-35, 139-41, 194, 196-97

Bush, George W., 56, 63, 98, 213, 216-17, 221

Calvin, John; Calvinism, 107, 130, 145, 162, 190

capitalism, 28, 86-87, 124, 141, 174

Catholic tradition, 31-32, 35, 99, 166

church, 24, 31-32, 35, 44-45, 64-65, 74, 76-80, 102-6, 108-10, 112, 136, 142, 165-67, 194, 198-200, 215-25

collect, xiii-xiv, 189

compassion, 207-9, 212

conservatism and liberalism, xv-xvi, 17-19, 21, 25, 28, 31, 35, 39, 50-52, 57-59, 61-63, 86-88, 91-96, 99-100, 133, 141-42, 178-79, 199-200, 213-25

Constantinianism, 53-54, 56, 59-63, 66, 72, 76, 78-81, 103, 109

Constitution, United States, 53-54, 58, 92

Creator and creation; creatures, 18-19, 28-30, 33-38, 44, 65, 90, 104-5, 111-12, 183, 199

cross of Christ, xviii, 22, 44, 65-66, 75-77, 135, 156-57, 160, 162-63, 210, 217, 219, 222, 224

241

Scripture Index

22:15-20	193	4:26-27	43	12:12-16	228
22:31-32	193	5:1-11	109	12:15	78
22:42	108	5:32	108	12:21	202
23:40	163	5:41	198	14:17	69, 228
23:41	163	7:51	108	15–16	69
24:34	112	8:14-24	108	15:5-6	78
24:35	135	8:18-24	109		
24:49	105, 230	9:26	230	**1 Corinthians**	
24:52	230	10:9	38	1:18-25	159
		11:30	230	1:21-25	65
John		12:25	230	2:3	65
1:14	106	13:34	43	3:10-15	xiv
1:45-46	222	13:35	43	4:20	70
3:16-17	206-7, 212	15:4	230	6:20	112
4–5	70	19:1-7	108	10–11	132-33
6:69	43	20:22	109	10:3	133
7:37-39	105, 216	21:14	109	10:4-5	43
8:42-44	106	21:17	230	10:5-7	133
11:49-50	163			10:11	65
14:6	xi	**Romans**		10:16	133
15:5-6	201	1–4	69	10:18	133
16:7-8	45	1:1	70	10:20-22	133
16:13	104	1:3	70	10:25-27	133
17	107	1:9	70	10:28-29	133
17:26	45	1:16	70	11:18-20	133
18	163	1:18-25	179	11:21-22	133
20:21	197	1:28-32	103	11:26	133
		2:5	6	11:27	133
Acts		2:24	31	11:29	133
1:8	109	4:24-25	163	11:30	133
1:8a	106	5–14	69	11:32	133
2	104	5:1-5	219	11:34	133
2:4	108	7:24	187	13	74, 198
2:16-22	170	8:26-27	112	15	76
2:17	65	8:39	195	15:45	105
2:22-36	191	9:17	38	15:45a	104
2:22-37	43	9:31-33	164	15:50	65
2:25-33	43	10:3-4	77	16:19-20	104
2:38	108	10:6-7	111		
2:38-39	44	10:6-10	78	**2 Corinthians**	
2:42-47	135	10:9	111	2:9-16	200
3:14-16	43	11:7	77	4:13	22
3:17-26	191	11:34-36	112	5:16-21	156
3:18-26	170	12:3-13	202	5:17-19	155

250